On-Stage
AND
Off-Stage

English Canadian Drama in Discourse

Albert-Reiner Glaap with Rolf Althof (eds.)

On-Stage
AND
Off-Stage

English Canadian Drama in Discourse

Albert-Reiner Glaap with Rolf Althof (eds.)

BREAKWATER

BREAKWATER
100 Water Street
P.O. Box 2188
St. John's, NF
Canada
A1C 6E6

The Publisher gratefully acknowledges the financial contribution of the Canada Council which has helped make this publication possible.

Published in co-operation with Cornelson University, Germany.

Canadian Cataloguing in Publication Data

Main entry under title:

On-stage and off-stage

Includes bibliographical references.
ISBN 1-55081-117-7

1. Canadian drama (English) — 20th century —
History and criticism. * 2. Theatre — Canada —
History — 20th century.   I. Glaap, Albert-Reiner.
II. Althof, Rolf.

PS8163.067 1995   C812′ .5409   C95-950101-0
PR9191.5.067 1995

Contents

Presenting Authors and Their Work

Touching on Quebecois Drama

Introduction

Canada having become a model of a multicultural society, a mosaic of different ethnic groups, races and nationalities, it goes without saying that a pan-Canadian concept, an all-embracing metaphor as a yardstick to measure by what is "specifically Canadian" is now out of the question. Nationalism has given way to globalism. In this day and age, the variety of the Canadian mosaic finds its expression in a cultural and literary polyphony, and Canadian playwrights, like playwrights anywhere, write about issues relevant to human beings in general.

This publication addresses readers not only in Canada, but also in other English-speaking countries and in areas in which English is the second language spoken. It was put together primarily for those who have a great interest in, but do not know much about, English Canadian playwrights and their work. It sets out to provide contextual knowledge, focuses on some of the better known playwrights of the 1970s and 1980s, points out recent trends and thus mirrors stages in the development of Canadian drama. It is a panoramic view of what has been going on in the past thirty years and has led to the present state of Canadian drama. Its emphasis is on the playtexts and the playwrights, not on the most recent theatrical developments in very special fields or the grave funding problems for theatres in Canada. In this respect, *On-Stage and Off-Stage* is different from publications which have been written for readers who are familiar with both the development of Canadian Drama and the works of the most prominent playwrights. In other words, it is the "what" more than the "how" that this book is about, the plays as such and their context more than their theatricality and production aspects, which may be dealt with in another volume. The book does not aim to achieve anything complete. It goes without saying that more or other authors could have been considered. But *On-Stage and Off-Stage* tries to approach Canadian theatre and drama from the angle of those who are trying to become insiders or "outsiders inside" the field of Canadian drama and, for that reason, has had to moderate its needs.

On-Stage and Off-Stage is subdivided into four sections. Brief surveys of the development of Canadian drama from 1606 until 1949 and of the theatre in English-Canada after World War II are followed by a critical assessment, "Assigning Value and Place in Canadian Drama", in the first chapter of this volume. Native Drama, Women's Drama, Theatre for Young Audiences and drama in Newfoundland are subsumed under the heading of "Tracing Specific Developments" in the second section. The central chapter comprises thirteen essays on established and "up and coming" English Canadian playwrights with special emphasis on some of their plays. Although *On-Stage and Off-Stage* is a book on English Canadian drama, its concluding chapter ("Touching on Quebecois Drama") provides glimpses of playwriting in Quebec since 1980.

This book is a collaboration of two German editors, some twenty experts and a publishing house in Newfoundland. As yet, most of the experts on Canadian drama are Canadian scholars. No one outside Canada could and should ever pretend to "know it all." What the German editors of this book had in mind was to publish a collection of essays on the grounds of their knowledge of what has not been done but should be done in and outside Canada for those interested in getting basic information about English Canadian drama.

The first idea for this book came out of a number of questions: Why has Canadian Drama so far played hardly any role in the multi-faceted European theatrical life? Why do directors and dramaturges in the German-speaking countries know so little about David French, Michel Tremblay, George Walker, Tomson Highway or Judith Thompson, to name but a few of the great number of contemporary playwrights in Canada? Why, on the other hand, have Sam Shepard, David Mamet and other American dramatists become so popular over here? Albert-Reiner Glaap discussed these questions with artistic directors at German theatres, who, when being asked why they had never thought of putting on Canadian plays in their respective theatres, asked him in return:"Are there any?" That was at the turn of the decade, and it occurred to Glaap that something should be done to make Canadian plays known in the German-speaking countries.

Needless to say, a lack of knowledge about Canadian theatre in Europe before the early nineties was also due to the fact that this is a relatively young theatre. There had been theatrical activities in Canada before, but those were, until the 1970s, confined to either Canadian plays put on by Canadian amateurs or non-Canadian plays mounted by touring companies from Britain and the USA which staged whatever had gained popularity on Broadway in New York or Shaftesbury Avenue in London. What can be termed "professional Canadian theatre" came into being only after the 1967 Centennial.

Another reason for European theatre people's indifference to Canadian drama was, and partly still is, the great popularity of British plays in and outside Britain. "Plays in English" were almost exclusively "British plays", i.e. plays written by authors in Britain. Why should Canadian plays be of interest to European theatregoers—plays which are set in the prairies or in the fishing villages of Newfoundland or thematize the well-known stereotypes of Canada? Due to the fact that Canadian plays are hardly known, people who are interested in theatre in various European countries have never had a chance to find out that contemporary Canadian playwrights do not merely write about specifically Canadian, but also about universal topics.

In 1992, a collection of essays was published by Cornelsen in Düsseldorf (Germany) under the title of *Das englisch-kanadische Drama*. This book has paved the way for detailed research in German universities and has initiated activities in our theatres. For *On-Stage and Off-Stage*, a few articles, which—in the German edition—were meant to provide background information for those who were totally unfamiliar with theatrical life in Canada, have been taken out. Seven new essays on more recent achievements and plays have been written specially for this book.

We would like to express our sincere gratitude to our Canadian colleagues and friends who have kindly and most willingly contributed to the book and without whom this publication would not have been possible. Special thanks are due to the whole Breakwater crew and to Carla Kean in particular, for being such an untiring and painstakingly working "travelling companion." Last, but by no means least, we are indebted to the Canadian playwrights, who and whose works form the central part of *On-Stage and Off-Stage*. They are representatives of the many other dramatists all over Canada who have presented and are increasingly presenting us with their works. Apart from being eye-opening stage plays, these plays are windows on the Canadian world for those who endeavour to be more than "outsiders inside."

Recently, when Albert-Reiner Glaap asked a Canadian friend, a specialist in Canadian drama, what he considered to be specific features of Canadian drama as opposed to drama in other cultures, his answer was: "Certainly its subtle irony, which is self-depreciating, but also gentle; its quirkyness. A Canadian play with its quirky tilt at this or that makes people think. Most American plays don't have that."

A "Resource Guide to the Arts," entitled *Theatre in Canada* (Canada Communication Group, Ottawa: 1993, 2.) contains the following lines about Canadian theatre:

> However, at this time when theatre in Canada is faced with an economic crisis, it is being forced to re-evaluate what it has been, what it has become, and why it exists. This re-evaluation is undoubtedly leading to the formation of a more Canadian theatre—a theatre that is here because it reflects Canada and does not feel the need to look to the United States or overseas for hit plays and sense of values. To achieve this, we must build on what has happened in the past with our pioneering Canadian playwrights, actors and directors. But now the theatre must open its doors to include all Canadians and not remain the almost exclusively white, male-dominated profession of the past.

We, the editors of this book, would like to add that it is high time for Canadian theatre and drama to get the interest it deserves also of theatregoers in Europe and elsewhere. *On-Stage and Off-Stage* is trying to make a modest contribution to this undertaking.

A.-R.G./R.A.

Anton Wagner

"The Quintessence of Canadianism:" Canadian National Drama 1606-1949

"The soul of Canada—does the idea seem strange to you? Does it embarrass you to have it mentioned?" Robertson Davies asked in 1987 in the 100th anniversary issue of Canada's most important cultural magazine, *Saturday Night*.[1]

Davies, whose plays and novels are characterized by the exploration of the individual and national Canadian psyche, quickly affirmed that "I am convinced that Canada has a soul." "Can you seriously think," Davies queried, "that Canada, unlike every other country in the world, lacks an essence that is the outcome of the history it has undergone, the races who have lived in it, the unique land and climate that are its geographical being?"[2]

For much of the 20th century, Canadian painters, poets, playwrights and novelists have attempted both to characterize and to forge the Canadian individual and national "essence" through their art. When the Royal Commission on National Development in the Arts, Letters and Sciences, appointed in 1949 by Prime Minister Louis St. Laurent, issued its seminal *Report* in 1951, it noted the vital importance of the Canadian playwright in developing a distinct Canadian cultural life.

"The drama has been in the past, and may be again, not only the most striking symbol of a nation's culture," the Massey Commission stated, "but the central structure enshrining much that is finest in a nation's spiritual and artistic greatness."[3]

Reviewing a production of Robertson Davies' *Fortune, My Foe* in 1949, Herbert Whittaker declared in Canada's national newspaper, the *Globe and Mail*, that "without too much exaggeration, I think, one could label *Fortune, My Foe* as Canada's first national play."[4]

Whittaker justified that claim by pointing out that *Fortune* had been published the previous year, a rarity for Canadian drama until the early 1970s, that the play had already had half-a-dozen other productions, and that it was about to be produced outside of Canada, in Norway, a production the Canadian consulate in Oslo actively discouraged, believing that Davies' comedy reflected unfavourably on Canada's cultural development.

Above all, it was the content of *Fortune, My Foe* which marked the work as a truly national play. Through its dramatic situation in which a talented young professor must choose whether to remain in Canada or follow a brighter future in the United States, Davies' comedy probed Canada's national cultural identity, satirized English Canada's colonial attitudes toward Great Britain, and examined the role of the arts and education in Canadian society.

Herbert Whittaker's slight hesitation in proclaiming *Fortune* as Canada's *first* national play stemmed from his awareness that a considerable number of Canadian plays had been written and produced prior to 1949. The question remained, however, whether any of these pre-World War II Canadian plays and playwrights had made a lasting impression on the nation's cultural consciousness.

Lacking Whittaker's active participation in the Dominion Drama Festival in the 1930s, for example, the critic Nathan Cohen all too readily dismissed the Canadian pre-1945 amateur theatre movement. In a 1948 review, Cohen declared of Canada's first major twentieth century dramatist, "about two decades ago, the plays of Merrill Denison were widely hailed as representing the quintessence of Canadianism; today, only suffering students recollect them." [5]

In the 1920s, Merrill Denison (1893-1975) *had* been widely perceived as the leading Canadian dramatist. Lawren Harris, the most prominent member of the Group of Seven painters, called his 1923 play anthology *The Unheroic North* "the first authentic, entirely indigenous literary work done by a Canadian." [6] The editors of the 1924 *Highways of Canadian Literature* similarly perceived Denison's realistic and satirical plays as "a significant beginning of creative Stage Drama in Canada." [7]

Yet Denison was himself only one of a series of playwrights and directors in English and French Canada who had attempted to create an indigenous national theatre and drama. [8] For three-and-a-half centuries, beginning in colonial French Canada in the early 1600s, virtually insurmountable cultural and economic obstacles confronted these efforts to establish an indigenous theatre.

In Quebec, the Catholic church vehemently opposed the attendance at live theatre until well into the twentieth century. [9] Canada's sparse population, dispersed over a vast geographic area, made professional theatre production uneconomical for local companies. For over a century, beginning in the 1850s, the demand for live theatre in Canada's urban centres was largely satisfied by professional touring companies from Great Britain, the United States and France. The financial and artistic resources of these touring companies, with their star performers such as Sarah Bernhardt, Henry Irving and John Martin-Harvey, high production values and constantly changing repertoire, discouraged indigenous theatre activity from maturing beyond the amateur level.

Despite these obstacles, theatre historians nevertheless can point to a considerable number of plays which constitute a body of pre-1945 Canadian national dramatic literature. One of the first theatrical presentations in the New World, Marc Lescarbot's 1606 masque *Le Théâtre de Neptune en la Nouvelle France* (*The Theatre of Neptune in New France*), already dramatized a central theme developed by poets, novelists and playwrights two-and-a-half centuries later: the attempt to establish civilization in the immense, untamed North American wilderness.

Lescarbot (c. 1570-1642) resided only one year at Port Royal, Acadia (present day Lower Granville, Nova Scotia). Eight months after the staging of *The Theatre of Neptune* on November 14, 1606, the French colonists were forced to return to France, having lost their monopoly of the fur trade.

France was also the country of origin of French Canada's first major dramatist, Joseph Quesnel (1746-1809). Following his capture by the British off Nova Scotia in 1779 while transporting provisions and ammunition from Bordeaux to the American revolutionaries in New York, Quesnel was the first artist in Canada to create a body of work consisting of music, poetry and a variety of dramatic works.

The most popular of these was his opera comique *Colas et Colinette ou Le Bailli Dupé* (*Colas and Colinette or The Bailiff Confounded*), produced in 1790, 1805 and 1807. The first original dramatic composition published in Canada, in 1808, *Colas and Colinette* has been periodically revived since the early 1960s.

Of equal interest, because of their subject matter, are two of Quesnel's unproduced dramatic works. Written in 1800-1801, his farce *Les Républicains français ou La Soirée du cabaret* (*The French Republicans or an Evening at the Tavern*) bitterly satirized the excesses of the French Revolution. In a gentler vein, his comedy *l'Anglomanie ou le Dîner a l'anglaise* (*Anglomania or Dinner English Style*), written in 1802-1803 satirized the social pretensions of Quesnel's contemporaries prepared to reject French culture and traditions for the latest English fashions and customs of the ruling colonial government.

French-English conflict is also the focus of the historical drama *Le Jeune Latour (The Young Latour)* by Antoine Gérin-Lajoie (1824-1882) staged and published in 1844. Set during the British conquest of Acadia in 1629, *The Young Latour* dramatizes the French Canadian struggle to preserve the French language, culture and traditions from British political and cultural oppression. Produced only seven years after the French Canadian rebellion of 1837, Gérin-Lajoie's heroic portrayal of his central character made a strong impression on French Canadians whose memories of the 1837 uprising were still vivid.

That unsuccessful rebellion also provided the subject matter of several popular dramas by the poet Louis-Honoré Fréchette (1839-1908). His comic political melodrama *Felix Poutré*, dramatizing Poutré's escape from being hanged by the English following the rebellion—by feigning madness—became an immediate success after its première in 1862. The production of Fréchette's romantic melodrama about the leader of the 1837 uprising, *Papineau,* led him to be acclaimed in 1880 as the "Father of the national theatre" by the French Canadian press.

In these and other dramas such as *Jacques-Cartier ou le Canada vengé (Jacques-Cartier or Canada Revenged)* of 1879 by Joseph-Louis Archambault (1849-1925) or *Riel* by Elzéar Paquin (1850-1947), published only a year following the execution for treason of the Métis leader in 1885, nineteenth century French Canadian playwrights invoke the struggles of great historical and political figures to emphasize the need for continued political action to preserve their French culture and heritage.

Many of these plays cited, particularly those in the nineteenth century, contain elements of wish-fulfilment or themes of reconciliation between French and English Canada. These themes of reconciliation are frequently themselves composed of a synthesis of an envisioned ideal world, ultimately a free Quebec, and actual reality, the defeat of the 1837 rebellion and existing English political oppression which must be resisted.

In Fréchette's *Felix Poutré*, for example, the rebellion, though defeated, has been exalted. Through the heroism of individuals, ideals and a political alternative have been clearly presented which preserve the possibility for future action.

As in French Canada, dramatic sketches satirizing politicians and government corruption appeared frequently in the partisan press in English Canada from the end of the eighteenth century onwards.[10] But because they were not required to struggle for their own cultural survival, playwrights in nineteenth century English Canada could achieve public recognition for literary romantic and historical verse dramas with non-Canadian settings meant to be read rather than actually staged.

The most prominent of these writers and their works include Eliza Lanesford Cushing (1794-1886) and her romantic tragedy *The Fatal Ring* (1840); the biblical *Saul* (1857) by Charles Heavysege (1816-1876); and the poetical tragedies by William Wilfred Campbell (1858-1918) published at the end of the 1800s. For Campbell, as he states in the preface to his collected·*Poetical Tragedies* (1908), Shakespeare was "still the great dramatic poet of the modern world." Campbell asserted that his historical tragedies dealt with "those eternal problems of the human soul which all of the world's thinkers have had at heart."[11]

Only just prior to the confederation of French and English Canada in 1867 do plays with contemporary Canadian political themes appear on stage and in print in English Canada. The first of these were the political burlesques *Dolorsolatio* and *The King of the Beavers*, by the anonymous "Sam Scribble," staged by the Amateurs of the Garrison at the 2,000-seat Theatre Royal and published in Montreal in 1865.

Nicholas Flood Davin (1843-1901) published *The Fair Grit or The Advantages of Coalition*, a farce satirizing Prime Minister Mackenzie, party patronage and the partisan press, in 1876. Sarah Anne Curzon (1833-1898) also completed *Laura Secord, the Heroine of 1812* in 1876 but only saw her historical drama published in 1887 "owing to the inertness of Canadian interest in Canadian literature at that date."[12] *Tecumseh*, the verse drama about the great Indian leader opposing the Americans before the War of 1812, by Charles Mair (1838-1927), was published in 1886.

The most accomplished of all these nineteenth century political works is William Henry Fuller's *H.M.S. Parliament, or The Lady Who Loved a Government Clerk* staged and published in 1880. Based on Gilbert and Sullivan's popular *H.M.S. Pinafore, or The Lass that Loved a Sailor*, *H.M.S. Parliament* satirized the Conservative government's protectionist economic National Policy, Prime Minister John A. Macdonald, government bureaucracy, patronage and political opportunism. Premièred at Montreal's 1,800-seat Academy of Music on February 16, 1880, *H.M.S. Parliament* was toured by the E.A. McDowell Comedy Company to thirty Canadian cities in Quebec, Ontario, Nova Scotia, New Brunswick and as far as Winnipeg, Manitoba, then the longest professional theatre tour ever undertaken in Canada.

While a number of other Canadian plays received amateur and professional productions at the end of the nineteenth century, it was primarily the Little Theatre movement in the 1920s and the Dominion Drama Festival in the 1930s which stimulated indigenous playwriting and play production on a nation-wide level. These movements were in part themselves the result of an increasing national consciousness and cultural nationalism which began to make itself felt at the beginning of the century.

The critic Fred Jacob, in his June 1914 *Canadian Magazine* essay "Waiting for a Dramatist," for example, declared that Canada's literary and cultural development was being retarded by the lack of indigenous dramatic writing. Jacob noted that while Canadian prose writers were beginning to gain reputations on an international level, "Canada still lacks a dramatist, and it will not be possible for us to claim that our self-expression is complete until some aspect of the life of the nation has been placed behind the footlights."[13]

Roy Mitchell, the first artistic director of the University of Toronto's Hart House Theatre, the most important of the Canadian Little Theatres, similarly called on Canadians to create their own meaningful dramas and theatre art instead of relying on commercial theatre productions touring from the United States. "The most ancient principle of the arts is that it is better to use what you have, to build with native stone, to carve in native woods.... Art is a native growth which, to be strong, must arise generation by generation from the soil of its own people," Mitchell declared in his *Creative Theatre* published in 1929.[14]

Merrill Denison was the most important playwright produced at Hart House Theatre in the 1920s. Already in his first play, the one-act comedy *Brothers in Arms* (1921), Denison satirized the over-romanticized depictions of the Canadian north and backwoodsmen popular in fiction and Hollywood film treatments. Yet while Denison was debunking the search for "romance in the land of Robert Service and Ralph Connor," with the dramas of his *The Unheroic North,* the Group of Seven painters and their supporters (a number of them leading figures in the Canadian theosophist movement) were recreating a new romantic perception of the Canadian landscape and its influence on its inhabitants.

For artists such as Lawren Harris, Arthur Lismer, Bertram Brooker and Roy Mitchell, ultimate reality was not to be found in Denison's quasi-realistic depictions of every-day life but in a more spiritual, metaphysical existence which could be evoked through stylization, abstractionism and mysticism. Central to their theosophic beliefs was the conviction of the paramount influence of the natural environment, particularly the "spiritual austerity"[15] of the Canadian north, as a stimulus to artistic creativity and a national consciousness which would not be narrowly parochial but which would be based on, and embody, universal experiences.

The non-realistic stylization, idealism and cultural nationalism of the Group of Seven directly influenced Herman Voaden (1903-1991), the most important Canadian playwright in the 1930s. Already in 1929-1930, Voaden organized a competition for one-act plays requiring an exterior northern setting and a mood or subject matter suggested by Canadian paintings. The aim of the playwriting competition was to stimulate interest "in the creation of a Canadian Drama and Art of the Theatre."[16]

In his Introduction to *Six Canadian Plays*, published in 1930, Voaden defined his concept of the distinct Canadian national theatre he would attempt to establish until the early 1940s. "By a Canadian 'Art of the Theatre' we mean a tradition in the staging of plays that will be an expression of the atmosphere and character of our land as definite as our native-born painting and sculpture," Voaden stated and went on to say:

> we shall have a new theatre art and drama here that will be an effective revelation of our own vision and character as a people...the vision and beauty of a new people in a new land.[17]

Voaden's own multi-media "symphonic expressionism," a striking combination of realistic, poetic and choral speech, music, lighting, dance and non-realistic movement and set design, ultimately was technically too complex and too mystical to establish itself as a national dramatic form. Though not published until after the mid-1970s, Voaden's symphonic expressionist dramas such as *Rocks* and *Earth Song* (1932), *Hill-Land* (1934), *Murder Pattern* (1936) and *Ascend As the Sun* (1942) nevertheless constitute an important contribution to Canadian experimental theatre and national drama.

While the amateur pre-World War II theatre movement did not enable playwrights to make an actual living from their stage writing, a number of talented dramatists did gain sufficient experience to establish themselves as major figures after 1945. The most prominent of these playwrights and works include Gwen Pharis Ringwood (1910-1984), whose *Still Stands the House* (1938), *The Rainmaker* and *Dark Harvest* (1945) vividly depict the struggle of men and women with nature on the Canadian Prairie; Elsie Park-Gowan (1905—), another Albertan dramatist whose comedy about war and peace, *The Last Caveman*, was toured by Sidney Risk's Everyman Theatre to seventy-five towns from Vancouver to Winnipeg in 1946-1947; and John Coulter (1888-1980), already an established writer in Ireland before coming to Canada in 1936, whose historical drama *Riel*, staged by the New Play Society in 1950, again dramatized the tragic death of the Métis leader in 1885.

A major bridge between the pre-World War II amateur and post-1945 professional theatre was the Canadian Broadcasting Corporation (CBC) which provided intermittent employment for hundreds of actors, playwrights and production personnel. Over one hundred original plays were produced by CBC Radio in 1937 and over three hundred in 1948. Throughout the 1940s, the CBC served as Canada's national "theatre on the air" and revealed the extent of indigenous creativity which could be developed with government financial support.

Radio also helped launch Quebec's first major post-World War II actor, director and dramatist, Gratien Gélinas (1909—). His comic character Fridolin was heard on radio from 1937 to 1941 and seen on stage at the 1,400-seat Monument National in annual satirical "Fridolinons" revues from 1938 to 1946. Through his immensely popular Montreal working class street-urchin character, dressed in suspender-hung short pants, loose socks, old sneakers and ragged Canadien hockey club sweater, Gélinas was able to explore both the comic and sometimes tragic aspects of the Québécois condition.

Out of the 1945 and 1946 Fridolinons sketches "The Conscript's Departure" and "The Conscript's Return," Gélinas developed his full-length drama *Tit-Coq* about the unsuccessful attempt of an illegitimate soldier to win the family and love he has never possessed. The première of the drama, at the Monument National on May 22, 1948, was critically acclaimed as the beginning of a national theatre in French Canada. An unprecedented audience of over 400,000 saw the French and English productions of *Tit-Coq* in Montreal and on tour in Canada and the United States.

Gélinas has himself remarked that there are many ways of using a stage to convey national sentiment but that "sentiment alone will not create a body of literature, a theatre. A literature expresses a nation which has found its personality."[18] Gélinas' own dramas and those of his successors such as Marcel Dubé (1930—) and Michel Tremblay (1942—) in Quebec and James Reaney (1926—) and David French (1939—) in English-Canada attempt to deliniate the individual and national psyche through dramatizations of family members in conflict with one another and their society.

When that Québécois and Canadian "essence" became more clearly established, and the new wave of national sentiment of the late 1960s began to ebb, playwrights such as George Walker (1947—) and René-Daniel Dubois (1955—) were once again free, like the poetic dramatists of the nineteenth century, to set their works in exotic non-Canadian settings and to dramatize "those eternal problems of the human soul which all of the world's thinkers have had at heart."[19]

NOTES

[1] Robertson Davies, "Keeping Faith," in *Saturday Night*, 102, 1 (January 1987), 187.

[2] Ibid.

[3] Royal Commission on National Development in the Arts, Letters and Sciences 1949-1951, *Report*, Ottawa: King's Printer, 1951, 193.

[4] Herbert Whittaker, "Fortune, My Foe," in *Globe and Mail*, November 28, 1949. Reprinted in Ronald Bryden with Boyd Neil (eds.), *Whittaker's Theatre: A Critic Looks at Stages in Canada and Thereabouts 1944-1975*, Greenbank, Ontario: The Whittaker Project, 1985, 17.

[5] Cited in Wayne E. Edmonstone, *Nathan Cohen: The Making of a Critic*, Toronto: Lester and Orpen, 1977, 98.

[6] Lawren Harris, "Winning a Canadian Background," in *Canadian Bookman*, 5 (February 1923). Denison's most important work in the anthology was the starkly naturalistic drama *Marsh Hay*, not produced until 1974.

[7] J.D. Logan and Donald G. French, *Highways of Canadian Literature*, Toronto: McClelland and Stewart, 1924, 336.

[8] A greater awareness and analysis of the achievements of these artists began to emerge only in the mid-1970s with the founding of the Association for Canadian Theatre History and the Association d'histoire du théâtre du Québec in 1976; book-length histories such as Murray D. Edwards' *A Stage in Our Past: English-language Theatre in Eastern Canada from the 1790s to 1914*, Toronto: University of Toronto Press, 1968, *Le Théâtre canadien-français: évolution, témoignages, bibliographie*, Montreal: Fides, 1976; and the journals *Canadian Theatre Review* (1974—), *Canadian Drama/L'Art dramatique canadien* (1975-1990) and *cahiers de theatre Jeu* (1976—).

[9] See Jean Laflamme and Rémi Tourangeau, *L'Église et le théâtre au Quebec*, Montreal: Fides, 1979.

[10] For a discussion of this genre of "paradrama" in English and French Canada, see Leonard E. Doucette, *Theatre in French Canada: Laying the Foundations 1606-1867*, Toronto: University of Toronto Press, 1984 and Mary Elizabeth Smith, "Three Political Dramas from New Brunswick," in *Canadian Drama/L'Art dramatique canadien*, 12, 1, 1986.

[11] Wilfred Campbell, *Poetical Tragedies*, Toronto: William Briggs, 1908, 5.

[12] Sarah Anne Curzon, Preface to her *Laura Secord, The Heroine of 1812 and Other Poems*. Toronto: C. Blackett Robinson, 1887, 3.

[13] Fred Jacob, "Waiting for a Dramatist," in *Canadian Magazine*, 43, (June 1914), 142.

[14] Roy Mitchell, *Creative Theatre*, New York: John Day, 1929. Reprinted Westwood, New Jersey: Kindle Press, 1969, 143, 183.

[15] "Introduction," in Herman Voaden (ed.), *Six Canadian Plays*, Toronto: Copp Clark, 1930, xv.

[16] Ibid.

[17] Ibid. xxi, xxiv. Voaden's Introduction is reprinted as "Towards a Canadian Drama: A View From the Thirties," in *Canadian Theatre Review*, 28 (Fall 1980). See also Anton Wagner (ed.), *A Vision of Canada: Herman Voaden's Dramatic Works 1928-1945.* Toronto: Simon & Pierre, 1993.

[18] Laurence Sabbath, "Gratien Gélinas Speaks Out on Canadian Playwrights," in *Performing Arts in Canada*, 2 (Summer 1963), 27.

[19] Campbell, *Poetical Tragedies.*

Don Rubin

Creeping Toward a Culture:
The Theatre in English Canada after World War II

It was the nineteenth century French critic, Ferdinand Brunetiere, who first spoke of the fascinating relationship between periods of intense nationalism and periods in which one could say that a nation's drama takes some bold steps toward maturity. Utilizing in his 1894 essay, *The Law of the Drama*, that keyword of nineteenth century thought—Will—and identifying Will with the movement toward national selfhood, Brunetiere pointed out that:

> it is always at the exact moment of its national existence when the Will of a great people is exalted within itself, that we see its dramatic art reach also the highest point of its development, and produce its masterpieces. Greek tragedy is contemporary with the Persian wars.... Consider the Spanish theatre: Cervantes, Lope de Vega, Calderón belong to the time when Spain was extending over all of Europe, as well as over the New World, the domination of her Will.... And France in the seventeenth century? The greatest struggle that our fathers made to maintain the unity of the French nation was at the end of the sixteenth century.... The development of the theatre followed immediately.... I do not see a dramatic renaissance whose dawn has not been announced, as it were, by some progress, or some arousing of the Will.[1]

If one can accept Brunetiere's theory—and it does seem quite defensible (one could easily add the emergence of theatre in the United States which only occurred after the recognition of American selfhood following World War I)—one may just have a significant reference point for recognizing, understanding and assessing the impressive development of theatre in Canada in the first four decades following World War II.

I think most of those working in fields of Canadian social history would be willing to accept World War II as a starting point for purposes of identifying the roots of Canada's cultural nationalism of the late 1960s

---

and 1970s, a period quite extraordinary in its long-term impact and a period quite unlike any that had come before. This is not to suggest in any way that periods of Canadian nationalism (cultural, economic or political) had not existed before the 1960s nor is it to suggest that its roots really only begin in the 1940s. Studies are now being undertaken in Canadian scholarship which show clearly that these movements have a long, though not particularly glorious, history in the country. Because Canadian cultural nationalism of the 1960s and 1970s has been so significant, however, this discussion will limit itself primarily to the period since World War II. Certainly there was a national realization in the decades after the war that Canada did have some viable social, economic and cultural role to play in the world at large.

In attempting to determine some of the causes for this change, one could speak, of course, of the Canadian experience during the war itself when more Canadian men than ever before in the country's history found themselves in Europe, found themselves dealing with cultures that were either not easily recognizable to them or cultures in which they simply did not feel comfortable. Home, for these men, suddenly became more than just the place where one started from. Perhaps for the first time in Canadian experience, the soldiers and statesmen of that generation realized that they were not just displaced or second-rank Britishers or Frenchmen but that they were individuals with their own traditions, their own customs and, perhaps even more crucial, their own history. Colonialism dies hard, but clearly a colonial mentality takes even longer to dissipate. It was certainly on the battlefields of Europe that popular Canadian attitudes toward national self-esteem and self-awareness began to transform. It was through the Canadian troop shows that these men learned the simplest of lessons: even the subjects of their laughter were somehow different than those around them. Suffice it to say here, the war experience, the impact of that experience in homes from Atlantic to Pacific Canada and the new awareness of "being Canadian" laid the groundwork for a series of developments that would have the profoundest effect on Canadian cultural growth in the decades to come.

It was in the wake of this new Canadian awareness that Prime Minister Louis St. Laurent put forward to his Privy Council in 1949 a recommendation suggesting the formation of a Royal Commission. The Commission's job would be to examine national development in the arts, letters and sciences and make recommendations as to how the government could best encourage organizations in these fields "which express national feeling, promote common understanding and add to the variety and richness of Canadian life, rural as well as urban."[2]

Created that same year, this Royal Commission, headed by University of Toronto Chancellor Vincent Massey, travelled nearly 10,000 miles, held 224 meetings (114 of which were public), received 462 briefs and heard 1,200 witnesses in the course of its two-year study. Included were submissions from thirteen federal institutions, seven provincial governments, eighty-seven national organizations, 262 local groups and thirty-five commercial radio stations. A Nootka Indian, it was even pointed out, travelled 125 miles to tell them about the vanishing art of his race and suggested ways for keeping that art alive.

What the Commission ultimately recognized after hearing the same nationalistic cries over and over again was that Canada was fast becoming an empty shell. While it had managed to retain its own government, its own leaders and its own buildings through the years, there was precious little that could be called Canadian in many of those people, and precious little that could be called Canadian inhabiting those buildings. Canada, the *Report of the Royal Commission on National Development in the Arts, Letters and Sciences* suggested, was losing its culture, its arts, its artists and its scholars to its friendly neighbour to the south.

> From these influences, pervasive and friendly as they are, much that is valuable has come to us: gifts of money spent in Canada, grants offered to Canadians for study abroad, the free enjoyment of all the facilities of many institutions which we cannot afford, and the importation of many valuable things which we could not easily produce for ourselves. We have gained much. In this preliminary stock-taking of Canadian cultural life it may be fair to inquire whether we have gained a little too much.[3]

The Commissioners went on to point out that "our use of American institutions, or our lazy, even abject, imitation of them has caused an uncritical acceptance of ideas and assumptions which are alien to our tradition. But for American hospitality we might, in Canada, have been led to develop educational ideas and practices more in keeping with our own way of life."[4] Only a few pages later, they make the statement even stronger:

> a vast and disproportionate amount of material coming from a single alien source may stifle rather than stimulate our own creative effort; and passively accepted without any standard of comparison, this may weaken critical faculties. We are now spending millions to maintain a national independence which would be nothing but an empty shell without a vigorous and distinctive cultural life. We have seen that we have its elements in our traditions and in our history; we have made important progress, often aided by American generosity. We must not be blind, however, to the very present danger of permanent dependence.[5]

The final report of the Royal Commission was submitted to the Governor General in May of 1951 and was accepted by the government.

Not only was it accepted, it was distributed widely, it was read widely and, when Vincent Massey himself was soon after named the new Governor General of Canada, it became impossible for the government to ignore. Within six years, its most crucial recommendation was implemented:

> That a body be created to be known as the Canada Council for the Encouragement of the Arts, Letters, Humanities and Social Sciences to stimulate and to help voluntary organizations within these fields, and to foster Canada's cultural relations abroad.[6]

As for the Commission's specific comments on the state of Canadian theatrical art, comments based on a special report done for the Commissioners by Robertson Davies, it was pointed out that Canada was not deficient in theatrical talent,

> whether in writing for the stage, in producing or in acting; but this talent at present finds little encouragement and no outlet apart from the Canadian Broadcasting Corporation.... Facilities for advanced training in the arts of theatre are non-existent in Canada.... Professional theatre is moribund in Canada, and amateur companies are grievously handicapped through lack of suitable or of any playhouses.[7]

But, the Commission went on to say, from the evidence it was clear "that there is in Canada a genuine desire for the drama."[8]

> We have been repeatedly informed that the theatre could be revived if only federal subsidies could be secured for the erection of suitable playhouses throughout Canada and for parts of travelling expenses of Canadian professional companies.[9]

Continuing in this vein, it was further noted that the writing of plays in Canada "has lagged far behind the other literary arts...because of our penury of theatrical companies; these are few in number for lack of playhouses."[10]

The Massey Commission Report clearly becomes the first key to understanding the rapid rise of Canadian arts and arts organizations in the period following World War II. It is the major precipitating factor in the creation of the Canada Council which, in its turn, was to become the prime mover of arts organizations. And the prime task for the Council, the task it saw as most necessary at the time, was the construction of a chain of buildings strung out across the vast expanse of the country in which to house "culture."

For the record, the Canada Council was established by a government act in 1957 "to foster and promote the study and enjoyment of and the production of works in the arts, humanities and social sciences." Financed exclusively in those early years from death duties on the estates of two millionaires—Sir James Dunn and Izaak Walton Killam—the Council found itself in that first year with some $100 million.

Of this sum, roughly half was to be used for capital and building grants to Canadian universities; the remaining $50 million—or, more precisely, the interest that could be generated on that $50 million (approximately $2.6 million)—was to be used for grants to companies in the literary, visual and performing arts as well as to individual scholars and artists.

By 1970, the Council's budget—now assisted heavily by annual grants from the federal government—had risen to $32 million. Grants, in its first fourteen years of existence, had totalled some $104 million of which $60 million had gone to arts groups and individuals.

By 1985—with the arts and scholarly wings now separated into two separate organizations (the Canada Council for the former, and the Social Science and Humanities Research Council for the latter)—the Canada Council budget had reached $98 million with $16 million of that going into professional theatre activities alone.

In 1969, Canada's leading drama critic, Nathan Cohen of the *Toronto Star*, pointed out that

> nearly all of the professional theatres we now have in Canada have come into existence since the Canada Council was established—regional theatres in Winnipeg, Edmonton, Calgary, Vancouver, Fredericton and Halifax...the Shaw Festival, the Charlottetown Festival and Toronto Workshop Productions to name just a few of them.[11]

Cohen went on to point out that these theatres were not actually created by the Council (although a few did receive Council funding prior to beginning operations including Theatre Toronto, the St. Lawrence Centre in Toronto, the Neptune Theatre in Halifax and the Lennoxville Festival in Quebec). Rather, his point was that "conditions appeared in which serious theatre projects have been able, by and large, to obtain help from the Council for their continuation."[12]

Left out of this discussion so far—and just as important as the Massey Commission Report and the formation of the Canada Council as an influence on the long-term development of theatre in Canada during this period—was the establishment of the Stratford Festival in 1952-1953. Created by local Stratford businessman Tom Patterson with the help of innumerable theatre people in Canada and abroad (most notably, Sir Tyrone Guthrie), the impact of the Stratford Festival on Canada's emerging national theatre identity was staggering indeed. Begun as a summer festival producing only the works of Shakespeare, the Festival's first season attracted attention from across North America and Europe (thanks primarily to the presence of Guthrie, Alec Guinness and Irene Worth).

The first season began in mid-July of 1953 in a canvas tent and consisted of two plays—*Richard III* and *All's Well That Ends Well*—which ran for six weeks, attracted some 68,000 people and cost $157,000. The Festival today has three stages—an extraordinary 2,300 seat quasi-Elizabethan mainstage; a 1,200 seat proscenium house in downtown Stratford called the Avon; and a convertible space now called the Tom Patterson Theatre which began operation in 1971 in what was formerly a Badminton Club. Playing an eight-month season and operating virtually year-round, in 1987, Stratford drew an audience of 440,000 and brought in $9.5 million at the box office on a total budget of just over $14.5 million. Canada Council support for Stratford alone in 1986 amounted to $900,000.

Indeed, so significant had Stratford's cultural and economic impact become by the early seventies, there were those calling for the theatre to be subsidized not by the Canada Council, but by the Ministry of Tourism which was, in fact, already making grants to the Festival. The argument was that if the Canada Council ever had to cut Stratford's budget for either economic reasons or to find funds for other theatres, the city of Stratford would itself suffer severe economic ramifications (a situation that almost came to pass in 1981 when the Festival nearly closed down over its refusal to hire a Canadian artistic director). Yet Stratford—despite discomfort with its role as assumed leader in the development of a uniquely Canadian culture—has continued on through the years providing the Canadian theatre with, at the very least, a classical production standard second to none in the world.

As Nathan Cohen described this tripartite development of Canadian theatre since 1949:

> The Massey Report set down as a cardinal principle that the arts are a matter of governmental concern and by so doing, it fundamentally changed the government philosophy on the subject.... The Stratford Festival came along two years later to prove the Massey Report's point.... The Stratford Festival became the status symbol among opinion makers and intellectuals in Canada of the uses to which the arts could be put to give Canada an independent identity at home and abroad.... The establishment of the Canada Council followed inevitably from these events.[13]

Suddenly Canada had a theatre. Suddenly the government was in the theatre business. Suddenly major cities across the country were producing the classic plays from world dramatic literature with professional companies. Actors were being developed, technicians were being trained, designers were slowly appearing and very, very gradually Canadian directors were emerging. Even newspapers began hiring full-time theatre critics. Both Herbert Whittaker of the Toronto *Globe and Mail* and Nathan Cohen of the Toronto *Star*, began travelling widely at this time to report on developments beyond Canada's largest English-speaking city. By the late 1970s, the Southam newspaper chain had hired Jamie Portman of Calgary to do nothing *but* travel as Canada's first full-time itinerant arts reporter, commentator and theatre critic. Suddenly Canadians had an alternative to the second-rate touring companies which had been sent through a handful of major cities for so many years. And suddenly too, Canada had a fully-professional alternative to the innumerable amateur or pick-up professional companies which had struggled so bravely across the country in the pre-Canada Council years, companies which had for so long provided the country with its only real claim to indigenous theatre.[14]

By 1967—the celebration of the nation's Centennial—it had become apparent that Canada had a theatre in its midst. And for the first time in the history of professional theatre in Canada, it also was beginning to develop an infra-structure of some significance (I am thinking primarily of the Canadian Theatre Centre, established in 1956, a national communications organization linked to UNESCO's International Theatre Institute). The only question existing by this time, though, was one of that theatre's social, political and cultural identity: most of the theatre being produced in Canada was not Canadian. That is to say, it was not a theatre *of* Canada but merely one which existed *in* Canada.

The element that was obviously missing was the playwright, the writer who could speak clearly, firmly, intelligently and, perhaps most of all, passionately about the soul of the Canadian people who, after a hundred bizarre years, still found themselves together as a nation.

Critic Anton Wagner has written of the attempts to create a native drama prior to the Centennial in a series of volumes called *Canada's Lost Plays*. In that series, he identified a great number of playwrights who wrote from their own experiences in Canada. Among them, nineteenth century dramatists such as Nicholas Flood Davin (*The Fair Grit*, 1876), Sarah Anne Curzon (*Laura Secord*, 1876, and *The Sweet Girl Graduate*, 1882), William Henry Fuller (*H.M.S. Parliament*, 1880), and J.N. McIlwraith (*Ptarmigan*, 1895), and twentieth century dramatists such as Merrill Denison (*The Weather Breeder*, 1923), Herman Voaden (*Murder Pattern*, 1936), John Coulter (*The House in the Quiet Glen*, 1937), Gwen Pharis Ringwood (*Pasque Flower*, 1939, and *The Rainmaker*, 1945) and Robertson Davies (*Hope Deferred*, 1948). These were Canada's true play-writing pioneers and a national debt is owed to every one of them.

Unfortunately, virtually all of these writers were working in styles that had been developed elsewhere. As a result, their plays— with only a few exceptions—were depressingly derivative and dramatically dubious.[15] The few Canadian plays which did have wide commercial success actually achieved their fame in other countries, plays such as Mazo de la Roche's *Whiteoaks*, Brian Doherty's *Father Malachy's Miracle* and Patricia Joudry's *Teach Me How To Cry*.

This, of course, leads us back to the original question of national awareness and identity. It should have become clear by now that the Canadian identity—in theatre and otherwise—was, through this period and up to about 1967, essentially a colonial one, an identification with the founding countries (England and France) or, through an economic umbilical, to the United States. In each case, such identification dwarfed the less confident Canadian giant.

But I would suggest that when Canada and, in particular Montreal (French-language Canada achieved its cultural identity some years earlier) took upon its shoulders the burden of a World's Fair (Expo '67) at the same time that England and France were mired in national economic difficulties and the U.S. was having its world image tarnished by the shattering war in Vietnam, the seeds of national introspection as well as of national extroversion that had been sown less than two decades earlier began to grow.

I remember at that time attending a lecture at York University by one of the growing number of Canadian nationalists then appearing on the scene, Prof. Robin Matthews of Carleton University. I don't remember much about Matthew's lecture but I do recall that after his very persuasive arguments about the need for Canadians to be themselves and to speak with their own voices, he asked for questions. A student raised her hand and began by telling Matthews that she appreciated his comments very much but she didn't really understand them. "You tell me," she said, "that I am unique as a Canadian student. That I'm special, different. But I have to tell you that I don't feel different, Prof. Matthews. I believe that my problems and my needs and my concerns are essentially the same as students' in many parts of the world. I don't believe that I am really different than a French student or an American student or a British student. What makes me so unique?"

Matthews paused at this point and smiled. I remember the answer he gave and I've used it myself in the years since. "A French student," he said, "would never in a million years think he was the same as a British student. And a British student, would certainly never think he was the same as an American. And an American would never believe he was the same as a Canadian. Only you, only the Canadian thinks he's the same as everyone else. Start there." he said. "That perception alone makes you different than every other student in the world. That makes you unique." The student, I think was stunned by the logic of the answer, and the audience applauded wildly. For many of them that answer was enough.

It was Jean-Paul Sartre who once said that sometimes it is just as important to define yourself by what you are not as by what you are. Clearly, as Matthews suggested, the task of cultural and national self-definition in Canada would still be a negative one for a time. But self-definition—particularly in the cultural field—had clearly begun, led by the Massey Report, followed quickly by the creation of the Stratford Festival and the Canada Council, nurtured through the sixties and emerging finally during Canada's Centennial celebrations. It was essentially these elements which set the political and social stage for the cultural awareness and self-pride which characterized Canadian life in the seventies and early eighties and which has given Canadians since that time a clear sense that if they have something to say—in the performing arts, literature, radio, film or television—they will be heard.

It was these elements, too, which created the climate for a whole new generation to emerge of much more aggressive and militant artists than had ever before been seen in Canada. Among the key playwrights whose careers can be traced to and, indeed, through this unprecedented period of self-awareness are such names as George Ryga, John Herbert, David Freeman, Michael Cook, David French, Beverly Simons, James Reaney, David Fennario, Sharon Pollock, and George F. Walker to name just a few. And those who followed—writers such as Tomson Highway, Judith Thompson and Brad Fraser—have gone even further to assure audiences that self-awareness and self-expression, when celebrated in the lives of native people, women and those choosing to live alternative lifestyles, will never again be ignored in Canada.

Once upon a time, Canadian critics thought the goal of such theatrical ferment was to bring into being a Golden Age of Canadian Drama but such a notion no longer seems to have relevance. Indeed, language itself—the traditional root of dramatic literature—is giving way in the theatre to theatrical-ism and the whole notion of text and performance as independent elements in a balanced equation is coming more and more into question. Theatre is obviously becoming more filmic, more visually-oriented, with each new generation and Canada's contemporary artists—like so many others in the world—are assaulting the borders between theatre and the various forms of the visual arts daily. It grows increasingly unlikely therefore that Canada's theatrical history will ever produce a Sophocles, a Shakespeare, a Molière or a Calderón. In any event, that no longer seems the goal.

As for the forty years under discussion—years when Canada went from a colonial to a post-colonial society, years when its artists made the move from an essentially nineteenth century culture to a post-modern culture, years when cultural maturity was to a very great extent forced upon the country by a series of circumstances which will be analyzed for decades to come—one is forced to conclude simply that these years were extraordinary and that they did indeed produce a few important works which helped to illuminate a rather large corner of the world at a rather fascinating period of time in its history.

NOTES

[1] Ferdinand Brunetiere, "The Law of the Drama," in Barrett Clark's *European Theories of the Drama*, New York: Crown, 1918; newly-revised edition edited by Henry Popkin, 1965, 384-385.

[2] *Report of the Royal Commission on National Development in the Arts, Letters and Sciences*, 1949-1951, Ottawa, xi.

[3] Ibid., 13.

[4] Ibid., 15-16.

[5] Ibid., 18.

[6] Ibid., 377.

[7] Ibid., 195.

[8] Ibid., 195.

[9] Ibid., 197.

[10] Ibid., 196.

[11] Nathan Cohen, notes from a lecture given at York University, Toronto, December 2, 1969.

[12] Ibid.

[13] Ibid.

[14] The impact of non-professional companies, and especially the impact of the Dominion Drama Festival, during this period cannot be minimized, but since this essay is primarily concerned with the growth and development of professional theatre, the non-professionals, as important as they are, must be left out. An important book on the role of the amateur movement at this time is Betty Lee's *Love and Whiskey*, Toronto: Simon and Pierre, 1982.

[15] It might be noted here that Barrett Clark, the revered American dramatic scholar, had published a list of "major" Canadian dramatists as early as 1928 in his book, *A study of Modern Drama*, New York: Appleton, 466. Among the Canadian dramatists mentioned are Merrill Denison, Fred Jacobs, Isabel Ecclestone Mackay, Duncan Scott, Marion Osborne, H. Borsook, Britton Cooke, Carroll Aikins, L.A. MacKay, Leslie Reid, Mazo de la Roche, Lyon Sharman, T.M. Morrow, and a gentleman named Merton Stafford Threlfall. It would appear that Clark had culled his list almost directly from authors included in the following volumes published in the twenties—*Canadian Plays from Hart House Theatre* edited by Vincent Massey in two volumes, Toronto: Macmillan of Canada, 1927 and *One Act Plays by Canadian Authors*, Montreal: Canadian Author's Association, 1926.

Alan Filewod

Critical Mass:
Assigning Value and Place in Canadian Drama

I. "A Pious Aspiration"

In an important but now generally forgotten essay written in 1922 entitled "The Prospects of a Canadian Drama," Vincent Massey made the point that:

> It is, of course, almost as easy to be witty about the Canadian drama as about the Canadian navy. They each, at the moment, seem to represent a well-meaning but rather insignificant effort to complete our national equipment—to suggest a pious aspiration rather than reality. The Canadian drama, as a matter of fact, at present represents no more than twelve or fifteen produced plays. On this slender foundation, what can be built? The inquiry has all the romance of an uncharted voyage into unknown seas. (Massey 197)

Massey argued that a canon of Canadian dramatic literature would only develop as the corollary of a "Canadian free theatre"—free of commercialism and free of the New York syndicates that controlled most Canadian playhouses. This was a conviction he carried through his subsequent diplomatic career; three decades later it would be a cornerstone of his arguments in favour of public funding in the arts when he was appointed to head a royal commission on cultural policy. The result of that commission was of course the Canada Council and the subsequent renaissance in Canadian theatre.

Massey was keenly aware that there must be such a thing as "Canadian Drama" but he had trouble defining it. Like many critics of the day, he believed that a nation is known by its literature, and drama, he believed, is "the highest and most difficult" of the literary forms. (195) Massey foresaw the canon as an instrument of national culture which expresses and distils the essential qualities of the national psyche. The nation is the condition of the drama; the drama is the proof of the nation.

Having established that drama is a necessary attribute of national culture, and that a dramatic literature proceeds from a lively and committed theatre, Massey posed his key question, which in the end he was unable to answer:

> Now to turn to a more difficult subject: the materials of a Canadian drama. What are its essentials? Must the plays be by a Canadian? Must they be about Canada? They must surely have something more than Canadian authorship. (206)

Keenly aware that the drama he spoke of was still an "aspiration," Massey answered his own question with a proposition that was more accurate than he might have thought:

> We shall find, however—indeed we know it already—that Canada is a unit only in a political sense—otherwise it is still a magnificent abstraction. In the elements out of which drama is made—manners and social customs and atmosphere—there are several Canadas, for a country so scattered geographically, and composed of so many types, diversified in their origin, is bound always to reveal great provincial divisions. (207)

Nevertheless, he wrote, "It would be comforting, of course, to feel that whatever the diversities of material, a characteristic feeling, manner or style was possible that could be called Canadian." In the seventy years since Massey proposed diversity as the condition of the future drama, we have seen this pious aspiration more than fulfilled, in large part because of the policies his royal commission proposed to the government in 1951. Not only are the plays more diverse than Massey could have foreseen, but so, too, are the Canadas they reflect. Massey's central questions remain valid: what is Canadian about Canadian drama? Does Canadian drama prove the existence of a Canadian national culture? In one important sense, one of Massey's fundamental convictions has been disproved by history. "True Canadianism," he maintained, would emerge from the "common cultivation of the things of the mind" by English and French speaking Canadians. In literature and the arts, the two linguistic cultures have effectively separated into distinct national communities; when we speak of Canadian culture today, we refer to English Canadian vis a vis Quebecois.

No-one can say with certainty how many new plays are produced by English Canadian theatres every year. In 1989, the last year for which figures are available, the Canada on Stage project listed the activities of some 350 theatre companies, a figure which the editor admits may be conservative because it includes only those companies the project could identify and record. Many Canadian theatre companies are "one-off" troupes performing in fringe festivals and play development programs and consequently their activities go unnoticed by the critical press. But the figure of 350 companies suggests that an estimate of perhaps 1,000 new Canadian plays every year may be valid.

Of the approximately 1,000 new plays produced by Canadian theatre artists in a year, a small number find productions in subsidized theatres with union (Equity) actors. In all, perhaps five to ten percent of them go on to second productions. It is a dispiriting irony that a play which receives productions in three or four theatres across Canada, and which, after years of preparation, earns the playwright two or three thousand dollars, is considered a hit.

Of these thousand plays performed in a given year, perhaps fifty might find their way into publication, whether it be as a single text from one of the few playtext publishers, one of several texts in an anthology, or in a theatre magazine, such as *Canadian Theatre Review* and *Theatrum*. Publishers have very different reasons for selecting texts but they have in common an eye to the market, and for that reason usually select plays that have had some impact in the theatre. The publication of plays makes subsequent productions more feasible. Perhaps more importantly in the long run, the plays that are published (as opposed to the 95% that are not) join and expand the canon of Canadian drama.

The published canon of Canadian plays is the basis of the academic discipline of Canadian drama studies, which is instituted in a number of university drama departments and programs, in critical journals, such as *Theatre Research in Canada*, *Jeu: cahiers du théâtre* and *Canadian Theatre Review*, in scholarly organizations, such as the Association for Canadian Theatre Research and the Societé québécois des études théâtrales, and in the publication of critical monographs. The task of this discipline, as in any critical field, is to explain patterns of meaning and development and to examine the relationship between the theatre as a cultural practice and the literature it produces. But if the study of Canadian drama is based on the published canon, we are left with the uncomfortable awareness that the patterns and cultural narratives we define in that canon may not be representative of the much larger number of Canadian plays that remain unpublished. This is the first problem in the phrase "Canadian drama:" the fact that the canon proposes inclusivity but practices exclusion.

The critic sifts through a body of material (in this case playtexts) and by defining patterns, seeks to impose coherence on an otherwise undifferentiated mass. Critical methodologies and theories vary radically but they share a common purpose of assigning place and value. These are the mutually corollarative imperatives in literary and dramatic criticism. Placement establishes categories and attempts to set each work against others so that the juxtaposition will reveal its particular qualities. The assignment of value can either determine or proceed from placement: value establishes a hierarchy in which particular texts are promoted (or demoted) according to how well (or poorly) they express the determinants that define placement. Thus placement defines "kinds" of plays; value determines which are "best" or "most representative" of their "kind."

This mode of reasoning is virtually impossible for critics to avoid, because criticism itself began as an exercise in categorization; Aristotle categorized literature in the same way as he did plants. But if it is impossible to avoid, it is nevertheless problematic because placement and value must either reflect immanent, objective qualities or reflect the ideological and cultural experience of the critic. Until recently, most critics throughout history have accepted that there are verifiable, objective standards by which plays can be assessed and placed. Through the course of the present century that attitude has been inverted; today most academic critics would argue, to greater or lesser degree, that the standards by which art is valued and placed are themselves cultural products, and that artistic criticism is an ideological project.

Perhaps the most important ideological condition to be attached to drama has been the concept of the nation and national culture. This raises the second problem with the phrase "Canadian drama:" "Canadian," as Massey recognized, is neither an objective description nor a categorical imperative. If anything it is an ideological coding in a constant state of transformation. Like the country itself, the use of "Canadian" in this context is the unstable site of constant renegotiation.

It is increasingly apparent that we live among numerous cultural matrixes, of which the nation is merely one; and the formation of identity cannot be reduced to simple determinants. Thus the pluralism of contemporary drama resists neat categorizations: as soon as we speak of Canadian drama we must then deconstruct the term, to explain what Canadian may contain and preclude. How can any selection of published playtexts be stabilized—placed and valued—in terms of their nationality, when their publication is itself the result of a long process of selection and accident, and when they articulate very different, often conflicting, understandings of Canada, as a nation and a system of intersecting cultural communities? If the canon is an ideological project, how can we refer to it to explain "Canadian drama?"

To explore this question, I want to first define the "Canada clause" of "Canadian drama" in a material/structural sense which identifies as Canadian those plays that come out of theatre practice in Canada. This is useful primarily because it dodges the questions of citizenship that vexed many theatre practitioners as recently as 1967 when Eddie Gilbert, then artistic director of the Manitoba Theatre Centre, complained that

> I don't see how a play can be Canadian. I mean, what is a Canadian play? Is it a play written by a Canadian, is it a play written in Canada? What happens if a Canadian writes a play in Bermuda? Is that a West Indian play or a Canadian play? The whole issue seems to me to be a total red herring. (Chusid 14)

Locating "Canadian" in terms of a productive relationship with Canadian theatre practice means therefore that we needn't worry whether Canadians George Hulme (who lives and works in England) and Bernard Slade (in the United States) ought to be included in the canon of Canadian drama.

Having narrowed the field, we are still left with a remarkable pluralism, expressed by hundreds of professionally produced plays. So vast a diversity makes it impossible to generalize about Canadian drama. But there are some points of commonality, and they lie in the material theatrical practice from which these plays emerge. The conditions that govern the theatre also govern the playwright by establishing a field of possibilities. In that sense, if a national drama articulates characteristics of the nation it is because the nation, through the institutional structures of cultural policy, shapes imagination. The extent to which imagination shapes the nation (the question that most concerned Massey) is, I submit, unanswerable.

II. Critical Mass

The question at hand then is whether it is possible to symptomize common elements in Canadian drama when we examine the question of nationality in the context of the productive relations of theatre practice and dramatic literature. Given that any selection of texts for examination must be arbitrary, it is clear that we can choose the texts to best illustrate the conclusions we have in mind. For that reason I have relied on the regulating mechanism of the theatre itself to make my choice. Every year the theatre community across the country legitimizes itself through the institution of awards ceremonies. In every major city, the theatre community has established a mechanism to signal its taste for "best" or "outstanding" play: the Doras and Chalmers awards in Toronto; the Jessies in Vancouver, the Sterlings in Edmonton. For playwrights the biggest prize is the Governor General's Award for Drama (which carries a substantial monetary prize). The GG award is implemented through the Canada Council which convenes a jury of three people drawn from the theatre (usually a critic, a playwright and a director) to read all of the plays published in book form in the award year and to choose a winner. My field of texts then is the four finalists for the 1992 Governor General's Award for Drama. Although it is impossible that any four texts can symptomize a culture, the differences and similarities expressed by these plays may be as reliable an index as any of the general state of Canadian playwriting.

The problem of place and value surfaces as soon as the texts are introduced, because the precedence in which they are named and described implies a progressive sequence. Given this problem, the critic might choose to list the plays according to the celebrity of the play-wrights, or the theatrical success of the plays, or in some kind of thematic, ideological or formal progression, or simply by taste. My choice is to approach these plays according to a thematic spectrum, because my reading of them shows a definite range of cultural analyses that reflect on the larger issue of national experience. All four plays address questions of identity, human volition and, in the larger sense of the term, ideology. But the formulations they propose are markedly different, occupying a spectrum from the mysticism of Judith Thompson's *Lion In The Streets* to the empiricist materialism of *The Noam Chomsky Lectures*.

Lion In the Streets is the third play for Thompson to be nominated for the Governor General's Award, and although unlike her two pre-vious finalists it did carry the prize, it confirms her enduring place in the front rank of Canadian playwrights. As in her previous plays, the action takes place in a shadow world where characters struggle to articulate the searing images that tear them apart and where the very act of thinking can be painful.

In all of Thompson's plays, plot emerges out of the conflict of brutal social forces and interior obsessions; typically these conflicts manifest in characters desperately attempting to maintain a sense of coherence and control in their lives. *Lion In The Streets* represents a new develop-ment in Thompson's dramaturgy however; it is the least restrained by plot but at the same time its intricate structure is an effective restatement of the fragmented inner experience of her characters.

The play's title derives from the recurring image articulated by the choral figure of Isobel, the ghost of a nine-year-old girl, the child of Portuguese immigrants, who was murdered in a random act of violence by a stranger seventeen years prior to the events of the play. Isobel is trapped in an eternal present of fear and flight from the stranger who killed her, and her quest is to find redemptive solace. This quest provides the dramaturgical structure of the play, which is written without scene divisions.

As Isobel reaches out to the people who pass her by, we follow their overlapping lives, a device which gives the play its apparent "relay" structure (modelled distantly on Schnitzler's *Reigen*): a series of character encounters unified sequentially by the projection of a character from one scene into a different set of circumstances in the next, from which (following Isobel's gaze) a different character continues onward. In each case, seemingly stable characters are revealed to be trapped in their personal hells. Beneath the relay structure, a hidden, more subtle arrangement reveals itself. *Lion In The Streets* is not simply a tag-team sequence; it is a circle of violence which mirrors—and indeed takes its meaning—from Isobel's attempts to free herself from her own cycle of violence.

The lion of the title surfaces in each of the scenes, but takes very different forms, sometimes externally imposed but more often released from within the particular character's psyche. The invasive pressure of the invisible world that plays so important a role in all of Thompson's plays is in this case given outward dramatic form. Isobel's perception provides the play with a cage in which the lions stalk, in often harrowing and extreme forms.

Thus simple dramatic situations explode into crisis that transforms cliché into a revelation of the fragility of social order. Early in the play, for instance, Isobel has revealed herself, as a lost and frightened child, to a caring woman named Sue. Immediately we follow Sue to a dinner party where she confronts her husband and his lover. This loaded situation, the grist of a thousand melodramas, quickly upsets our expectations. Sue precipitates a confrontation that begins as a breathless attack on her husband's infidelity:

> YOU TOOK A VOW! In a CHURCH in front of a priest and my mother and your mother and your father and you swore to LOVE and honour and cherish till DEATH DO US PART till DEATH DO US PART BILL, it's your WORD your WORD. (22)

The tension revealed in Sue's speech pattern is representative of Thompson's recurring technique in which characters have to struggle to articulate rage. All of Thompson's characters move in and out of private worlds that are constructed through language; at the same time, language marks the social environments through which the characters have passed. The less adequate language reveals itself to be to mediate those environments, the more closely Thompson's play actually succeeds in articulating the inarticulate, primarily through directives for the actor planted in rhythm, in repetition and even in typeface.

For many playwrights this level of tension and rage might emerge in the climax of a scene, but Thompson's particular genius lies in her ability to create credible events which begin in extreme crisis and develop into psychodramatic horror. Within moments of this outburst Sue is publicly humiliating herself, imploring Bill with memories of desire, and losing her public persona in orgasmic self-immolation:

> (*Music beats louder, filling the room, and* Sue *begins a slow striptease*)
> And whooosh...and...close to you, you're hard...and far away and...turn...and whoosh...and...let...my...hair...down...you—love my hair whoosh and...zipppper...whoooo down so slowwwww turn and turn...you watching lying on the bed and ease...off my shoulders you love my shoulders, elegant ohhhh Billy, and. down. Over my body the soft silky down and whooooooooooooooooo whooOOOOOOOO Billy. Take me home, Billy, take me home and let's make mad passionate love! Please. (24)

This is only the first of the six "relay" episodes in the play, each of which is punctuated by a brief bridging encounter or by Isobel's attempts to intervene. In subsequent scenes, we see a nursery school teacher confronted by parents who criticize her for giving sweets, in a meeting that quickly moves from polite restraint to screaming hostility and class hatred; a young man—who may or may not be a figure of mystical retribution forces a priest in a confessional to admit his long suppressed desire; a woman lunching with a friend attempts to confide that she has cancer—"Shadows...that's what they call them...and it is...the very worst thing it could be, and the...kind, the kind is of the bone" (34)—; a young woman interviewing a woman with cerebral palsy for a newspaper story viciously beats her in a rage that shocks her even more than it does her taunting victim; a young man shows up unexpectedly at the office of a former high school friend to punish him for their youthful flirtation; and finally, by threatening to cancel their impending wedding, a man violently forces his wife to relive the rape she suffered six years previously. In an act that reveals him as no less abusive than the rapist, he demands that she "admit" that the rape was her fault:

> SHERRY: And...and...I lie there for hours, passed out, all my blood pouring out onto the cement.
> EDWARD: But happy, right? You finally got it GOOD.
> SHERRY: Until the lady's putting out her garbage!
> EDWARD: And you told her the truth, didn't you?
> SHERRY: What?
> EDWARD: That it was all your fault.
> SHERRY: What?
> EDWARD: That you teased the poor guy, that you wanted him to power you, it was the sexiest hottest sex ever you wanted to be HAD. (61)

In all of these scenes, the lion stalks both within and outside; male violence against women, traumatic rage and cancer are equally lethal and omnipresent. The dangers of the invisible world, which in Thompson's previous plays are situated in the fragmented psyche, here approach a Mephisphelean construction of hell. Not surprisingly, *Lion In The Streets* concludes on an enigmatic redemptive note. In all of the scenes, the perpetrator of violence is discovered to be driven by fear and guilt that cannot be communicated through language. The humanism of this position does not imply forgiveness; in its way, the morality of the play is biblically stern. But the revelation that the lion is itself a figure of trauma leads to the possibility of understanding. Following the episode of the abusive fiancé, we meet the man who killed Isobel seventeen years previously. In one of the most dispassionate monologues in the play, he explains that he "done her a favour" and killed her quickly when he "stepped out of the twister cause that's what it's like when you're doing something like that, you're inside a twister" because "she touched me okay?"(62)

This final meeting releases Isobel, who after confronting the lion, addresses the audience as an adult:

> I want to tell you now a secret. I was dead, was killed by a lion in long silver car, starving lion, maul maul maul me to dead, with killing claws over and over my little young face and chest, over my chest my blood running out he takes my heart with, in his pocket deep, but my heart talk. Talk and talk and never be quiet never be quiet. I came back. I take my life. I want you all to take your life. I want you all to have your life.

> (*Players sing a second, joyful chorale, walking off.* Isobel *ascends, in her mind, into heaven. The last thing we see is her veil. End.*) (63)

Isobel's mystic redemption breaks the cycle of violence and the circularity of the play, but leaves us with an unresolved question. Does Thompson imply that violence is an inexorable human condition that can only be reconciled through the perfect knowledge that comes with death? Behind the redemptive celebration that closes the play there seems to be a chilling despair that subverts its mysticism.

Dianne Warren's *Serpent in the Night Sky* falls into a more recognizable mode of dramaturgy, grounded in realism and family conflict, and it is shaped with the sense of restraint that seems characteristic of much contemporary playwriting from the Prairies. Like *Lion in the Streets*, *Serpent* turns on a mystical figuration, but one which is contextualized within the characters themselves rather than materialized in the performance.

Of the four plays under discussion, *Serpent in the Night Sky* is the most conventional in its structure, in that it fulfils most closely the expectations generated by a realist plot. The novelty of the play is not therefore to be found in its formal structure, but rather in the playwright's ability to create characters and to write sharp, emotionally compressed dialogue. *Serpent* takes place in a rural community in northern Saskatchewan, where Duff, a young taxi-driver, has brought Joy, a teen-age runaway who has fled an abusive family in the United States, to his rustic shack. There Joy meets Duff's older sister Stella and her husband, the brutish Gator. Two other characters enter the action: Duff's mother Marlene, and a local eccentric known as Preacher.

The apparent stability of this society is quickly upset as Duff's hopes for a simple life with Joy become the site of a violent struggle that develops mythic overtones. Each of the characters is aligned clearly in a struggle against the patriarchal order personified by the violent, domineering Gator. The notion of patriarchy as systematized violence recurs throughout the play, and is intensified by its association with the United States—not only Joy, but Preacher as well has fled across the border; in Preacher's case, the play implies, it was to avoid the Vietnam war. Preacher spends his nights on top of his "church," scanning the skies through a telescope for signs of the cosmic snake that swallows the moon and obliterates light from the world. His obsession with the mythical serpent is a traumatic legacy of his flight from the United States:

> Everybody said you should steer clear of the big east and west coast crossings so I picked Montana. I crossed at Willow Creek, just north of Havre. Nothing to it. I could have snuck a whole busload across. It was maybe 6 o'clock in the morning. Still dark but there was a big moon. And damned if I didn't see an eclipse. I pulled my bike over on the side of the road and watched it. It was half an hour, maybe forty minutes before you could see the moon again. I was watching it, and I was thinking...it was weird, the way it got so dark...I was thinking this snake had swallowed the moon...you know how you see pictures of them with these giant bulges in their guts. Anyway, this snake had swallowed the moon and the nights were never going to be the same again. (*Pause*) I cried. I did. I actually cried. I sat by the side of the road, the first night of the rest of my life and cried. I cried, Stella. (56)

Preacher's snake is more than an obsession; as he comes to realize, it is materialized in the domestic violence and terror inflicted by Gator. Like Preacher, Marlene has also fled but the only borders available to cross in her flight from oppression are those of home and family. For years, Marlene has been living on her own in the bush, emerging only rarely to leave rabbits and game at Duff's doorstep. For Marlene, retreat into a solitary life spent walking in the woods is the only answer she has to a past of domestic violence.

A swaggering good ol' boy who ruthlessly controls those around him but offers nothing in return, Gator is a malevolent but highly theatrical character. He demands subservience from Stella and Duff, and receives it for very different reasons. Stella, who attempts to conceal her obvious pregnancy, is the wage earner in the family and her attempts to resist Gator through verbal combat only reinforce his hegemony; Gator likes "tough women." But Stella is a fighter who by the end of the play will have developed the strength and the self-esteem needed to defy him. For his part, Duff is a willing accomplice, eager to serve as Gator's sidekick, and desperate for words of praise. Duff is on the verge of manhood, but his complicity in Gator's patriarchal order is not yet confirmed. Thus he is the real site of the central struggle in the play, for which Joy provides the catalyst.

Joy's arrival on the scene is one of two events that trigger the revolution that upsets Gator's rule of terror. Duff and Joy plan to marry but when Duff confides to Gator that he offered her money, Gator convinces him that she is "a whore, for Christ's sake. Duffo, you've gone and got yourself involved with a whore" (60). Unaware that Gator has already attempted to rape Joy, Duff breaks off the engagement but realizes as she packs her bag that he has made a mistake. When he asks her to sleep with him one last time, she punishes him by demanding money; he complies, vaguely aware that she is forcing him to accept the consequences of his accusation.

The other critical event is explained through exposition: Stella has won a lottery ticket, which she plans to use to buy a trailer for Marlene. Gator persuades her to buy a truck instead, planning to use it in his own criminal schemes. The lure of the truck brings Marlene into the action, and in the final scene, she joins with Stella, Joy, Preacher and finally Duff to drive Gator away. In the end, Preacher performs his own version of a wedding service, giving the play a classically comic ending that unites the young lovers in a world free of the impediments that stood in their way:

PREACHER: Okay, okay, I don't have much time. Let's get this moving.

DUFF: We don't have any witnesses. Don't we need witnesses?

PREACHER: No. What do you need witnesses for? Okay. Let's see. Turn two whirls.

DUFF and JOY: What?

PREACHER: Whirls. Whirls. Circles. Come on. Come on. Snap this up. I'm a busy man. (*Pause*) Turn around, for heaven's sake. (*Pushes them in circles.*)

JOY: I don't have any papers.

PREACHER: What?

DUFF: You don't have to tell him that.

JOY: I don't have a visa or anything like that.

PREACHER: Trivialities. I don't believe I heard that. Come on, people. Don't waste my time.

DUFF: See, I told you Preacher's church is different.

PREACHER: Do this.

(Preacher *holds his two hands up, palms outward. Moves his hand in two circles.* Joy *and* Duff *do the same.*)

PREACHER: Now repeat after me. Bliss. (*Pause*) Say it. Come on, come on.

JOY and DUFF: Bliss.

PREACHER: All right.

DUFF: Is that it?

PREACHER: That's it. (66)

The wedding scene shows *Serpent in the Night Sky* to be a comedy of triumph and celebration. At once a feminist country 'n' western comedy and a serious depiction of the politics of male violence, its strength lies in Warren's acute ability to integrate a mythic fable of women's empowerment in the raunchy, often humorous, confines of realist localism.

The third text to be discussed, *The Noam Chomsky Lectures* by Daniel Brooks and Guillermo Verdecchia, developed in performance over two years, and its inclusion in the list of Governor General Awards finalists is a welcome gesture of recognition that "drama" must also describe those plays that do not conform to traditional expectations of plot and mimesis. *The Noam Chomsky Lectures* is described by its authors/performers as a "table play," a form used by several avant-garde companies in the English-speaking world (such as The Wooster Group in New York and Open City in Australia). The premise of a "table play" is simple: in a format that may derive from television talk shows and theatrical lectures in equal measure, the performers sit before the audience and, in this case, use direct address and slide projections to shape their performance discourse. Although this format is easily accessible to an audience, it is also the case that some viewers—and reviewers—may be puzzled by its refusal to abide by the conventional "rules" of drama. The performers defuse the crisis of expectation at the beginning of the play:

BROOKS: First let me state that *The Noam Chomsky Lectures* is a perpetual workshop, an unfinished play, a fourth draft, a work in progress; hence you are a workshop audience, an unfinished audience, a fourth-draft audience, an audience in progress; hence this is not a real play, you are not a real audience—so let's all sit back and have a whale of a good time… (12)

Because the performances of *The Noam Chomsky Lectures* changed and adapted to the political events they addressed, they were rarely the same. Consequently, the text records a particular phase in the history of the performance. At the same time, the published text (which includes over twenty pages of footnotes and a bibliography) offers an archaeology of the play's own performance history.

The title of the play is deceptively accurate. The authors set out to explicate the ideas of the American social philosopher and media critic Noam Chomsky, who in his many books has argued that the corporate concentration of the mass media perpetuates a false ideology of democratic choice in a world where (as he explains in his important study *Manufacturing Consent*) actual choices are restricted by an invisible totalitarianism.

The published text begins its explication of Chomskyian principles with a response to the reviews of previous performances in a gesture that reveals the critic-performer relationship to be metonymic of the larger critique of journalism and the myth of media objectivity that Chomsky provides.

> VERDECCHIA: Daniel and I will be making some "chaotic gestures"and using some "bizarre indigenous instruments" to borrow two phrases from *Globe and Mail* theatre critic Ray Conlogue, or as he's known in some circles...
>
> SLIDE: This show is convincing evidence of the need for an Esthetic Police —Ray Conlogue, *The Globe and Mail*, June 13, 1990.
>
> ...Constable Conlogue. One of the more bizarre indigenous instruments we will be using is the Artstick. [*He holds up an elaborately decorated bamboo stick.*]
>
> SLIDE: When a work resolutely refuses to view the world in anything but naive us-versus-them terms, it is not a play but a polemic and the playwright but a pamphleteer. —Alex Patterson, *Metropolis*, February 1, 1990.
>
> It will be used by either Daniel or myself whenever one of the performers crosses that fine line between art and demagoguery. A demonstration.
>
> BROOKS: Okay, let's talk about this Gulf War. Why didn't Bush let sanctions against Iraq work? I'll tell you why. He wanted a war, he wanted to end the talk about a peace dividend, he is seeking the legitimization of war and the elevation of the United States to the status of world mercenary policeman—
>
> VERDECCHIA: [*strikes the table with the Artstick*] The Artstick. Article 51 of *The Noam Chomsky Lectures* Charter states: "When hit with the Artstick, the speaker is effectively silenced." (13)

But as the authors warn, in their typical self-mocking and ironic manner, *The Noam Chomsky Lectures* is more than a "post-modern push-up." The satire of the play may be most engaging and acute when interrogating the aesthetic and political assumptions of the media reviewers who criticized the show, or when analyzing the topology of avant-garde theatre in Toronto (including a hilarious "sexual flow chart" of Theatre

Passe Muraille), but the "lectures" in the title is no misnomer. The play consists of several interrelated lectures, on art and politics, on corporate capitalism and the mass media, and most importantly, Canadian complicity in American foreign and ideological policy. Performed at the time of the Gulf War, it is an angry challenge for Canadians to "disobey, disrupt and dissent." (62)

In effect the performance itself fulfils these directives—by disobeying notions of art reinforced by critics, by disrupting the expectations we bring to theatrical performance and by dissenting against the very proposition that we live in an informed society. The self-referential mockery of the performers themselves adds to their critique by constantly reminding us that the authority of the performer is based on power that we are trained not to question in the theatre. Although Brooks and Verdecchia subvert their own authority so that *The Noam Chomsky Lectures* will not replicate the conditions of information manipulation that it critiques, the charm and wit of the performance tend to reinforce the authority of the performers; we are not persuaded to their point of view by their argument but by their satiric rhetoric and sassiness. The authors close the play with a final joke on the structures of power in performance:

> BROOKS: What we'll do now is show you one last slide. We will turn to the slide, and the lights will go to black as we exit. We ask that you consider the slide in the dark. When any one of you has had enough, you will yell, "Light!" The lights will come up and the show will be over.... (65)

This apparent abrogation of the power to invoke closure is another illustration of Chomskian principles. As the audience ponders the final quotation from Chomsky, they may feel that it has been empowered but in fact it has been presented with a very simple choice that excludes alternatives. They may sit in growing discomfort, or call for the lights. In either case the choice has been stipulated for them already by the performers. The apparent power to choose is in fact no more than the obligation to follow orders. This simple, sly gesture recapitulates the thesis of the performance of *The Noam Chomsky Lectures*.

The last play to be looked at is the text that won the 1992 Governor General's Award, John Mighton's *Possible Worlds*. In fact, as the award is technically conferred for the published book, this discussion should also include the second play in the volume, *A Short History of Night*. However of the two, the former strikes me as most interesting and useful to the present discussion, for reasons of formal innovation and thematic relevance.

The plays discussed to this point have been ordered by their mutual relationship along an axis that moves from mysticism to materialist empiricism. *Possible Worlds* moves beyond materialism, to the domain of quantum physics—which is not without its mystical aspects. It is at once the furthest removed from and closest to *Lion in the Streets*. John Mighton is a teacher of mathematics who has written few plays and has not yet had a major popular success. His first play, *Scientific Americans*, was a finalist for the Governor General's Award in 1990; his award for *Possible Worlds* (his second published text) places him in the anomalous position of a playwright who although not well known enjoys high critical esteem.

All of Mighton's work to date explores the ramifications of contemporary scientific philosophy on our understandings of reality. In his formal innovations, he disproves the now orthodox Brechtian approach that equates science with materialism. In his *Short Organum for the Theatre*, Brecht argued that the theatre for the scientific age must be investigative, empirical and analytical. Mighton in contrast attempts to dramatize the confusing ambivalences of modern sub-particle physics, in which the very notion of reality (and thus of realism) is understood as a human construct we impose to make sense of a contradictory and chaotic universe.

The plot of *Possible Worlds* is simple to the point of minimalism but its actions are paradoxically complex. It begins with a pair of detectives investigating a series of bizarre murders, some in locked rooms; in each case the victim's brain has been mysteriously removed. Parallel to the detective scenes we are introduced to a man and a woman, George and Joyce, who commence a love affair that seems to slip through phases of reality. Every time George and Joyce meet, the basic circumstances of their lives have changed inexplicably. We are led to assume that we are meeting this same couple in alternate worlds, a common motif of science fiction. This simple explanation seems to be confirmed by George's obsession with the idea of overlapping realities:

> I'm talking about possible worlds. Each of us exists in an infinite number of possible worlds. In one world I'm talking to you right now but your arm is a little to the left, in another world you're interested in that man over there with the glasses, in another you stood me up two days ago—and that's how I know your name. (23)

As George's possible worlds begin to overlap in rapidly shifting phases, the detectives of the first scene encounter a scientist who studies the phenomenon of consciousness with the disembodied brains of rats. The rat brains are encased in metal boxes and connected to wires that stimulate the cortex with simulations of reality. A light on the box flashes whenever the disembodied rat thinks it is pressing a lever for food. The scientist explains that he has dozens of such rat brains because:

Some biologists think that natural processes create fields of information.
I'm seeing if a group of brains, in isolation, can learn something faster after
one of them has learned it. (26)

As the detective comes to believe that just as the rats cannot even imagine their predicament, so is he facing an enemy beyond imagination, the two narrative tracks converge. The detective explains to his assistant that the scientist also had human brains connected to his devices, one of which was George. He explains to Joyce, who we learn is George's wife, that the scientist

...was never able to get more than rudimentary consciousness going.
There's a light that flashes occasionally but we don't know what it means.
Your husband probably isn't aware of who he is. Penfield described it as
a kind of fluctuating dream state. Very discontinuous. (72)

The final scene reverts to Joyce and George, who are sitting by the edge of the scene, as a light flashes in the far distance. On the level of plot, the ambiguities of the play seem to be resolved by the suggestion that we have participated in George's disembodied dream state throughout the play. But on another level, the questions that confronted the detective at the beginning are never answered. How were the victims murdered in locked rooms? How were their brains removed? Behind the apparent resolution of plot, Mighton leaves us with ambiguities that support the detective's conjecture: perhaps all the characters are caught in a disembodied field of information; perhaps there is another agency at work which the very structures of our brains prohibit us from conceiving. Just as in quantum physics, every answer opens up a host of greater puzzles. *Possible Worlds* is a provocative attempt to probe the very limits of philosophy, and while such an attempt by definition must fail because it cannot transcend human consciousness, it provides an enthralling dramatic reflection.

III. How Many Canadas?

If we look to these four plays to characterize Canadian drama, we are faced with a range of choices as diverse as the country itself. Like all texts, these plays invite analysis from different perspectives that describe differing, perhaps conflicting, notions of what Canada and Canadian mean. Whether analyzed in terms of gender, of class or race, each reading will reveal valuable insights into contemporary Canadian society. And like the plays themselves, each of these readings challenges Massey's proposition of "true Canadianism." In fact the plays can be read to reinforce whatever construction of Canadian culture the particular critic has experienced.

There is, however, one material reflection of Canadian society that all four plays embody which is pertinent to the discussion of the

Governor General's Awards. As in most western cultures, the institution of the theatre as an art form and industry in Canada legitimizes a hierarchy of value. The theatre is a publicly subsidized art in Canada but it has long been accepted as appropriate that funding should be distributed unevenly between large and small theatres. The scale of disproportionate funding is vast, ranging from the millions of dollars given annually to such large theatres as the Stratford Festival and The Canadian Stage Company, to the mere thousands given in project funds to avant-garde troupes on the fringe. This system is one that has developed without planning but finds its usual rationale in the proposition that large theatres stand as civic and national showcases, which are invigorated by the waves of innovation that spread out from small theatres. Disproportionate funding is justified by the simple proposition that cream rises to the top.

Considered in these terms of material culture, no play is a neutral artefact. The four plays discussed here typify this principle—each of them is a consequence of a specific set of productive relations in the theatre. By their example, the real accomplishments of Canadian playwriting has little to do with the assumptions of cultural policy inscribed in the funding of theatre.

In any country, public funding of arts and culture functions to support the ideological premises of the state. In Canada, the humanist vision of a unified Canadian culture articulated by Massey eighty years ago and materialized in public policy four decades later bears little relation to the actual creative state of Canadian drama. To the bureaucratic mind, it may be that the increasing number of Canadian plays is a balanced reflection of the funding of Canadian theatres. But all four of these plays originated in small theatres that account for a small fraction of theatrical funding, and none has been seen on the stage of a large theatre. And despite the assumptions of regional culture that underlie that funding, three of the four (the exception being *Serpent in the Night Sky*) originated in the theatrical cosmopolis of Toronto.

In their thematic concerns and formal differences, these four plays argue against the notion of an organic, unified Canadian culture. It is more useful to reflect on their differences, which only begin to hint at the diverse cultural experiences that Canada embodies. Indeed, some of the most important and urgent differences, particularly of ethnicity and race, are barely suggested in these plays. The relevance of difference as a mode of perception is reinforced by the material practice from which the plays emerge: their provenance in small, underfunded theatres, which contradict the fundamental assertion behind public funding, also resists the imposition of totalizing narratives of "true Canadianism."

BIBLIOGRAPHY

Brooks, Daniel and Guillermo Verdecchia. *The Noam Chomsky Lectures*. Toronto: Coach House Press, 1991.

Chusid, Harvey. "Nationalistic Labels Stifle Development." *The Stage in Canada / La Scène au Canada*, May 1967, 9-18.

Massey, Vincent. "The Prospects of a Canadian Drama." *Queen's Quarterly* 30, (December 1922) 194-212.

Mighton, John. *Possible Worlds* & *A Short History of Night*. Toronto: Playwrights Canada Press, 1992.

Thompson, Judith. *Lion in the Streets*. Toronto: Coach House Press, 1992.

Warren, Dianne. *Serpent in the Night Sky. Canadian Theatre Review* 63 (Summer 1990).

Drew Hayden Taylor

The Re-Appearance of the Trickster: Native Theatre in Canada

In 1986, there was perhaps one working, produced, Native playwright in all of Canada. Today, it can safely be said that a good two dozen experienced and talented Native playwrights can be found writing for the stage, and that number may well double in less than half as much time. All this in less than ten years.

With that in mind, it should also be noted strenuously that Native theatre, in one form or another, is much older than that scant few years. It is as old as this country, as old as the people who have been here for thousands of years, as old as the stories that are still told today. It is merely the presentation that has changed.

While the proscenium stage may be new to the North American continent, the art of telling stories with voice and mannerisms is certainly old hat amongst the aboriginal people of Canada. For example, Nuu-chah-nulth of the West Coast have for centuries used such theatrical devices as trap doors, masks, smoke effects and props to help illustrate their religious dramas.

Most amazing perhaps is the fact that the heart and soul of what was in those early dramas and stories is very much evident in the work of the 20th Century contemporary storyteller.

Tomson Highway, perhaps Canada's most well-known Native playwright, was quoted, in the late 1980s, as saying "Nanabush is still around, he's just passed out underneath a table at the Silver Dollar. It's up to us, the artists, to kick him in the ass and wake him up." And that conceivably is exactly what Native playwrights are attempting to do.

And while the physical manifestation of Nanabush, the trickster, appears in precious few plays, his spirit permeates almost all work

---

presented as Native theatre. That is because Nanabush, known in various parts of Canada as Nanabozho, Weesageechak, Glooscap, Crow, Raven, Coyote, etc. is at the centre of our mythology. Most of the legends in this country revel in the tales of this fabulous character, a trickster character that often does as much harm as he does good.

Highway was referring to the now drunk Nanabush being banished by the introduction of Christianity, alcohol, bureaucratic government, and English to name a few things. Due to an over-zealous non-Native cultural majority, Nanabush lost his hold on the imagination of his people.

As Tomson Highway put it, "the trickster stands at the centre of our dream life, as opposed to the European context where the central figure is an agonized individual. European mythology says we are here to suffer; our mythology says we are here to have a good time." It is through his adventures and escapades, that the trickster teaches us lessons, morals, values, and warns us of good and evil, usually in a humorous but intelligent manner.

And so as the Native people of Canada were an oral culture, well skilled in story-telling and verbal narratives, the tales of Nanabush were passed down from generation to generation through the art of story-telling. It should therefore be no surprise that many consider this to be the start of Native theatre in Canada; it has been around for thousands of years. For what storytellers worth their merit, can't help but breathe life into the tale they tell and for all intensive purposes, act them out.

It isn't such a long journey from telling stories around the camp-fire to telling stories on a stage. And the process, it could be said, helped sober Nanabush up.

For over the last one hundred years or so, Nanabush and his stories were the victim of a governmental attempt to eradicate all existence of him or his activities. It was only the strength and belief of his people that kept him alive in the Native equivalent of the underground.

But with the coming of the last half of this century, many felt it was time for his re-appearance. The years of inactivity had left him a broken, drunken shell of his former self. It would take a lot to make him care again.

Canada got its first taste of contemporary Native theatre in 1967, though many would argue *The Ecstasy of Rita Joe* doesn't qualify as Native theatre. It was written by a non-Native named George Ryga but it told for the first time the grittily real story of Canada's Native people. In this case, a young girl named Rita Joe who goes to the city.

Unlike in many earlier plays involving Native characters, there are no romantic or noble savages in this story. It is an unsettling story with a sad ending. But for the first time, Canadians were awakened to the social realities of the urban Indian within the context of a theatrical play. Noted Native actor Chief Dan George was an integral force and presence in the first production. And ironically, the only "authentic" Native in the cast.

The text later became a staple of high school and university English/drama courses, and eventually a ballet was created incorporating and translating the story into dance. *The Ecstasy of Rita Joe* was one of the first influential and original pieces to come out of Canadian theatre in general.

It was almost ten years later before there was another substantial appearance of what could be called the New Native Theatre. James Buller, president of the Association for Native Development in the Performing and Visual Arts, wanted to develop a play that was written, produced, directed and performed by Native people. In fact the whole production team was Native including the stage management and designers.

The play, *October Stranger*, was written by George Kenny in collaboration with Denis Lacroix and had its première at the Sixth International Amateur Theatre Association Festival in Monaco in 1977. Results were mixed due to the space the company was given necessitating a re-blocking of the piece and reception of the audiences because they were not the stereotypical "Indian" that were anticipated. According to the cast, they were expected to bring "their feathers and their furs and their drums."

After the Festival, Buller and Lacroix realized that their play did not fit into any of the Festival's categories. This prompted them to create and organize the World Indigenous Theatre Festival. In 1980, the first Festival was held at Trent University in Peterborough, Ontario and brought together many people of many cultures, attracting delegates from as far away as the Caribbean, the South Pacific, Scandinavia and the United States. The Festival saw the emergence of a large pool of Native talent, including Spiderwoman Theatre from New York (a feminist theatre group of mainly Native women), Tukak Teatret from Denmark (Inuit of Greenland) and graduates of the Native Theatre School in Ontario.

It is important to note it was shortly after this Festival that Canadian Native theatre began forming into a creative force of its own. Canada's first known professional Native theatre company was officially formed in 1980. This Sioux Lookout (Ontario) based company was called Northern Delights. Several soon-to-be-known artists were influenced and/or involved in various ways with this early company.

Their early material consisted of works mainly by a non-Native writer, then as confidence built along with experience, they expanded into dramatizing legends for the stage. The company toured for a few years before the people involved went their separate ways and ended up being involved with several new Native companies being set up.

Specifically two have helped shape and foster the face of modern, contemporary Native theatre. In 1982, a company was formed in Toronto by a loose association of friends and professionals. Their function was to collectively create plays that maintained and strengthened the pride and identity of Native peoples by providing a unique artistic platform for the expression of traditional and contemporary Native themes. This company was called Native Earth Performing Arts Inc. During the early years the company produced such shows as *Who am I?: Wey-Can-Nee-Nah* and *Double Take: A Second Look* which explored key social issues facing Native people. It was during this time that several key figures in the further development of Native theatre made their appearance with Native Earth. Tomson Highway, a Cree from Brochet, Manitoba, joined the group as musical director and his nephew, Billy Merasty, performed as an actor. Highway spent a few years with Native Earth before he left in 1985 to take up the Artistic Directorship of another company located on Manitoulin Island. This company, De-Ba-Jeh-Mu-Jig (a word that means storytellers in Cree/Ojibway) Theatre Group was founded in 1984 by noted artist Shirley Cheechoo.

Since their inception, both companies have been at the vanguard of the development of Native Theatre. Native Earth Performing Arts, with its emphasis on the urban experience and decidedly sophisticated productions in a fixed space, while De-Ba-Jeh-Mu-Jig Theatre Group excelled at presenting the rural or Reserve experience to many Native and non-Native communities as it toured.

The history of both companies is very intertwined with personnel, talent and scripts going back and forth on a regular basis. Larry Lewis, the dramaturge/director behind such Highway creations as *The Rez Sisters* and *Dry Lips Oughta Move To Kapuskasing*, later took over the helm of De-Ba-Jeh-Mu-Jig Theatre Group once Highway left the company, and ushered in a whole new generation of writers, actors and tech people.

In the spring of 1986, Tomson Highway took over the position of Artistic Director of Native Earth Performing Arts Inc. in Toronto. This was the major turning-point in the history of Native theatre. Up until this point, most of the aboriginal theatre seen had been viewed with a sort of anthropological or sociological interest but seldom was it seen as legitimate and innovative theatre for the masses.

Under Highway's stewardship and armed with a new mandate, the company's first production was a little known play written by Highway that practically all the theatres in Toronto had refused to consider. It was the story of seven Native women and their passionate hobby, a game known as Bingo. It was called *The Rez Sisters* and it took Toronto by storm, and later a national tour did the same for the country.

This one play put Native theatre on the map. From then on Native Earth Performing Arts was considered a force to be reckoned with in the Toronto theatre scene. It won numerous awards for Highway and set the stage for its sequel, *Dry Lips Oughta Move To Kapuskasing* about the reaction of seven Native men to the news of a national Native women's hockey league. He is currently working on the third instalment, a full scale musical named *Rose*, in a cycle of seven plays.

Other writers were introduced to the theatre scene via the company. One of the earliest and most successful was Daniel David Moses, author of such critically acclaimed work as *Coyote City* (a woman gets a phone call from her dead lover asking to meet her in a bar) and *Almighty Voice and His Wife* (the historical and then surreal story behind the famous Cree warrior).

Other plays and writers produced by Native Earth Performing Arts include *Diary of a Crazy Boy* by John McLeod, the story of a boy undergoing treatment at a psychiatric institute who calls upon the help of his shamanic ancestral spirits in his struggles with his doctor. Another highlight for the company was *Moonlodge*, a one-woman show by Margo Kane highlighting the journey of a young Métis girl raised in a non-Native home struggling to find her heritage.

Son of Ayash by Jim Morris is a return to traditional storytelling material as it was adapted from the Cree/Ojibway legend of the hero, Ayash, with a few contemporary twists. Other Native Earth productions include *Night of the Trickster* (a story about rape) by Beatrice Mosionier, *Lady of Silences* (described as a Native noir play) by former Native Earth Artistic Director Floyd Favel, *Fireweed* (a man deals with being Catholic, gay and Native) by William Merasty.

Most recently Native Earth has produced *Generic Warriors and No-Name Indian* (an examination of the warrior spirit through the ages) by Ben Cardinal and *Diva Ojibway* (a drama/opera about love, betrayal, and trapping) by Tina Mason.

But perhaps one of Native Earth's greatest accomplishments is the *Weesageechak Begins to Dance Festival*. First held in 1989, the festival provided the opportunity for first time playwrights to work with experienced actors and dramaturges in a professional workshop setting, the result having been the high level of quality scripts available for Native Earth and other companies to choose from. Many if not most scripts workshopped over the last half dozen years have gone on to full scale productions.

Artistically, De-Ba-Jeh-Mu-Jig Theatre Group wasn't far behind—with such innovative creations like *Respect the Voice of the Child* by Shirley Cheechoo and William Merasty, a story about a young girl whose medicine gifts made her an outcast, and *Shadow People* by Shirley Cheechoo, a devastating tale about teen suicide.

De-Ba-Jeh-Mu-Jig Theatre Group also produced the first version of the Jim Morris script, *Ayash*, based on the traditional story. Two plays written by Shirley Cheechoo and Alanis King were produced back to back. *Nothing Personal* was a penetrating but shallow view of very bored lives. *Nanabush of the Eighties* was an all-Native country and western musical.

Further productions included *Toronto at Dreamer's Rock* (an initiation story about three adolescent Native boys) by Drew Hayden Taylor, *Lupi the Great White Wolf* (the dramatization of a local legend of a boy magically transformed into a ravenous wolf by his grandmother) by Esther Jocko, and *The Bootlegger Blues* (a comedy about a fifty-eight-year-old woman who has to bootleg 143 cases of beer for the Church) also by Drew Hayden Taylor. The company has received its own share of rewards and recognition.

This is, however, not to say that Native theatre was happening only with these two companies and only in Ontario. Native theatre companies were being created and running in cities and Reserves all across Canada.

Between 1986 and 1991, a company called Four Winds Theatre operated out of the Hobemma Reserve located in Alberta. Again, many of the plays created dealt with social issues important to their community.

Awasikan Theatre did some imaginative work for a few years before it disappeared in the early nineties. Originally a Native puppeteer company, it became the only professional theatre company in Winnipeg, Manitoba.

In 1988, Sen'klip Native Theatre Company, outside of Vernon, British Columbia was formed by expatriates of Spirit Song Theatre. Named after Coyote, one of the manifestations of the trickster, their material tends to deal with the legends of the Okanagan people in that area.

Up in the far North of Baffin Island, Tunooniq Theatre has become Northern Canada's most famous and influential theatre company. Formed in 1986, the company has a good history of thought provoking theatre dealing with matters important to the Inuit people.

Several new Native theatre companies have been formed in the last few years. Margo Kane, Vancouver based actress, singer, director and teacher is the founder of Full Circle First Nations Performances. The Sweetgrass players opened their first show, *Dance Me Born*, on April 29, 1993 in Calgary after six years of trying to start their own company.

Spirit Song Native Indian Theatre Company, out of Vancouver, is mainly a theatre school for young Native actors. As well as student productions, Spirit Song has produced plays on a semi-professional basis. Their list of public performances over the past ten years is rather modest. Unfortunately, the company was forced to close its doors in 1994.

The Native Theatre School, breeding ground of some of Canada's best Native actors, was founded in 1974 and is still running strong. But recently, a change in title and mandate has refocussed the company. Christened "The Centre of Indigenous Theatre," the company now works with refining already experienced Native actors rather than providing training for first time performers. They are also constantly developing an original and truly unique aboriginal performance style.

It is also important to note that Native plays are not only regulated to being produced by Native owned and run companies. Plays such as *The Rez Sisters, Toronto at Dreamer's Rock, The Bootlegger Blues*, amongst others, have been produced at mainstream theatres from Sydney, Nova Scotia to Victoria, British Columbia. Writers like Tomson Highway and Daniel David Moses have had direct commissions to create plays for non-Native companies.

Jessica, by Linda Griffiths and Maria Campbell, loosely adapted from Campbell's autobiography *Halfbreed*, was developed and rehearsed for 25th Street House Theatre in Saskatoon and later rewritten for Theatre Passe Muraille in Toronto. *Princess Pocahontas and the Blue Spots*, a show about the history of Native women in the Americas, was written and performed by Monique Mojica for Nightwood Theatre and Theatre Passe Muraille Backstage.

It should also be mentioned that Native plays tend to have certain characteristics that can be plotted. Possibly the most obvious feature of Native theatre is its need to explore and examine social, environmental, or historical issues. This is not of course to say that non-Native theatre doesn't do this. But within the classification of Native Theatre, this particular aspect well defines the medium.

Looking back at traditional storytelling, the legends and fables being told were more than that. They were the history, the culture, the essence of who those people were. A culture can best be examined and explained through its folklore. And much if not all the folklore was passed down through these stories.

And more often than not, these stories were more than simple time wasters designed to keep the children amused. Within the heart of these stories were parables, allegories, moral issues, deep and complex metaphors, historical information, philosophies and impressive understandings of the human mind. All elements of good theatre.

So it should be no surprise that with the extension from camp-fire to stage, many of these storytelling aspects would naturally be included in the plays of today. Some within the community would argue a Native play by definition must examine or interpret concerns of the people. And with the recent history of Native people being one of oppression and pain, the newly re-acquired voice of the people would be questioning that history and the current repercussions that are affecting aboriginal people today.

Regarding this matter, Highway likes to quote Saskatchewan Cree Lyle Longclaws who once said "Before the healing can take place, the poison must be exposed."

Plays like *Night of the Trickster, The Rez Sisters, Moonlodge, Diary of a Crazy Boy, Generic Warriors* and *No-Name Indian, Toronto at Dreamer's Rock,* etc., all have at their core, fundamental questions that the writer is posing to the audience.

In fact, if you look at the majority of Native plays objectively, many have one specific characteristic. *The Rez Sisters, Night of the Trickster, Jessica, Moonlodge, Dry Lights Oughta Move to Kapuskasing, Fireweed,* even *The Ecstasy of Rita Joe,* all in one way or another, deal with the concept of rape. In *Night of the Trickster,* there are several rapes that occur at varying intervals throughout the two acts.

This is for several reasons. The most obvious being the tragically high levels of sexual abuse faced by Canadian Native women. Since many of these plays reflect what is happening in the community today, this is one of the most important issues Native playwrights feel must be confronted on stage.

The second reason being the metaphoric implications of a cultural rape. In *Dry Lips Oughta Move to Kapuskasing,* Dickey Bird Halkett, suffering from "Fetal Alcohol Syndrome," attacks and rapes with a crucifix, Patsy Pegamagobow who spiritually is Nanabush and is pregnant with the child of one of the last traditional people left in the community.

The rape is horrific on two counts. The image of the pregnant woman being raped with a crucifix had many audience members in tears. But the concept of Christianity and alcohol raping Nanabush and traditionalism is lost on no one. History is filled with cases of Native spirituality and beliefs being driven underground or stamped out by these two forces.

And while early Native theatre primarily relied on the dramatization of legends, or didactic morality plays, experience and success in the Canadian theatre world provided Native playwrights with the opportunity to experiment with various styles and forms of theatre.

The Bootlegger Blues, by Drew Hayden Taylor, is a Native interpretation of a classical English sex farce. *Diva Ojibway* by Tina Mason had many comic and tragic elements of classical opera. The last act of Moses' *Almighty Voice and his Wife* is quite absurdist in structure and Highway's new play, *Rose*, promises to be a big spectacle of a musical.

There is an old Cree saying that says "many of us have died, many of us are living today, but most of us have yet to be born." The same can be said for Native Theatre. The last eight years have brought about a revolution in the Native artistic community and the birth of a new theatre industry. Most of us are dying to see what will happen next.

Nanabush is now sober, awake and waiting to go onstage.

Susan Bennett

Diversity and Voice:
A Celebration of Canadian Women
Writing for Performance

This article can start with a happy and certain fact: there are now more women involved in producing more theatre than at any time previous in the history of Canadian theatre. Canadian women playwrights (the latter word a term I want to use in the broadest sense, to include all kinds of writers for performance) are seeing and making their work on all kinds of stages across the country and, indeed, in many venues far from the national borders. Because of the strength and number of women's performances, I cannot hope, far less claim, to offer a comprehensive account of their contributions to contemporary Canadian theatre; what I want instead to chronicle is something of their emergent history and to suggest a multiple trajectory of interest which finds particular expression in this historical moment.

As other histories of women's theatre have indicated,[1] the post-1968 growth of the Women's Movement provided a context for the development of much more work by, for and about women (some feminist, some ambivalently so, some not, some resolutely not) on both mainstream and alternative stages. It is the last twenty-five years or so, as a more or less global phenomenon, that has brought into both stage production and academic focus a subgenre under the umbrella of theatre recognized as something specific to women.[2] In Canada, the organization of such work is perhaps complicated by the particularities of specific regional interests which concentrate the arts, like so many aspects of the apparently Canadian cultural experience, in the provinces of Ontario and Quebec.[3] It is nonetheless true that a contemporary history of women's dramatic writing in Canada can locate performances across the map and, when the focus is narrowed to more local geographies, they can be located both within and without theatre buildings in every region. And those maps are not just the literal ones produced by the cartographer; there are also those which might chart the diversity of identity positions that represent Canadian women across race, class, ethnicity, sexuality, age and other positionalities. At the interstices of identity and place, the strength of Canadian women's writing for performance finds both voice and presence.

But before celebrating the diversity of such work, it is perhaps worth re-marking this contemporary history onto a more conventional (linear) record of playwriting in this country. In other words, it is important to remember the foresisters to women writing today. Yvonne Hodkinson has pointed out in her useful introduction to *Female Parts: The Art and Politics of Female Playwrights,* the many, largely unsung and unremembered women who contributed to the emergence of drama and theatre in Canada. Nineteenth-century playwrights Eliza Lanesford Cushing and Sarah Anne Curzon wrote resisting, transgressive plays, subtly reworking the melodrama form to speak of their own cultural experience.[4] In the earlier part of the twentieth century such different women as Dora Mavor Moore (whose labours established a professional theatre in Toronto)[5] and Gwen Pharis Ringwood (whose writing for and work with the little theatre movement in the West brought women-centred theatre to all kinds of new stages)[6] provided a model history of how women in Canada have made it happen—not always or not often on the main stage of existing theatres, but by inventing forms and creating theatres where their work might develop and explore an aesthetic which engaged with the lives that they found themselves living. Moreover, as the pageants and performances around women's suffrage issues ably demonstrate,[7] women have also long known the efficacy and necessity of entering their creative work into the political arena so as to bring visibility to their hopes, concerns and oppressions. If the contributions of these many gifted women are only now beginning to be documented and analyzed, and names such as Elizabeth Sterling Haynes and Elsie Park Gowan[8] remain woefully unfamiliar, it is nonetheless important to locate contemporary energies in a continuum of activity, to see (in Canada as elsewhere) a women's dramatic tradition.

The 1970s, however, brought an intensity of interest in women's theatre and many women playwrights who might now be thought of as the senior, accomplished representatives in the field were then trying to find theatres and other performance spaces interested in producing their work—or, at the least, agreeable to them producing their own work. Writers such as Sharon Pollock, Joanna Glass, Margaret

Hollingsworth and Carol Bolt created works with perspectives that challenged notions of what Canadian theatre and drama was and could be, even as some of this earlier work now seems tentative in its interest in what might be termed a feminine aesthetic.[9] At the same time, the first spaces which would proactively encourage women's dramatic writings were coming into existence, although and once again it should be noted that their commitment to a women's project was not always obviously foregrounded. Catalyst Theatre in Edmonton, for example, has consistently produced scripts for and with women, and had key artistic direction provided by women (Jan Selman, Jane Heather, Ruth Smilie among others);[10] yet its primary commitment is to a broader field of social action theatre. Furthermore, as Cynthia Grant's account of Nightwood Theatre makes evident, "[w]hen we established the company in 1978 we were very anxious that people not consider Nightwood a "women's theatre." Personally, I wished to have a career as a director, *not* as a woman director. Although I was already clearly defined as a feminist, I knew the derogatory, second-class implications of such terms." (45) Nightwood, of course, went on to become Canada's most significant producer of women's theatre, has been proactively feminist, and the venue where so many of the contemporary writers considered here had some of their first work produced.

With these frames in mind, I want to impose three categoric designations on contemporary writing for performance by women and to gesture towards the kind(s) of diversity that such multivalent writing produces, and is produced by. Most obviously in what I have suggested is a tradition in women's writing in Canada, I want to examine some contemporary plays, texts that both retain and examine the possibilities of the conventional form. Beyond that, I will examine the emergence of a performance art tradition (even if that seems something of a contradiction in its terms) as well as the development of collective theatre writing and performance.

Plays and Playwrights

The merest glance at the membership list for the Playwrights Union of Canada indicates just how many women are writing and, moreover, how prolific so many of them are. It is still the case, even with all the achievements of those women writers and practitioners in the 1970s and through the 1980s, that only a small percentage of women writing for theatre see their work professionally produced. Full productions of new works by women remain noteworthy simply by their occurrence. While many more plays by women are receiving attention, so many of these scripts are not supported beyond the workshop or staged reading. With that caveat in mind, it is not unreasonable to name Judith Thompson as one of Canada's foremost playwrights—female or male. Her plays (including *The Crackwalker, White Biting Dog, I am Yours,* and *Lion in the Streets*) have not always enjoyed critical enthusiasm or, indeed, respect, but her gripping creations of what one critic describes as "a surreal day-dream or nightmare spill[ing] into a naturalistic picture" (Adam 22) have brought her Governor General's Awards for Drama, productions of her texts both across and outside Canada, and considerable academic attention. Thompson's representation of people who struggle to articulate themselves, along with situations that impinge on that articulation, bring to theatre audiences a compelling dramatization of aspects of the world that we (as a hegemonically white and middle-class realization of the gaze) are otherwise efficiently trained to screen out. Robert Nunn suggests that Thompson's plays "are increasingly bold journeys into the abyss of the unconscious" (27)—and these are apparently journeys that audiences and academic readers are anxious to make. Her remarkable contribution is to provide an innovative and provocative aesthetic which attempts to account for generally invisible aspects of contemporary Canadian life.

Yet if Thompson's plays flatten out aspects of gender difference in order to explore a universalized psychic debilitation, then many other contemporary women playwrights have brought on to the stage their relationship to dramatic tradition precisely in terms of the gendered body. Many of their plays insist on entering into visibility the specificities of women's histories. Writers such as Jackie Crossland (*Collateral Damage*), Deborah Porter (*No More Medea*) and Anne-Marie MacDonald (*Goodnight Desdemona (Good Morning, Juliet)*) have turned to the canonical texts of dramatic literature and insisted on their own precisely female, re-readings. Others have taken as their subjects women little known and less recognized in history and brought the women's stories to the stage: specifically Canadian are Mary Vingoe's *Living Curiosities: A Story of Anna Swan* (which imagines the world inhabited by Anna Swan, a seven-feet-ten-inches tall, nineteenth-century Maritime woman who by virtue of her amazing height found herself at the age of seventeen one of Barnum's exhibits in New York City) and Wendy Lill's *The Fighting Days* (which explores the friendship of Frances Beynon with well-known suffrage activist Nellie McClung). Banuta Rubess' plays have also often turned to women's obscurity in history. A short radio play fantasizes the life of Isabelle Eberhardt, the nineteenth-century, Swiss-born writer and adventurer. Her *Tango Lugano* tells the story of Aspazija Rainis, a Latvian political revolutionary—a play which Rubess produced in Riga after the dissolution of the Soviet Empire (see Much and Rudakoff 51-52).

That Rubess returns to the experience of her Latvian background (her parents came to Toronto in the 1950s) is indicative of many contemporary women playwrights' particular interest in the cultural formation of their identities. Monique Mojica's powerful *Princess Pocahontas and the Blue Spots* counterpoints popular received images of Native women (always inaccurate, inevitably abusive) with the stories that Native women have always told and which have provided a non-linear but sustaining history. The high farce of Princess Buttered-on-Both-Sides not only draws a white audience's attention to Hollywood and other misrepresentations of Native peoples, but at the same time marks our on-going complicity in the maintenance of these images/stories. And an unmistakable part of her critique is directed at the white feminist who has insisted on a univocal feminism. As the Contemporary Woman #1 in Mojica's play describes it, "So many years of trying to fit into feminist shoes. O.K., I'm trying on the shoes; but they're not the same as the shoes in the display case. The shoes I'm trying on must be crafted to fit these wide, square, brown feet. I must be able to feel the earth through their soles." (58) The play claims a strong, but heterogeneous Native identity. If nothing else—and there *is* much else—*Princess Pocahontas* demonstrates how rare it is, still, for women of colour to see their realities on any stage and, as part of that, celebrates a recognition of the power of diversity in/as identity.

Djanet Sears, who directed the first workshop production and dramaturged the first full production of Mojica's *Princess Pocahontas*, raises her own complicated series of questions concerning identity. A one-woman show, *Afrika Solo*, explores the cultural condition of hegemonic whiteness. Djanet (raised in the United Kingdom and Canada of Jamaican and Guyanese parents), irrespective of that background and her own skin colour, discovers that she was "white" in the way she perceived the world. The play takes the form and the story of a quest, Djanet's own discovery of her roots and, as a result, her coming to terms with (her) identity. As Joanne Tompkins rightly suggests, "*Afrika Solo* does not occupy the usual colonial split of enunciation (of imperial centre and colony), rather it focuses on a multi-vectored site of enunciation, all violence of which must be accounted for in the construction of Djanet's 'Canadian' cultural heritage." (36-37) Once again, H/history is invoked not only to expose the fractures around gendered positionality, but to remark the colonial imperative of our Canadian heritage which hovers, yet, to restrict expressions of identity and selfhood.

And Audrey Butler's *Black Friday?* (in *Radical Perversions* 13-65) collapses labour history in Cape Breton into a classic coming-out story of lesbian identity. As Butler herself writes in the introduction of *Black*

Friday? "[m]any people have asked: why the question mark? ...Through the process of writing the play I began to perceive one of the characters as Black. Why? For me there was a clear connection between homophobia, racism, and the system that destroyed Terry's father. The title transcends a real historical event (my intention when I started the play) and encompasses issues I have been struggling with as a white working-class dyke" (*Radical Perversions* 12). As with *Princess Pocahontas,* part of the attraction to *Black Friday?* resides simply in making visible the otherwise invisible through the focus of a dramatic text.

The plays mentioned here represent only a few of the many exciting and innovative works women are producing for the Canadian stage. But they represent an active assertion of women's (counter)history, of the making and remaking of an aesthetic which asks new questions of the art form known as drama, and solicits new processes by and through which audiences recognize the form. And if these writers have transgressed, in the most productive sense, the container of the play, other women have sought other less text-based expressions for their ideas and concerns.

Performing Women

As Lenora Champagne explains, "[t]he performance-art form has subversive origins and tendencies.... Contemporary performance has precedents in the avant-garde movements of the early twentieth century that challenged established standards and definitions of art and sought to shake up social conventions with shocking, outrageous behaviour in public appearances." (xi)[11] It is hardly surprising, then, that this is a form that many women have chosen seemingly instead of conventional theatre. Given the history of exclusion in mainstream theatre, it must have often seemed easier to invent a new form and to pursue new venues for radical work. Moreover, women have often made it an explicit aspect of their performance strategy to seek out non-traditional audiences.

Both *Princess Pocahontas* and *Afrika Solo* were Nightwood Theatre "plays" and both, to differing extents, divert their energies from the conventions of theatre and drama, to explore form(s) that will more readily realize the complex ideas they are endeavouring to stage. Yet both, I think, retain some connection with conventions of the play, the shape of that performance. ahdri zhina mandiela's *dark diaspora in dub* was likewise first produced by Nightwood Theatre, but this text bears far less resemblance to the kind(s) of structures we generally identify as a play. *dark diaspora* was developed with a collective choreography and mandiela's dub poems were performed by seven women representing internal voice, shape and sound.[12] The work has also been performed as a solo show, with and without live musicians, and is available as a print text and as an audio recording. mandiela's performance poetry is full of rage, calls to empowerment, and celebration for women of colour. *dark diaspora* performs a strong and pointed challenge to the conventionality of both form and subject matter in others' (play) texts. The writer states in the prefatory material to the published text of *dark diaspora in dub* that she envisages her work performed by up to fifty women. Even if only as fantasy, this possibility gives testament to the remarkable sight/site a theatre stage occupied by so many women (of colour) would undoubtedly be.

Margo Kane's *Moonlodge* looks "to explore and mine the stories from within my [Kane's] experience" (Kane 26) and so, like Mojica's *Princess Pocahontas*, it records a history that has carried orally but which has in so many ways been denied by "Canada." *Moonlodge* has been performed in venues such as Native Earth Performing Arts in Toronto, the Banff Centre for the Arts in Alberta and the Vancouver East Cultural Centre, but it is important to note that it has also been seen by Native and Inuit communities across Canada. I offer here a long description by Kane of that experience, but one I think worth repeating for its sense of the community in/as performance:

> I join my relations in their evening circles over tea and bannock smeared with red, red jam. As mosquitos and flies vie for our attention, the young and old alike sing, with hand drums and crickets as accompaniment. Babies swing in hammocks. Dogs wander in and out, sometimes curling at our feet, then sneaking off together to chase down the night animals beyond our circle of light. Poetry, songs, memories and stories are shared. It is a place to give a first reading of a new poem, to receive encouragement for a new piece of progress. Sometimes I am coaxed to participate; other times I bring out material to be read aloud by those gathered. I need to hear it spoken by them. I want their impressions and advice. Often I just want to give something of myself....
>
> It is at times like these that I feel a strong sense of belonging. For all my wanderings, in and out of urban cities and towns, here the connection to tribal family and nation is reaffirmed. It is where my relations gather and my ancestors smile at me through their faces. (26)

Notions of land and place are so crucial to Native beliefs and practice, and Kane's *Moonlodge* marks those connections as a powerful performative, one that is offered as a gift to her nation. For the non-Native audience, as with Mojica's play, there is the invitation to listen—a contract from which we might learn much.

Other performance work draws more specifically on a visual arts context in which to frame issues by, for and about women. Such a context has, as Champagne suggested, its roots in the provocative 'acting out' of the so-called avant-garde movements in this century. An example of such 'acting out' is *Lies About Betty and The Truth about Zucchini*, a multimedia performance piece by Lori Weidenhammer.[13] In this work, Weidenhammer stages a plethora of domestic rituals, emphasizing through comic exaggeration the often ridiculous logic enforcing women's quotidian experience. The video segment of *Lies About Betty* imagines a "holiday from misogyny" and, like her earlier work *The Saskatchewan Lawn Ornament Opera*, suggests a serious social critique behind the melodramatic farce of her performance elements.

Shawna Dempsey and Lorri Millan, performance collaborators based in Winnipeg, have created the kinds of revisionist feminist histories that were highlighted in the plays of some of the more conventional writers. Dempsey and Millan, however, do not start with a written text but instead create the object which they eventually animate. The object functions, they suggest, as "a visual metaphor for the paradox we find ourselves in politically." (Bennett and Patience 9) *Mary Medusa* worked from the construction of a wig of snakes to articulate the imagination and assumptions of a contemporary corporate woman whose body carries the legacy of the Medusa myth. More recently, they have created a series of unlikely dresses—an arborite housewife's dress, a stained glass window dress of the Virgin Mary, a saran-wrap dress for the contemporary feminist and so on—through which to explore questions of identity as an embodied practice. As I have discussed at some length elsewhere, all of Dempsey and Millan's work "explores and exposes those systems of exchange in which the female body has functioned as the currency for its Other's power and as the material evidence for a stability of reference to the so-called objective world." (Bennett 37)

The performance of a counter-currency for female bodies—one of lesbian eroticism and desire—has brought much attention to the work of the Vancouver-based collective Kiss & Tell. *True Inversions*, a live performance incorporating video and audiotapes, slides and music, explores "the view that sex and the world are intricately complicated.... Sexual pleasure is interrupted by, framed by and simultaneous with concerns about AIDS and safer sex, sexual abuse, male violence, pleasure, sexism, friendship, love, racism, state control of our bodies and our art, political disagreement, television, coming out to our families...all of these things are part of our sexuality. And still there is joy which we affirm alongside our pain." (Publicity material. First set of ellipses indicating omitted material; second set of ellipses in the original.) A development of their well-received interactive "photo-event" "Drawing the Line,"[14] *True Inversions* both celebrates lesbian identity *and* re-marks the diffuse and complicated territory of its possible constructions.

While Weidenhammer, Dempsey and Millan, and Kiss & Tell use a multi-media approach to performance through which to interrogate the assumptions of more traditional, linear arrangements of enacted text, Karen Hines has chosen another marginalized dramatic genre—clowning—on which to script a performance of her female body. In *Pochsy's Lips*, Hines as Pochsy performs a part-spoken, part-sung monologue which explores the dilemma (to quote the first two lines she sings): "falling apart,/But everyone's falling in love." (38) Like Weidenhammer's transformation of the domestic into artistic ritual, Hines/Pochsy manipulates the hospital bed and I.V. unit to play partner to her enactment of a 'sick world.' And in the story she tells, Pochsy is wildly funny, but always in that potentially sad and tragic mode of clowning. And the performance ending brings not the usual resolution: for a comedy where women fall in love usually bespeaks marriage; in *Pochsy's Lips* she simply cannot be saved by love or anything else and dies.

The performance work of these Canadian women, above all else, has its emphasis on the body as the bearer of culture's scripts. With diverse and often contradictory strategies for its realization, women's performance art makes explicit the spectator's gaze and poses the crucial question: how do I look?[15] At a time when visibility politics has consumed much of the energy of feminism(s), the prevalence and directness of these women's performance speaks to "an effort to recover, or postulate, a prediscursive body, a critical effort to free the female body from its overdeterminations as a body saturated with sex, site of pleasure for (an)other, subjected and devoid of subjectivity." (Hart in Hart and Phelan 5)

Collective Creation

A third and important aspect of this map of contemporary women's writing for performance in Canada is the work of women's collectives. As Lynda Hart has noted, "[c]ollective authorship was an extremely important concept in early feminist companies of the 1970s and 1980s." (Hart and Phelan 6) While some earlier collectives no longer exist, others have developed and broadened the notion of "collective" to encompass a number of performance and writing strategies which address particular community and women's issues. Kiss & Tell, whose *True Inversions* I have already mentioned, are one such example: alongside a core group of three members, the collective has added other women as their various projects dictate which, it would seem, allows both a freedom and a renewal of energy. While Kiss & Tell's work has been focussed on lesbian visibility, collective performance by women in Canada has addressed a multiplicity of social and artistic concerns.

Perhaps the most notable and, indeed, successful of these is Toronto's The Company of Sirens. This company started in the mid-1980s and involved many women who had previously been associated with Nightwood Theatre. Much of their work is produced as the result of commissions (such as *The Working People's Picture Show* for a convention for the tenth anniversary of Organized Working Women; *Shelter from Assault* for the Ontario Ministry of Education Family Violence Prevention Initiative Programme; *Whenever I feel Afraid* on violence against women for Metropolitan Toronto high school audiences).[16] A measure of the company's success is its recent division into a main company and one directed at productions for young audiences, as is the fact that they have been performing more than three hundred shows a year. Using the presentational style common to much popular, touring theatre and engaging/empowering audiences in post-performance discussions, the Siren's work is often seen—and engaged—by many more spectators than number the usual audiences for plays and, particularly, for more performance-oriented art. In this way at least, it is interesting to consider that the Company of Sirens might well be Canada's most significant women writers/performers.

But I want to end this incomplete survey of women's theatre work in Canada in the city where I live and work. Calgary, a city of less than one million people, has had for some seven years a women's theatre collective in the name of Maenad. This group came into existence to produce the work of one of their founding members, Rose Scollard,[17] but has since that time staged each season two full productions of new plays by women and a three-week "New Voices/FemFest." Many of Maenad's playwrights (who devote a minimum of six weeks to participation in the rehearsal and production process) have been found in Calgary though others have been drawn from across Canada. The festival has showcased many different types of local performance work, alongside presentations by women from England, Germany, Japan and the United States. And this company's history is, in effect, a microcosm of what I have charted here. Maenad's history, in a sense typical of the complex trajectory that I have tried to suggest, characterizes contemporary Canadian women's writing for the stage.

Among Maenad's work there is *Aphra*, co-written by founding members Rose Scollard, Nancy Cullen and Alexandria Patience, a play which retrieves Aphra Behn from the margins of (theatre) history; *Dance Me Born,* written by Alice Lee and co-produced with Sweetgrass Players, which was in 1993 the first full-length script by a Native woman to be produced in Calgary—an all the more remarkable fact when it is remembered that the city is almost entirely enclosed by Native land. The 1994-95 season opener, Gisele Villeneuve's *Oldest Woman in the*

World, brings to the spotlight a woman whose age would usually mean that there is literally no role for her, on the stage or anywhere else.

And this is what Canadian women writing for performance are doing in/as the theatre. These women have rewritten the parameters for the cultural experience of "theatre;" they have, in short, reinvented the term. Many wonderful playwrights whose work I have not considered here—all the ground-breakers from the 1970s along with "newer" names like Pamela Boyd, Yvette Nolan, Sally Clark, Joan MacLeod, Janis Spence, Colleen Craig, Cindy Cowan and others—make Canadian theatre stronger and more diverse than ever before. Other artists, some of whom I have mentioned here, use more visual arts, cabaret settings, fringe festivals, women's festivals to reimagine women's bodies and the way(s) that we might see them. In so many communities, inside and outside of Canada's major urban centres, women are claiming their own performance spaces, some of which they name as theatres and some not. We can celebrate that seeing the work of Canadian women playwrights is, in the 1990s, an easier task. More of it gets done (though even more of it should) and it doesn't always mean paying at least $35 for a seat.

Writing for performance by Canadian women is not only strong and diverse; it is in more places and spaces than ever before. A cause for celebration, indeed, and—I hope—a cause, too, for some optimism for where it will surely lead us.

NOTES

[1] See, for example, Michelene Wander's, *Carry on, Understudies*, London: Routledge, 1986; Lizbeth Goodman's, *Contemporary Feminist Theatres: To Each Her Own*, London: Routledge, 1993; and Charlotte Canning's *Feminist Theatres in the USA*, London: Routledge, 1995.

[2] To some extent, to speak of women's theatre is to echo the tenets of cultural feminism. And an effect of that is to bring together a disparate collection of writers whose only commonality might in fact be their biological make-up. It is possible, too—or at least this article takes as one of its assumptions that it is—to celebrate a diversity of positionality which speaks to an inclusive, diverse and contradictory women's theatre. The relationship between a category defined as women's theatre and one defined as feminist theatre is both complicated and problematic. In either case, production of histories seems to me to pose questions that theatre historians have not yet grappled with in an entirely satisfactory way. For an account of some of the historiographical problems in accounting for feminist theatre, see my "Feminist (Theatre) Historiography/Canadian (Feminist) Theatre: A Reading of some Practices and Theories" in *Theatre Research in Canada*, 13, 1/2 (Spring/Fall 1992), 144-151.

[3] Theatre work in Quebec is discussed in another article in this collection. Here I'd like to make two notes. One is that women's theatre in Quebec has had a particularly rich and interesting history, drawing on French feminisms and European avant-garde performance styles that give, I think, a different shape and expression to much of the work Quebecois women have produced. The second is an emphasis of the first: while much of the work I include here has commonalities with work produced in Quebec, the difference—or, to pick up on the most common adjective summoned in support of Quebec's sovereignty— its distinct nature makes its inclusion in my own discussion both too complicated and, indeed, inappropriate. I should also record this article's restriction to writing in English, a fact which excludes contributions as important as Antonine Maillet's long and brilliant career in the Maritimes and works by Native women which primarily utilize their own languages to tell their stories.

[4] Heather Jones' "Feminism and Nationalism in Domestic Melodrama: Gender, Genre and Canadian Identity" in *Essays in Theatre*, 8, 1, November 1989, 5-14 provides helpful prolegomena to this area.

[5] An important biographical account of Dora Mavor Moore's huge contribution to the development of professional theatre in Toronto which emphasizes her experience precisely as a woman has been written by Paula Sperdakos. The biography is forthcoming from ECW Press.

[6] Anton Wagner's "Gwen Pharis Ringwood Rediscovered" in *Canadian Theatre Review*, 5, (Winter 1975), 63-69 offers an interesting account.

[7] See Kym Bird's "Performing Politics: Propaganda, Parody and a Women's Parliament" in *Theatre Research in Canada*, 13, 1/2 (Spring/Fall 1992), 168-193.

[8] See Hodkinson's introduction as well as Moira Day and Marilyn Potts' "Elizabeth Sterling Haynes: Initiator of Alberta Theatre" in *Theatre History in Canada*, 8, 1 (Spring 1987), 8-35; Anton Wagner's "Elsie Park Gowan: 'Distinctively Canadian'" in *Theatre History in Canada*, 8, 1 (Spring 1987), 62-82; and Moira Day's "Elsie Park Gowan's (re)-*Building of Canada*, 1937-1938: Revisioning the Historical Radio Series through Feminist Eyes" in *Theatre Research in Canada*, 14, 1 (Spring 1993), 3-19 for accounts of both women's contributions to Canadian theatre.

[9] The possibilities of a feminine (or, more explicitly, a feminist) aesthetics constitute a fraught, if interesting, debate among contemporary theorists. It would seem to me that many Canadian women now writing for performance quite deliberately construct a counter-aesthetic which is absolutely committed to the engagement of an interested spectator. Yet the risk that such an identification always already contributes to women's marginalization is an argument that cannot be too easily dismissed. See Rita Felski's persuasive account in *Beyond Feminist Aesthetics: Feminist Literature and Social Change*, Cambridge, MA: Harvard University Press, 1989.

[10] The Women's Circle project of Catalyst Theatre is recorded in *Canadian Theatre Review*, 69 (Winter 1991), 5-14.

[11] Despite the usefulness of Champagne's definition, the distinction between a play and a work of performance is often hard to draw. For the most part, the publication of a script appropriates it for the category of a play, although a text like Monique Mojica's *Princess Pocahontas* is not legible in terms of conventional dramatic structure. Other work I have tended to organize as performance. An exception here is ahdri zhina mandiela's *dark diaspora*; my inclination, despite its publication, to retain the category "performance" to describe this work is its flexibility— mandiela performs it with and without a supporting cast, with and without live music, and it exists not only as a published script but also as recorded music.

[12] See my review of *dark diaspora in dub*, as well as Mojica's *Princess Pocahontas and the Blue Spots*, Robert More's *Patches* and Wendy Lill's *Sisters*, in *Canadian Theatre Review*, 75 (Summer 1993), 82-83.

[13] Performance art is generally thought of as a marginalized form—yet paradoxically most of it is produced very much in the centre: New York, London, Los Angeles, Montreal. Lori Weidenhammer extends the marginality to include geography and, indeed, to stage geography since much of her work addresses precisely her coming from Cactus Lake, Saskatchewan where she still resides. Shawna Dempsey and Lorri Millan, discussed later in this article, started in Toronto, but now live and work in Winnipeg. It is tempting to suggest that Canadian women performance artists—some of them at least—have made the most of what Lynda Hart suggests is "certain advantage that is produced alongside their marginalized status. In that sense they are in limited but important ways 'unbound,' achieving a fluidity of movement simultaneously inside and outside dominant discourses" (in Hart and Phelan, 6).

[14] For an interesting and thoughtful review/analysis of "Drawing the Line" see Marusia Bociurkiw's "The Transgressive Camera" in *Afterimage*, 16, 6 (January 1989), 17, 19.

[15] I am indebted to the anthology *How Do I Look?* and especially Teresa de Lauretis' article "Film and the Visible" (see especially page 233) in that anthology for drawing attention to the significance of this question. The anthology is produced by the Bad Object-Choices collective and was published by Bay Press in Seattle in 1991.

[16] See Kym Bird's account of the Sirens' work for a fuller discussion of some of their performance strategies. Also Maria DiCenzo's interview with Cynthia Grant, one of the company's Artistic Directors, brings to attention many important issues.

[17] Susan Stone-Blackburn's interview with the founding members is useful for its charting of the group's mandate and history.

BIBLIOGRAPHY

Adam, Julie. "The Implicated Audience: Judith Thompson's Anti-Naturalism in *The Crackwalker, White Biting Dog, I Am Yours,* and *Lion in the Streets.*" In Much, 21-29.

Bennett, Susan. "Radical (Self-)Direction and the Body: Shawna Dempsey and Lorri Millan's Performance Art." *Canadian Theatre Review* 76 (Fall 1993), 37-41.

———— and Alexandria Patience. "A Dialogue on the Expression of Sex and Self in the Political Theatre of the Body." *i.e.: a magazine of contemporary culture* (December 1992), 9-10.

Bird, Kym. "The Company of Sirens: Popular Feminist Theatre in Canada." *Canadian Theatre Review* 59 (Summer 1989), 35-37.

Butler, Audrey. *Radical Perversions: Two Dyke Plays.* Toronto: Women's Press, 1990.

Champagne, Lenora. *Out from Under: Texts by Women Performance Artists.* New York: Theatre Communications Group, 1990.

Crossland, Jackie. *Collateral Damage.* Vancouver: Press Gang, 1992.

Dempsey, Shawna and Lorri Millan. *Mary Medusa. Canadian Theatre Review* 76 (Fall 1993), 42-57.

DiCenzo, Maria and Susan Bennett. "Women, Popular Theatre, and Social Action: Interviews with Cynthia Grant and the Sistren Theatre Collective." *ARIEL* 23.1 (January 1992), 73-96.

Grant, Cynthia. "Notes from the Front Line." *Canadian Theatre Review* 43 (Summer 1985), 44-51.

Hart, Lynda and Peggy Phelan (eds.). *Acting Out: Feminist Performances.* Ann Arbor: University of Michigan Press, 1993.

Hines, Karen. Pochsy's Lips. *Canadian Theatre Review* 75 (Summer 1993), 36-46.

Hodkinson, Yvonne. *Female Parts: The Art and Politics of Female Playwrights.* Montreal: Black Rose Books, 1991.

Jansen, Ann (ed.). *Adventures for (Big) Girls: Seven Radio Plays.* Winnipeg: Blizzard Publishing, 1993.

Kane, Margo. "From the Centre of the Circle the Story Emerges." *Canadian Theatre Review* 68 (Fall 1991), 26-29.

Lill, Wendy. *The Fighting Days.* Vancouver: Talonbooks, 1985.

MacDonald, Anne-Marie. *Goodnight Desdemona (Good Morning, Juliet).* Toronto: Coach House, 1989.

Mojica, Monique. *Princess Pocahontas and the Blue Spots.* Toronto: Women's Press, 1990.

Much, Rita. *Women on the Canadian Stage: The Legacy of Hrotsvit.* Winnipeg: Blizzard Publishing, 1992.

Nunn, Robert. "Spatial Metaphor in the Plays of Judith Thompson." *Theatre History in Canada* 10.1 (Spring 1989), 3-29.

Rubess, Banuta. *Oblivion: A Story of Isabelle Eberhardt,* in Jansen, 1-24.

Rudakoff, Judith and Rita Much. *Fair Play: 12 Women Speak. Conversations with Canadian Playwrights*. Toronto: Simon & Pierre, 1990.

Scollard, Rose, Alexandria Patience and Nancy Cullen. *Aphra. Theatrum* (September/October), 1991.

Sears, Djanet. *Afrika Solo*. Toronto: Sister Vision Press, 1990.

Stone-Blackburn, Susan. "Maenadic Rites on Stage in Calgary." *Canadian Theatre Review* 69 (Winter 1991), 28-33.

Thompson, Judith. *The Other Side of the Dark*. Toronto: Coach House, 1989.

Tompkins, Joanne. "Infinitely Rehearsing Performance and Identity." *Canadian Theatre Review* 74 (Spring 1993), 35-39.

Vingoe, Mary. *Living Curiosities: A Story of Anna Swan*, in Jansen, 25-50.

mandiela, ahdri zhina. *dark diaspora in dub*. Toronto: Sister Vision Press, 1991.

Joyce Doolittle

Theatre for Young Audiences

June 1987, Calgary, the rodeo capital of Canada, home of the Calgary Exhibition and Stampede, hosted its first *Calgary International Children's Festival*. Its bright calendar of events carried this message from producer JoAnne James:

> Join us for five days of non-stop fun in June when we invite the young and the young-at-heart to participate in an exuberant event in downtown Calgary. Children's festivals have become joyful annual celebrations in Vancouver, Edmonton, Toronto and Halifax for years. Now it's Calgary's turn....

> Some of the world's finest entertainers for children will offer you a program jam-packed with "something for everyone." From provocative theatre and spellbinding puppets to hilarious unicyclists and fascinating magic, we've got it! Join your children in a flight of fancy with groups from Italy, Belgium, U.S.A., the Netherlands, and Australia, plus acclaimed Canadian performers from Wolfville, Nova Scotia to Victoria, British Columbia. Fifteen artists/companies will present 100 mainstage performances....

> Thanks to corporate and government support we have been able to keep our ticket prices low....

> Join us as we offer to the children of southern Alberta an opportunity to experience excellence from around the world....[1]

That such a festival can flourish is a tribute to four decades of hard work by underpaid, dedicated artists who believe in the significance of theatre's 'poor sister'—theatre for children.

Canada's professional theatre for young audiences is a post World War II phenomenon. Until that time there were various groups formed to allow children to act; also, the Junior League, a women's service club, produced and performed plays in schools. Adult amateur companies put on occasional pieces designed for children during school holidays.

After the war professional theatre for the young in English Canada grew concurrently with adult theatre. The beginning was Holiday Theatre of Vancouver. In 1953, the same year that the Stratford Festival opened in Ontario, Joy Coghill and Myra Benson set a pattern of family entertainment for weekends and vacations—hence the name, Holiday, for their company. Later they added the school tours which have since become an important fact of life in theatre for the young in this vast landscape. Because of its late beginning children's theatre in Canada was not inhibited by the tyranny of the proscenium arch, a factor that has no doubt contributed to the success of the travelling productions which visit schools. Millions of young Canadians see their first live theatre as captive audiences in school halls and gymnasiums. It is a tribute to the imagination and ingenuity of playwrights, directors and designers, and to the talent and energy of actors and stage managers, that these arid halls, so innately hostile to theatre, are transformed, for fifty minutes, into another world. However, in truth, it must be told that slipshod, predictable pieces, indifferently performed, do continue to undercut the credibility of the genre.

As regional theatres were established in the 1960s they followed the model of Winnipeg's Manitoba Theatre Centre (1958) and included a children's theatre in their mandate. By the 1990s, most of these had disappeared. In tough economic times, the priority was to keep the adult programs alive. Both Calgary's Alberta Theatre Projects (1972) and Saskatchewan's Globe Theatre (1966) in Regina, originally formed to present works to young audiences, no longer do so. The Citadel Theatre of Edmonton has cut its Citadel on Wheels/Wings (1968) and replaced it with occasional mainstage family productions. However, some companies specializing solely in work for the young have flourished. In 1977, Young People's Theatre of Toronto (1966) became the first Canadian theatre exclusively for the young to have its own building. In 1991, Kaleidoscope Theatre for Young People (1974) of Victoria, British Columbia, opened its own performing space.

There have been several 'fashions' in plays for young audiences in Canada. Early companies performed adaptations of fairy tales; those of Charlotte Chorpenning (USA) and Nicholas Stuart Grey (UK) were popular choices. Participation plays, written to include spontaneous but guided 'helping' from the audience were popular in the 1960s. Brian Way's 1959 tour of Canada to introduce his technique of teaching drama through improvisation influenced many teachers. Plays he wrote for his London, England, touring company dominated the repertoire of the Globe Theatre in its early years.

Paddy Campbell wrote some of the first Canadian participation plays. *Chinook* (1967, 1973), about how the chinook wind got its name, and *Too Many Kings* (1968, 1973), in which an apprentice mistakenly summons three monarchs, are typical. Another is *Almighty Voice* (1970, 1974) by Len Petersen. It tells the story of the Cree Indian, Almighty Voice, who is forced into hiding after he steals a cow to feed his starving people. Children in the audience are invited to take sides as Cree or Mounties, and a discussion of issues raised by the play frequently follows performances. Many of Rex Deverell's plays for the young, written for the Globe when he was playwright-in-residence, include participation. Among them are *Sarah's Play* (1975), about a little girl who finds having one's wishes come true is a mixed blessing and *Melody Meets the Bag Lady* (1982, 1984) in which an eccentric vagrant is transformed into a borgeoise matron, only to be changed back again when the children effecting the change regret her loss of 'character.' Audience participation, including coming onto the stage to physically help the performers, is encouraged in the children's plays of Calgary's Loose Moose Theatre (1976) whose scripts are often the result of group improvisation, using techniques of Theatre Sports for which the Loose Moose Company and their founder, Keith Johnstone, are internationally famous.

Some well-known Canadian authors have written plays for children; perhaps the most famous is a version of L.M. Montgomery's novel, *Anne of Green Gables*, a musical by Norman Campbell adapted by Donald Herron (1965, 1972). The production sells out every year at the Charlottetown, Prince Edward Island festival and has toured internationally.

However, it was only with the 1967 Canada Centennial celebrations, which led to the commissioning of new scripts and 1970s federal 'make-work' schemes, that a large body of new works were written, performed and published. Federal funds encouraged the creation of new plays through the establishment of companies with a distinctly regional bias, such as Alberta Theatre Projects which 'brought western history to life' and Mermaid Theatre which used Mic Mac legends of Eastern Canada for its first successes. Federal 'job creation' funds launched Playwrights Co-op, now Playwrights Union of Canada, an important project whose inexpensive and immediately accessible publishing policy made multiple performances of new plays possible. Also, in 1971, the Canada Council began funding specialized children's theatre companies for the first time. Thus, increased performances and publication opportunities nurtured many playwrights and led to the creation of varied styles.

Most endeavors for the young have a whiff of education about them. With its reliance upon schools for tour bookings, theatre for young audiences often fits productions to the aims and content of the school curriculum. Theatre in Education, or T.I.E., begun in England, is the most honestly named of many attempts, world-wide, to accommodate both art and education. Ideally, members of a T.I.E. company are trained actors/teachers, the performance of a script being only the centrepiece of a package of teaching services which includes both preparation and follow-up. T.I.E. proved too costly for most centres and was modified by Canadian companies, but follow-up materials prevail.

Theatre in Education was the forerunner of the issue play, the most recent style in theatre for the young, where theatre pieces attempt to bring current life problems out into the open through dramatic metaphor. The Green Thumb Theatre under its playwright-director, Dennis Foon, was an early contributor to and advocate of issue-oriented theatre. Foon said his theatre had "the goal to give children the tools to cope better with a world that has become increasingly confusing and complex."[2] Foon's *Skin* (1985) deals with racial prejudice. His *Feeling, Yes, Feeling, No* (1982) is designed to equip children with strategies against sexual assault. Other issues addressed have included immigration, poverty, learning disabilities and peer pressure. Green Thumb's current artistic director, Peter Zednik, continues the philosophy begun by Foon, who is now a free lance playwright and director.

Theatre Direct is another company committed to T.I.E. principles which has produced several issue plays including *Friends* (1984) by Tom Bentley-Fisher (with Patricia Grant) about day-care, and *Getting Wrecked* (1985) by Tom Walmsley about drug abuse. *Getting Wrecked* won a Dora Mavor Moore award for the best play for young people in 1986 and their production of Ojibway playwright Drew Taylor's *Toronto at Dreamer's Rock* won the Chalmers award for the best play for young audiences in 1992.

But not all plays are issue oriented. The top Chalmers award in 1986 went to *Running the Gauntlet* (1985), Duncan McGregor's story of the effect of the war of 1812 on children, written for Carousel Theatre of Ontario. Jim Betts' four plays for Young People's Theatre weekend family series have been popular all over Canada. His *Mystery of the Oak Island Treasure* (1983, 1985) won the 1983 Chalmers award and was nominated as outstanding new play by the Dora Mavor Moore Awards.

Two prairie companies formed during the 1980s are producing a blend of classic and topical work. In Winnipeg, Manitoba Theatre for Young People, under the direction of Leslee Silverman, was recognized by the Canadian Institute of the Arts for Young Audiences for the production of *Comet in Moominland*, directed by Graham Whitehead. In Calgary, Duval Lang leads Quest Theatre, whose work has ranged from classics such as Rick McNair's *Merlin and Arthur* to Clem Martini's *The Field*, which deals with racial discrimination.

The most encouraging sign of a mature repertoire of plays for the young is having some playwrights produce a large body of successful works for the genre. Rex Deverell, Dennis Foon and John Lazarus are writers whose scripts have been widely performed, published, and include a wide variety of styles and subjects.

Although many theatre workers begin their careers in school touring companies, training in the field is scarce. Drama departments at the universities of Calgary, Waterloo and Victoria do include under-graduate courses in theatre for young audiences and Calgary and Victoria offer a master's degree in Theatre in Education. But the National Theatre School does not offer special courses in acting, directing or designing for the young.

Once rare, but now in growing numbers, other professionals— directors, designers, administrators are devoting careers to theatre for the young, and in some cases having profound effect on the style of their companies. This is true of directors Duval Lang of Quest Theatre, Maja Ardal of Young People's Theatre and Elizabeth Gorrie of Kaleidoscope. Gorrie's lyrical gifts have developed a distinctive style for her company. Working with the barest essentials in set pieces, costuming and props, and relying on movement, transformations and imagination, she has created productions of great beauty and power. In Vancouver, Elizabeth Ball has created a series of pieces for children based on Shakespeare called *Suddenly Shakespeare* that has been enthusiastically received.

Reliance on school bookings, which might be considered a limitation, has given theatre for the young some advantage over adult companies. There is great affection for the troupe that arrives packed in with its props in a van. There is often more tolerance for difficult, controversial content and unusual, innovative staging from schoolteachers close to today's children and their complex concerns than from their parents, who more often take their children to the theatre for "entertainment." Children who regularly see school touring productions often become sophisticated theatregoers. But providing an audience for tomorrow is not the goal:

> The development of future audiences is not a concern because the present young audience is considered to be a valid, important entity in itself—whether or not they choose to go to the theatre when they grow up is up to them.[3]

A high quality of production, a growing repertoire of consequence and a body of dedicated career specialists have raised Canadian theatre for the young to a world class level. A landmark in Canada's progress in theatre for the young was the first of the international festivals, The Vancouver International Children's Festival, 1978. Since then, every year about a dozen foreign companies and individual performers have joined twice as many Canadian companies to present a ten-day-event in Vancouver. The Canadian Children's Festival Association, formed in 1990, represents festivals that now operate every spring in Calgary, Edmonton, Prince George, Toronto, Winnipeg, Regina and Quebec City. A comparison in the quality of work performed, once to Canada's disadvantage, now leads to a higher profile abroad and more respect at home. The pattern of international festivals developing across the land provides a welcome forum for an exchange of ideas amongst dedicated workers in the field who are usually too busy to reflect upon issues larger than this week's tour and next year's budget. The stimulation arising from seeing the best of the world's products is inevitably reflected in future Canadian plays and the visits here by foreign companies offer useful hints on how better to tailor our plays for trips abroad. As a result of appearances at Canadian festivals, several Canadian groups have been invited to appear abroad.

Canada's young companies enjoy a worldwide network of audiences. While most adult companies close down for the summer months, their counterparts in theatre for young audiences are often performing abroad. For the rising generation, companies devoted to theatre for the young are truly major cultural ambassadors.[4]

NOTES

[1] JoAnne James, Festival Brochure of the Calgary International Children's Festival 1987. Unpaginated.

[2] Dennis Foon, "Theatre for Young Audiences in English Canada," in Anton Wagner (ed.), *Contemporary Canadian Theatre; New World Visions*, Toronto: Simon and Pierre 1985, 253.

[3] Ibid.

[4] The current catalogue of Playwrights Union of Canada, 54 Wolseley Street, 2nd Floor, Toronto, Ontario, M5T 1A5 provides up to date lists of published plays and anthologies for young audiences.

BIBLIOGRAPHY

Canadian Theatre Review. (Particularly CTR 10 and CTR 41).

Canadian Children's Literature. (Double issue 8-9).

Canadian Children's Literature. (Double issue 57-58).

Davis, Desmond. *Theatre for Young People.* Musson: Don Mills, 1981.

Doolittle, Joyce (ed.). *Eight Plays for Young People.* Edmonton: Newest Press, 1984.

Doolittle, Joyce (ed.). *Playhouse—Six Fantasy Plays for Children.* Red Deer: Red Deer College Press, 1988.

Doolittle, Joyce and Zina Barnieh. *A Mirror of Our Dreams: Children and the Theatre in Canada.* Vancouver: Talonbooks, 1979.

Hamill, Tony (ed.). *Class Acts: Six Plays for Children.* Toronto: Playwrights Union of Canada, 1992.

Rubes, Susan (ed.). *A Collection of Canadian Plays, IV.* Toronto: Simon and Pierre, 1975.

Playwrights Canada (no acknowledged editor). *Kids Plays.* Toronto: Playwrights Canada, 1980.

The writer thanks Jan Truss, who helped with the original version of this essay in 1987 and JoAnne James, who provided valuable information for the update in 1992.

Denyse Lynde

Newfoundland Drama:
An Ever Changing Terrain

The history of drama written in Newfoundland can best be evoked by the rugged and rocky coastline of the province. Frequently striking, occasionally breath-takingly dramatic and always the focal point for the release of violent energies, the coastline like the drama that springs from these shores is an enduring testament to the wild and exuberant natural life of this North Atlantic island. From the early fifties to the present, a notable succession of waves have broken upon it. Thus the old amateur tradition of British and American plays in the towns, and the concert tradition in the countryside, gave place in the sixties to the indigenous drama of such major figures as Michael Cook, Tom Cahill, Al Pittman, and Grace Butt; they in turn were partially displaced in the seventies by the explosion of the Mummers, CODCO, and the associated vogue for the collective; by the late eighties a new wave of playwrights duly emerged to freshly define the present. Beneath such radical change, however, remain the enduring foundations of a passionate commitment to the bleak, beautiful, and frequently terrifying land that gives it birth; people and concerns resurface throughout the period regardless of dramatic mandate or fashion.

With the 1967 Dominion Drama Festival call for Canadian plays, the vibrant and successful tradition of amateur theatre in Newfoundland pushed in new directions. Amateurs wanted local scripts and playwrights obliged. In the early seventies, two very different theatre troupes emerged, partly in reaction to the increasingly competitive nature of the amateur tradition, partly as a logical outcome of the concert tradition and partly due to the different agendas of the two groups of individuals. From the success stories of CODCO and the Mummers can be traced a long list of collectives produced by these two

---

companies as well as by Resource Centre For the Arts, Rising Tide, Sheila's Brush and others; collectives became the mainstay of theatre production on the Island from the late seventies to the mid eighties, although earlier playwrights continued to write for both professional and amateur stages. In the late eighties, various factors encouraged the emergence of the playwright once again, many of whom had been major players in the collective tradition.

The Dominion Drama Festival provided a major focus for amateur dramatics in the Province and, when the D.D.F. announced that the centennial year competition would be devoted to Canadian scripts, amateur groups across the country sought local material. Previous to 1967, the Newfoundland amateur theatre companies mainly produced American and British classics, but this all-Canadian Dominion Drama Festival mandate sent them scurrying for new material. Grace Butt, who had founded the St. John's Players in 1937 and had been writing plays for over two decades, was joined by Tom Cahill, Al Pittman and Michael Cook in the search for appropriate plays. They all turned to the Island, her people and history for their inspiration; the resulting plays are varied and rich.

Butt's own plays are not the least notable of the group; among them are *An Ear or A Fear*,[1] *To Toslow We'll Go*[2] and the *The Road Through Melton*.[3] Perhaps her strongest play and also her earliest, is *The Road Through Melton*, first produced by the St. John's Players in 1945. This play is a realistic portrayal of a small town local farmer's stand against what he perceives to be corrupt electioneering. Steve Martin decides to run as an independent for his community in a provincial election rather than follow the tactics of the Liberal Party. Steve believes that the ruling party plans to buy votes with the promise of a new highway that is neither needed nor wanted. In the play, Butt considers the issues of personal and private integrity and the personal cost involved in maintaining such standards. *The Road Through Melton* is only one of several plays that Butt wrote which explores the individual coming to terms with a changing world. What gives this play its enduring quality are the carefully developed characters, well-crafted plot and universally unchanging tactics of politicians. Those of the forties could easily be campaigning today. Butt's contribution to the theatre continues through the nineties with the publication of *Persons*[4] in 1990. *Persons* is a collection of play excerpts, short stories and verse formerly published in a variety of sources and brought together here under one cover.

The 1967 Dominion Drama Festival witnessed the first production of Tom Cahill's *Tomorrow Will Be Sunday*[5] which garnered high praise from several adjudicators. In 1974, Cahill wrote *As Loved Our Fathers*,[6] a two-act play centred on the two referenda that took place in Newfoundland in 1948. Cahill presents a wide cross-section of Newfoundland society on the two evenings of voting. Con, a carpenter, is the chairman of the local committee working for independence but his aged mother-in-law is squarely behind Joey Smallwood and confederation. In the first act, his wife, Trese, admits that she too has joined Smallwood because of the promise of old age pensions and baby bonuses. At the close of the play with the confederation votes in the majority, Con discovers that he stands alone against his family.

Cahill uses the private sphere of family to explore the various tensions and issues that divided and, in some cases, broke long standing relationships during this tempestuous time of history. In a play dealing with passionate issues, Cahill manages to present each of these issues with feeling. On the one hand, the women care deeply for the young and aged. They believe that pensions and baby bonuses will make real change. This contrasts with the depth of Con's feelings about Newfoundland's independence. In the end, *As Loved Our Fathers* becomes both a passionate lament and at the same time a celebration of the dawning of a brave new day. In this play, there are no clear winners; confederation is assured but the ending sees Con in tears for the tremendous loss he feels. In the 1990s, this tale of the fight for independence or confederation remains tinged with both optimism and regret; the play asks as Con does: "...Do you realize you can't call yourself a Newfoundlander any more? In fifty years there won't be any such thing on the face of the earth!" (64) For Con, the final referendum outcome is the death of a way of life but typical of Cahill's play, this same result gives all the women new-found hope for the future.

Also in 1974, Al Pittman wrote *A Rope Against The Sun*.[7] Set in a fictitious outport town, Merasheen, Pittman's play, not unlike Cahill's, is a lament and a celebration of those "who once lived in the rugged perimeter of that forsaken Island." (iv) *A Rope Against the Sun*, reminiscent of Dylan Thomas' *Under Milkwood*, weaves the separate hopes, dreams and fears of a small outport's inhabitants. In song, narration and dialogue, Pittman presents us with a cast of unique individuals that, while tied to a specific place, assume almost mythic dimension. Specifically, Pittman colours the textures of this world with Newfoundland folklore and language, making it particular yet universal. The title of the play is explained by the local priest in a letter to his bishop:

> For all my sermons and prayers, they remain a very superstitious people. They believe it is bad luck to coil a rope against the sun, to purchase a broom in May, to meet a red-haired woman, to look over another's shoulder into a mirror, to come in one door and go out another, to cross knives on the table, to whistle on the water. (11-12)

The letter is never sent because the Priest knows he would be admitting failure; so he remains, feeling trapped in the community.

Also feeling an outsider is Michael, the local schoolteacher who no longer feels the community is as charming as he first thought it. He, too, longs for escape but, like the Priest, appears to be powerless to change his life. The play begins in the morning and charts the separate character's activities; however, as night draws in, fears and longings begin to dominate. From Mrs. Ennis' plea that her child be born when the sunkers are quiet to young Jennifer's self-questioning about nuns or boys to aged Jake's wish for death and Nell's tears of despair for her sterile life, the remote community with its isolated individuals appears in pain. The play is lifted from despair by the hopes and dreams of the young, characterized by Billy's thoughts of Jennifer: "You are soft like roses and white like roses and you are mine forever." (58) The final moments, however, remain bittersweet with the young generation continuing but both history and Pittman clearly marking the changes that will come. This outport with its beauty and hardship will be abandoned, but at what price? Cahill's Con would say the cost was too great, but here as in *As Loved Our Fathers*, the playwright chooses to celebrate the past, this time lyrically and romantically.

Less romantic but also exploring isolated Newfoundland are the many plays of Michael Cook. His first play, *Colour the Flesh the Colour of Dust*,[8] is set in St. John's in 1762 and recounts the capture of the British forces by the French and closes with the return of the British. This brutal period of Newfoundland history is told through the eyes of a British Lieutenant and his woman who are united at the opening by the hanging of a prisoner and are parted at the closing with the Lieutenant's death. Enclosed by these deaths is a horrible tale of betrayal, corruption and violence as the eighteenth century community scrambles to survive at any cost. Cook's approach to this broad story is itself panoramic. He writes with broad strokes, creating colourful character types who fill the stage.

In *Colour the Flesh the Colour of Dust* can be seen the first glimpse of one of Cook's recurring themes. Here, as elsewhere in his drama, he champions the sacred right of the individual to protect his personal integrity but, as is characteristic of Cook's work, the resulting cost is also explored. The Lieutenant will not escape his perceived duty to his country with his woman; he remains to fight and is killed by a bullet from his own lines. The woman finds his philosophy inadequate. For her, "the bravest people I know are the ones who will endure." (D42) Interestingly, it is these two attitudes that lie behind much of Cook's subsequent work: the ability to remain true to what one most values set against the powerful and attractive quality of endurance at any cost.

In his second play, *The Head, Guts and Sound Bone Dance*,[9] Cook, like Pittman, turns to an outport community for his setting but his play shares none of Pittman's nostalgia for a lost way of life. In this play, Cook explores the brutal cost of an individual's determination to hold on to his vision of the world. In what appears at first glance to be a traditional realistic drama, two old fishermen await the return of a son. As they wait, they reminisce and argue as they set about daily tasks dictated by their fishing stage. As the play progresses, it becomes apparent that the realism is embedded with ritualized behavior that reaches its climax when the Skipper casts the spell of the past so firmly over Uncle John that neither man hears the terrified cries for help from a child. When Absalom, the retarded son, returns with his pitiful catch of six fish, the grim reality of the old men's delusions are grotesquely made clear as they painstakingly celebrate the so-called harvest.

With Uncle John's wife's entrance, followed by Absalom's second entrance with yet another harvest, this time the drowned child, Uncle John is able to break free from the Skipper's terrible grip of the past. This painful yet achingly powerful drama closes with the Skipper, alone, resolutely completing his sterile celebration. Often interpreted as a slice-of-life outport drama, *The Head, Guts and Sound Bone Dance* is a highly stylized indictment of the human cost that can result when lives are shaped and controlled by mindless adherence to the past. Here, ritualization is used to create a truly Newfoundland dance of death.

In *Jacob's Wake*,[10] written in 1974, again a seemingly realistic portrayal of outport family is created but while Tom Cahill in *As Loved Our Fathers* celebrates the ambiguity of the past, here Cook is brutal in his analysis of the society that surrounds him and is damning in his thoughts for the future. Centring his action on one family, he recounts the failings of three generations. From the crippled Skipper confined to his bed to the drunken son, Winston, long suffering daughter-in-law, Rosie, and bitter daughter, Mary, down to the three grandsons, a corrupt politician, a crooked businessman and a defrocked priest, Cook sees no future for this family and, by extension, this society. The title refers to the drowned son, Jacob, but clearly points to the action of the entire play. *Jacob's Wake* is Cook's bitter and brutal condemnation of a world that has slid into addiction, corruption and self-complacency. A failure of traditional lifestyles with no acceptable alternative causes the Skipper, at the close of the play, to rise from his bed in a desperate attempt to steer his family out of the storm.

Cook again turns to history, an eighteenth-century sailor's diary, for his next play, *Gayden Chronicles*[11] and fashions what at first appears to be a high seas adventure. However, again, Cook's preoccupation with the individual's concern for personal integrity is felt. Here, Gayden's path to his final execution is explored and each turning point he reaches is questioned. In the end, he is offered a chance to join the establishment that he has fought against his whole life but he finds he must refuse: "I am my name and I will not give it to you." (74) Because he can read and write, he acutely felt and saw the injustice of the system and it is his literacy that becomes the heart of the play. Gayden appears as a man out of his times, at odds with the whole oppressive system, refusing to give in.

Cook's one-act plays, *Tiln*,[12] *Quiller*,[13] and *Theresa's Creed*[14] also deserve a mention. *Tiln*, clearly indebted to Beckett, is set in an isolated lighthouse, home of Tiln and Fern, two warring, reluctant companions, awaiting death and the end of the world. *Quiller* and *Theresa's Creed*, frequently performed as a double bill, are Newfoundland portraits, the former of an aged widower and the later of a middle-aged widow. In each play, the single character recounts a typical day and reminisces about the past. Again, unlike the plays of Cahill or Pittman, the characters find little in the present to comfort them; their past world is gone and modern times appear to have passed them by.

Cook continued to write for the theatre and radio. His several published and unpublished plays, radio dramas and arts commentary made him a major figure on the Canadian arts landscape until his death in Newfoundland in 1994. He, like Butt, Cahill and Pittman, contributed to the reawakening of drama in Newfoundland in the late sixties and early seventies and, although they all continued to create through the late seventies and eighties, the years 1972 and 1973 saw new forces coming together that would again reshape the theatrical landscape of Newfoundland.

Two of the most celebrated forces in Newfoundland drama emerged at that time; 1972 saw the formation of The Mummers Troupe and 1973 marked the beginning of CODCO. Throughout the seventies and early eighties, these two very different professional companies existed alongside the older generation of playwrights but gradually the collective theatre tradition began to dominate. Interestingly, the Mummers Troupe and CODCO, while forming at about the same time and from mainly the same background of amateur theatre and concert tradition, were radically different companies due to politics, style and approach. The Mummers Troupe developed a strongly pro-active political stance while CODCO choose to take on the perceived ills of society with their own, unique blend of wacky satire. By briefly examining the politics, process and products of the two groups, a sense of their unique approach to drama can be traced which, in turn, will shed some light on later collectives that dominated Newfoundland theatres.

In 1972, Chris Brookes, Lynn Lunde and John Doyle among others formed The Mummers Troupe[15] by researching, workshopping and developing their own version of the traditional mummer's play. The following year they staged and toured *Newfoundland Night*, "The Punch and Judy Show" and created *Gros Mourn*, which sprang directly from their collective response to the people of Sally's Cove who faced a park relocation policy made necessary by the new Gros Morne National Park. After touring *Gros Mourn*, Brookes assembled a cast to spend a few weeks in the mining town of Buchans in order to "create the *people's* history of Buchans." (115) The resulting play, *Buchans: A Mining Town*,[16] was a success not only in Buchans but in other mining areas in Newfoundland and Nova Scotia, and perhaps more significantly, at Toronto Workshop Production in 1975. The process, development and contribution of The Mummers Troupe has been analyzed by Alan Filewod[17] from the point of view of internal politics and government funding policy; equally compelling is the link between the Mummers' style of presentation and the traditional Newfoundland concert tradition. When asked about their performances in rural Newfoundland, Chris Brookes stated: "...I remember when we used to tour in the seventies, in the early seventies around the Island, it was sort of the kiss of death to advertise what you were doing as a play. We said it was a show or a concert...."[18] These early plays are characterized by the Troupe's search for politically relevant material. When they began to concentrate their activities in urban St. John's, shifts in policy based on audience, on company dynamics and funding begin to move the company in different directions. However, while the focus of their subject matter shifts slightly, their basic production approach appears to remain constant.

The Mummers Troupe was an exciting and active theatre company for ten years with several important collectives honed by the company. Briefly, in 1977 they produced *The Bard of Prescott Street*, a historical drama, followed by *They Club Seals, Don't They*[19] in 1977 and finally *Makin' Time with the Yanks*[20] in 1982. In the early days, the Mummers Troupe averaged five productions a year, developing new collectives, touring and remounting the traditional Newfoundland Christmas play. The company members changed over the years just as their approach to collective theatre evolved. For Filewod, the Mummers Troupe became the "most actively political theatre in English Canada" (Filewod, *Collective Encounters*, 151) but, by the late seventies, the Mummers, while continuing to produce quality material, were clearly moving in different directions and by 1982 Brookes felt "many Newfoundland actors were no longer interested in the kind of theatre which the Mummers presented. They'd cut their teeth on original political plays. Now they wanted to try their hand at other things: Joe Orton, Arthur Miller, Shakespeare." (Brookes, 1988, 223) The Mummers disbanded but their legacy to the drama of Newfoundland is felt today. Although some performers were drawn to scripted material as Brookes predicted, the different forms of collective creation that the Mummers had experimented with and developed were the major vehicle for several Newfoundland theatre practitioners throughout the rest of the eighties. Some had direct experience as former members; others had witnessed most of their work. The Mummers, along with the second very different company formed in the early seventies, CODCO, firmly placed Newfoundland theatre as a major player on the national cultural landscape and their work coloured subsequent activity.

The year after the Mummers Troupe was formed a very different company, CODCO,[21] was created. While Chris Brookes and the Mummers Troupe were initially politically motivated and issue-oriented, CODCO's first production, *Cod on a Stick*, indicated that this group of talented, versatile performers saw their world with different glasses. Their unique blend of zany and frequently black comedy demanded that its audience laugh at the grotesque reflection of themselves provocatively created. There is, however, a direct link to the Mummers Troupe; both companies, despite different approaches, were clearly political. Their art was used to demand change and response. In CODCO's first collective piece, they turned to their home province and exuberantly lampooned Newfoundlanders and government at the same time parodying the Toronto collective style of the early seventies.

Following *Cod on a Stick*, CODCO created *Sickness, Death and Beyond the Grave*, 1974, *Das Capital*, 1975, *Would You Like to Smell My... Pocket Crumbs*, 1975 and *Tale Ends* in 1976. The membership of CODCO shifted over the early years until by 1975 the members were Andy Jones, Cathy Jones, Bob Joy, Greg Malone, Diane Olsen, Tommy Sexton and Mary Walsh. However, after *Tale Ends* was produced, Bob Joy and Diane Olsen went their separate ways, leaving what would become a core group of performers consisting of Andy and Cathy Jones with Malone, Sexton and Walsh. Throughout the late seventies and eighties, Andy Jones, Cathy Jones, Greg Malone, Tommy Sexton and Mary Walsh pursued theatrical careers separately and collectively, occasionally mounting a CODCO revival. Then in 1988 CODCO moved to television,[22] performing weekly until 1993.

CODCO's black satiric form of humour is unique. Where did it come from? Was it merely a younger, less reverent, more cynical generation of artists who had no patience for a romantic view of the past? Certainly, a new generation was demanding to be heard. Perhaps too, the exuberant, at times, almost threatening mummering tradition that Brookes had found so attractive played its part as did the performance tradition of the concert. Finally, the fact that the group formed and created their first play because Paul Thompson in Toronto could not use them in *Them Donnellys* must be considered. These Newfoundland actors stood as observers, as outsiders to the Toronto collective scene and, because they were fine comic performers, their collective work took on an added richness and zest which no other company could match. Their confidence and brashness not only allowed them to lampoon themselves, their province and government but the whole collective creation tradition as they found it in the 1970s. When they finally disbanded in 1993 following Tommy Sexton's death, the remaining company members continued to enrich and complement Newfoundland drama by acting, directing and playwriting.

The late seventies and early eighties saw the creation of several new theatre companies; most of the work produced in this period was collective. However, in 1977, Rising Tide Theatre was established and this company while producing collectives like *Joey* and *Daddy What's A Train*, chose also to produce a variety of scripted work from different sources. Developing mainly collective plays were the Resource Centre For The Arts and Sheila's Brush. Membership between these two companies remained relatively fluid with CODCO performers such as Mary Walsh directing for the Resource Centre For the Arts and the Mummers and generally performers moving from group to group on a project basis. Collectives developed during this period gradually moved away from the issue-oriented stance that had previously dominated. Increasingly, collectives turned to history for inspiration and, not unlike Butt, Cahill and Pittman, these collectives celebrated the life and people of the Island. The membership of Rising Tide Theatre, initially under the leadership of Donna Butt and David Ross, worked independently of the Resource Centre For The Arts and found a home at the St. John's Arts and Culture Centre where collectives and scripted texts were performed.

During the late eighties, the landscape of Newfoundland drama again began to redefine itself. Once more playwrights began to emerge. In many cases these playwrights had experience in collective creation with the Mummers Troupe or CODCO or with The Resource Centre For the Arts, producers of *Terras de Bacalhau*,[23] directed by Mary Walsh in 1980, or Sheila's Brush, producers of *Jaxxmas*,[24] or Rising Tide, producers of *Joey*. The number of original plays produced in Newfoundland in the late eighties and early nineties was substantial; always a fertile theatrical landscape, now dominated by several versatile playwrights, Newfoundland drama had renewed itself again. Playwrights Ray Guy, Janis Spence, Pete Soucy, team Greg Thomey and Brian Hennessey, Ed Riche, Berni Stapleton and Liz Pickard are only a handful of those working in the province but a brief discussion of some of their work will indicate the range and variety of drama being created.

Ray Guy, satirist and commentator, has written three plays to date, *Young Triffie Been Made Away With*,[25] *Frog Pond* and *Swinton Massacre*. His predominately biting, black comic approach is shared by Janis Spence, also playwright of three texts, *Chickens*, *Catlover*[26] and *Walking to Australia*. Something of the zany, off-the-wall humour of CODCO appears to lie behind much of Guy and Spence's work but what is different in these plays is the placement of the bizarre, uncanny and absurd within an apparently realistic world with three-dimensional characters. The result is a skewered and distorted vision that becomes painfully funny. From Young Triffie's murder in *Young Triffie Been Made Away With* to Edwin's bizarre homecoming in *Catlover*, the playwrights constantly tease and stretch realistic conventions. For Guy, no member of society remains untouched and every imaginable sin is exposed. For Spence, the individual's sense of self and home is examined and exposed. Guy ends his text with a group crucifixion, allowing his characters to vindicate past wrongs; Spence sends her main character out into the world, allowing a freedom from responsibility.

Another approach is found by playwrights Soucy, Riche and the Thomey and Hennessey team, who also share a comic vision, but all of whom firmly ground their texts in realism. Soucy's play, *Flux*,[27] and Thomey and Hennessey's play, *Hanlon House*,[28] both explore an odd couple relationship as two men, in the former an artist and a pipefitter, in the latter a father and son, attempt to realign their visions of the world, themselves and each other. In *Possible Maps* by Ed Riche,[29] the Performer also reassesses a relationship, this time with his deceased father. In each case, conflict arises from a failure of communication.

In *Flux*, the pipefitter cannot understand the artist or his work but, after careful contemplation, he finds he can articulate his conclusions which the artist, in turn, can appreciate. In *Hanlon House*, the father wants his son to get married and settle down while the son complains of the boredom of his well-paying job at a weiner factory. Neither can make the other understand but the affection of a lifetime sustains them both. In the end the son gives his father a going-away gift, a dustbuster, and the appropriateness of this gift for the fussy old man confirms the basic understanding the two share. The Performer in *Possible Maps* recharts his relationship with his father through maps. The very personal journey through the past allows him to assess, value and finally begin his own journey, free from the phantoms of the past. In each case, conclusions become affirmations and suggest that a new passage will begin.

Moving in a very different direction are the plays by Berni Stapleton and Liz Pickard. Stapleton's *Woman in a Monkey Cage*[30] and Pickard's *The ALIENation of LIZZIE DYKE*[31] both explore women in society but their approaches, method and conclusions are radically different. In *Woman in a Monkey Cage*, a captured Newfoundland woman must explain herself to unseen, possibly alien, watchers. The text is a taunt, tightly drawn drama that rises above more commonplace confessional drama. The woman discusses her roles as daughter, mother, wife, caregiver and hair stylist and attempts to explain herself to an unsympathetic audience. Just as the Performer in *Possible Maps* finds himself confined by maps and mapping, the woman here is actually caged by lighting and her own story. The Performer, however, receives confirmation of self and strength from his story; the woman in *Woman in a Monkey Cage* finds no such satisfaction or salvation.

Not so in Liz Pickard's *The ALIENation of LIZZIE DYKE*, another one-woman play, where Lizzie recounts her madcap life through song, narration and dialogue with the assistance of sound, slides, videos and lights. This multi-media performance piece recalls the eccentric life of Lizzie and her triplets, Andromeda, Electra and Persephone or Andy, Elly and Percy for short. She reminisces about her life in Paris, her childhood at a Convent school, her unhappy adolescence and her first lesbian encounter. After a long series of arrests and confinements, she is finally rescued by Magenta Illuminous from the planet Karundia and a life of purpose begins in force. Liz Pickard's wacky sense of humour may find its roots in the work of CODCO but her own interest in music and multi-media theatre moves her work in another direction. In direct contrast to the stark simplicity of *Woman in a Monkey Cage*, Pickard carefully integrates the use of slide, video, music and lights into her carefully constructed stage picture. The solo performance becomes peopled by a complex and sophisticated mise-en-scene; the direct approach of the earlier collectives has been supplanted for a time.

Newfoundland drama continues to change and evolve. The amateur and concert traditions of the sixties are still popular vehicles. The collective work of the seventies and eighties continue in two ways. With the publication of *The Plays of Codco* and other collectives, these plays are being remounted. Collective creations are mounted by professionals[32] and special interest groups. Collective theatre remains part of the fabric of Newfoundland drama while playwrights continue to be encouraged and developed with Resource Centre For the Art's second space program and Rising Tide Theatre's workshopping program. A survey of drama over the last thirty years reveals that Newfoundland drama builds and renews itself. As each wave washes in, the past is not neglected nor dismissed but absorbed. The sixties set the stage for the activity of the seventies and eighties and from these exciting years came the playwrights who now hold the stage. What will come next is uncertain but based on the activity of the last thirty years, whatever it is will be exciting, stimulating and no less committed to Newfoundland than that which has gone before it.

Notes

[1] Grace Butt, *An Ear Or A Fear*, St. John's: Harry Cuff Publications Ltd., 1984.

[2] Grace Butt, *To Toslow We'll Go and Other Plays*, St. John's: Harry Cuff Publications Ltd., 1983.

[3] Grace Butt, *The Road Through Melton and Winter Scene*, St. John's: Creative Publishers, 1987.

[4] Grace Butt, *Persons*, St. John's: Harry Cuff Publications Ltd., 1990.

[5] Tom Cahill, *Tomorrow Will Be Sunday*, unpublished.

[6] Tom Cahill, *As Loved Our Fathers*, St. John's: Breakwater Books Ltd., 1974.

[7] Al Pittman, *A Rope Against The Sun*, St. John's: Breakwater Books Ltd., 1974.

[8] Michael Cook, *Colour the Flesh the Colour of Dust*, Toronto: Simon and Pierre, 1974.

[9] Michael Cook, *The Head, Guts and Sound Bone Dance* in *Three Plays*, St. John's: Breakwater Books Ltd., 1977.

[10] Michael Cook, *Jacob's Wake*, Vancouver: Talonbooks, 1975.

[11] Michael Cook, *Gayden Chronicles*, Toronto: Playwrights Canada, 1979.

[12] Michael Cook, *Tiln* in *Tiln and Other Plays*, Vancouver: Talonbooks, 1976.

[13] Michael Cook, *Quiller* in *Tiln and Other Plays*, Vancouver: Talonbooks, 1976.

[14] Michael Cook, *Theresa's Creed* in *Three Plays*, St. John's: Breakwater Books Ltd., 1977.

[15] For the fullest account see *A Public Nuisance. A History of The Mummers Troupe* by Chris Brookes, St. John's: Institute of Social and Economic Research, 1988.

[16] *Buchans: A Mining Town* in *Canadian Drama/L'Art dramatique canadien*, Vol. 13, No. 1, 1987, 73-116.

[17] Alan Filewod, *Collective Encounters*, Toronto: University of Toronto Press, 1987, 112-151. —Alan Filewod, "The Life and Death of the Mummers Troupe" in *The Proceedings of the Theatre in Atlantic Canada Symposium*, Sackville: Centre for Canadian Studies, 1988, 127-142. —Alan Filewod, "The Political Dramaturgy of the Mummers Troupe" in *Canadian Drama/L'Art dramatique canadien*, Vol. 13, no. 1, 1987, 60-72.

[18] Chris Brookes, in: "Discussion" in D. Lynde, H. Peters, R. Buehler (eds.), *Newfoundland Theatre Research: Proceedings*, St. John's: Memorial University, 1993, 108.

[19] The Mummers Troupe, *They Club Seals, Don't They* in Helen Peters (ed.), *Stars in the Sky Morning*.

[20] The Mummers Troupe, *Makin' Time with the Yanks* in Helen Peters (ed.), *Stars in the Sky Morning*.

[21] *The Plays of CODCO*, Helen Peters (ed.), New York: Peter Lang, 1992.

[22] Helen Peters, "From Salt Cod to Cod Filets" in *Canadian Theatre Review*, 64 (Fall 1990), 13-17.

[23] Resource Centre For the Arts, *Terras De Bacalhau* in Helen Peters (ed.), *Stars in the Sky Morning*.

[24] Sheila's Brush, *Jaxxmas* in Helen Peters (ed.), *Stars in the Sky Morning*.

[25] Ray Guy, *Young Triffie Been Made Away With* in Denyse Lynde (ed.), *Voices from the Landwash*.

[26] Janis Spence, *Catlover* in Denyse Lynde (ed.), *Voices from the Landwash*.

[27] Pete Soucy, *Flux* in Denyse Lynde (ed.), *Voices from the Landwash*.

[28] Greg Thomey and Brian Hennessey, *Hanlon House* in Denyse Lynde (ed.), *Voices from the Landwash*.

[29] Ed Riche, *Possible Maps* in Jason Sherman (ed.), *Solo*, Toronto: Coach House Press, 1994, 173-200.

[30] *Woman in a Monkey Cage* by Berni Stapleton in Denise Lynde (ed.), *Voices from the Landwash*.

[31] Liz Pickard, *The ALIENation of LIZZIE DYKE* in Denyse Lynde (ed.), *Voices from the Landwash*.

[32] Rising Tide Theatre is presently remounting past collectives and creating new texts for their summer festival in Trinty; Chris Brookes is scheduled to direct a collective in 1995 for the Resource Centre For the Arts.

Keith Garebian

Henry Beissel:
Tragicomic Moralist

The three best plays of Henry Beissel are poetic narratives based on brief episodes of concentrated action. The intellectual approach is truthful, the tone ironic. Mime, songs, and dance embody ideological points tersely as in epigrams. The radical scepticism about forms of reality all reflect an artistic sensibility that searches in human nature for what ought to be. *Inook and the Sun* (1973)[1] tells us that all things have their season under the decrees of fate. *Goya* (1976) tells us that the true artist must accept the burden of his life, and always be true to his own vision of reality. And *Under Coyote's Eye* (1978) is streaked with the suggestion that a man must find and keep his place in the order of things. In a fundamental sense, then, these are morality plays that eschew superficial "suspense." They seek to illuminate our understanding rather than to produce ephemeral excitement. There are marvellous theatrical devices, to be sure, but audiences are expected to be alert observers with active humane sophistication, rather than hypnotized spectators who react merely viscerally.

Beissel's plays are frankly theatrical and make no attempt to hide the strings of their artifice. They make their devices highly visible, and sometimes go all the way into the grotesque, caricature, and burlesque exaggeration. Beissel's irony turns away from the classical ideals of comedy and tragedy toward a more modern tragicomic texture that is serious, though of a questionable magnitude.

Although all his plays are quests and deal with principal characters at the edge of extinction, they are also, radically, modern queries about the estrangement of the self from the world. Reality—whether consisting of primordial patterns of life and death, the solitude of old age, states of mind, or the logic of events—becomes a crucible and, often, a trap, and the burden of survival and self-affirmation lies with the imagination.

Inook and the Sun expresses two basic dimensions of Inuit experience (the natural and the supernatural) with the help of a "delicate theatrical imagination"[2] that involves puppets (derived from the Bunraku tradition), masks, songs, dance, and mime. Ostensibly for children, it is an admirable blend of folk tale and poetry, fantasy and morality, and under its elemental conflicts ("summer and winter, light and dark, heat and cold, and the struggle to survive between them," 7) lies an implicit, crystalline belief in a cosmos that is not finally desolate. The boy Inook, who is eager to prove himself a man, is tested rigorously, but emerges with a maturity that redeems his travails. Out of compassion for his fellow Inuit in the land of the Aivilik who are starving and freezing in their stark, flat snowscape, he dares to pursue the sun. His reckless impatience is folly, but he is too young, too untested to have stature. He has yet to learn that between boyhood and manhood lies a "dangerous journey." (30) Quite apart from the fact that he invites retribution for having shot an arrow at the Spirit of the Caribou, he is fated to play his role in a contest against nature and its manifold spirits. Inook fights the Polar Bear that had slain his father, harpoons a seal, and is pulled underwater into the Hall of the Iceberg (haunt of Sumna, the ugly, imperious Goddess of the Sea) and the cave of the huge, blind, octopus-like Monster. He matches wits and prowess with a fox, flippant seals, and fierce sharks, solves Sumna's riddles, and frees the Sun from the throes of the Spirit of the Ice. Only after he has passed all his tests does Inook win merit as an emerging man, replete with just pride in bringing to his people the sun as his bride.

Although not written from within an Inuit perspective, *Inook and the Sun* does have a strongly developed sense of Inuit life and culture. The setting, lighting and costuming all make for a palpable arctic reality, with igloos, "a silvery ice-blue light of the rising moon," the noise of a "blustering wind," a flock of wild geese and wolves at close distance, and the "sinister cackle" and chant of "jet-black Raven." (11) The hunting game that Inook is eager to commence reinforces the idea of a primordial contest between man and nature. This is a harsh, bleak land, where the wind that drives "huskies of snow" across the tundra (46) is a "killer" that "jumps on the backs of animals and forces them to the ground." (14) It is also a land left at the mercy of the spirit world—represented by Masks for the various Spirits of the Caribou, Moon (male), Wind (male), Dream (female), Sumna (female), Ice (male) and Sun (female). The succession of episodes re-enacts rituals that establish principles of Inuit life—such as the fundamental precept of killing only for food and survival, the celebration of animal victims and the implicit belief in a cycle of nature.

But through all the fascinating evocations of Inuit life and with all his resources of theatrical illusion (shadow puppets, drums, rattles, clappers, black lighting), Beissel is able to insinuate an existentialism that fuses an antique world view with a modern ironist's. The first explicit manifestation of this occurs in the debate between the Moon and Wind in Episode 5. These antagonists—each accuses the other of envy (35)—moralize about the price of life, with the Moon charging that the mutable world is filled with suffering and melancholy, and the Wind finding consolation in life's joys. (34-35) Inook is mocked by the Moon even as he is warned by his staccato poetry about his sister Sun's fatal trap. (40) His trials and tribulations generate his sense of desolation. "I am a shadow/in a land of shadows" (39) is a line worthy of Beckett, and it undergoes only a subtle transformation when he passes underwater, for there he laments: "I am a shadow/in a sea of shadows." (63)

Yet Inook is a boy-trickster whose courage and wit rescue him repeatedly from consuming gloom. He is able to solve Sumna's largest riddle (61), and he cunningly eludes the sharks that guard (in yet another echo of classical legend) the entrance to the Great Hall of the Iceberg. (63) Although he is unable to rescue his father who is locked "forever into the eternal ice," (73) or strike the Sun with his harpoon (68), he is forgiven his impudence and rewarded for his courage. He succeeds in surviving all his tests, but his greatest success is the acquired wisdom of the world. He learns mutability—the principle that is ultimately affirmed by the tension between the play's naturalistic underpinnings and its overlayer of poetic symbolism. The world—even the dream world—is never subjugated; it is rationalized by Sumna: "No earthly shape or creature can last. That is the law. Everything must forever change and go on changing, Inook." (74) This is a philosophy that implies eternal transience and impermanence, but in this instance, man (who leaves his innocence behind him on his "dangerous journey") is able to dance with the spirits of his world. He is never wholly safe, however, as the Spirit of the Ice shows when it aims a harpoon at Inook but instead strikes the frozen Sun. (75) A balance of forces is eventually maintained, and the cycle of seasons and fortunes continues.

Under Coyote's Eye moves us to a different culture, but with an intense pessimism that looks back at the death of a civilization based on an historical incident in 1860, when six California settlers trapped a thousand Yahi Indians in a dead-end canyon and succeeded in killing them all, except for hardly a dozen. The play begins with the startling moment in 1911 when a middle-aged man, exhausted and delirious, appears outside a slaughterhouse in Oroville, California, and is eventually discovered to be Ishi, the last of his stone age tribe. The play is an exploration of his state of mind, and Beissel's dramatic structure, vivid with flashbacks, mixes "the actual, the remembered and the imagined"[3] in a single reality. There is no demarcation by scene or act in the episodic narrative, and reality is resolved into a sum of its various orders, mental states and consequences. There are superficial similarities with *Inook*: a trickster figure, diametrically opposed viewpoints, a belief in a cyclical destiny, chants accompanied by rattles, sacred decrees, the use of symbolic and mythological figures, a tension between man and his gods, the use of irony and two of Beissel's strongest preoccupations—metamorphosis and the human imagination.

Under Coyote's Eye is a more profound exploration of reality than is *Inook* and not simply because it is not a fable. The plight it presents is historically accurate, and a stigma on the white man's conscience. When we first see Ishi, he has already endured three years without the sound of another human voice: "The birds talk to each other. The trees talk to each other. Even the rocks talk to each other. But the canyons give me back only my own voice. The river gives me back only my own face." (1) His sister has drowned, as has the Shaman, Coyote has driven Ishi to despair by his deceptions and Rattlesnake, "a beast of ambush and poison," (3) is no solace. Although Coyote urges Ishi to return to Wowunupo, the grizzly-bear lair, where he can complete his destiny, (3) Ishi has no real choice, for to return would be to exacerbate festering memories of the Paleskins' slaughter of his people, whereas to continue his wandering would be to estrange him from the proper order of things. When he encounters the Sheriff who puts him in jail to spare him from murderous townsfolk, Ishi is grateful for a sympathetic human voice: "I don't know what he said, but there was something in the tone of it—it was like the patient rush of the river. I felt drawn to it. I felt like huddling over it as if it were a village hearth on a winter night." (19) The raw, unpremeditated poetry of his memory lends a special poignancy to his situation as a freak outsider among bloodthirsty whites.

But there is more in the play than simply the issue of genocide or isolation. Coyote and Rattlesnake both hold Ishi responsible for his suffering. Coyote accuses him of violating sacred decrees of custom by failing to burn his mother's corpse for fear the smoke would betray him to the Paleskins. "You left the spirit of your sister to languish in her corpse, you left a Shaman's spirit imprisoned in this rotting body—two spirits condemned by your impious lust for life." (15) Rattlesnake charges Ishi with an incestuous relationship with his sister and Eagle adds: "To break a taboo is to break with the world." (31)

This question of fracturing the cosmos is, in this play, a cruel irony, for Ishi is a man more sinned against than sinning in a world that seems intent on mocking and punishing him as a freak. There is no question that Ishi is abandoned by his gods. His dilemma is that his choice between the ancient taboos and the life of his people is really no choice at all. In a fundamental sense he is far more reasonable than his gods. He does not harm the Sheriff because "His death would not restore a single Yahi voice. The senseless circle of killing must be broken somewhere." (19) He cannot bear hiding in the canyon because it is "A home where no one is at home. We dare not be ourselves here." (22) And yet he is treated as if he were a violator—most of all by Coyote the chatterer who has a trick for every word and for every trick a face. The masks of Coyote are the mystery to which Ishi is ordered to submit, but behind the masks there is no real face—only a voice bent on an empty, cruel mockery of man. (46)

Eagle, who tries to draw everything upward into the realm of pure spirit, urges Ishi to listen "only to the voice of the spirit.... Go and talk to your solitude. Listen to the silence. There you'll find what you're looking for." (28) But this is unusual advice for a man who has been condemned to inhuman silence and whose spirit has been continually oppressed by the weight of evil in an apparently irrational world.

There is only a promise of escape from this cruel suffering when Ishi meets Waterman, the anthropologist who is intent on solving the puzzle of this Indian stranger. At first Waterman can find no magic code to break into Ishi's understanding. He tries various words and accents but to no avail, and when a sudden breakthrough is effected by the word *siwimi* (yellow pine), a rapport is established and then augmented by a "white" lie. When Ishi dances like a happy child and asks Waterman if he is a Yahi, the anthropologist lies that he is. (47) This lie stops Ishi from being a perpetual stranger in the world, and gives him at least the illusion of fellowship in a society that continues to regard him as a freakish spectacle—a man who has looked down the abyss of extinction without falling into it.

Perhaps with the moralist's sympathy for victims, Beissel strikes an elegiac note with Waterman's final address to the audience. His apotheosis of Ishi works more as unction for the white man's guilty soul than as a consolation for a doomed hero. "He saw," says Waterman of Ishi's delight in technological inventions, "that we lacked wisdom and that there was much that is false in our world." (48) Indeed, but how did this save him from becoming a requiem for a civilization? The chaos of Ishi's experiences is resolved with a composure that declares its own emptiness.

Beissel's most sophisticated play is *Goya*, which is also his technical and metaphysical breakthrough. Continuing Beissel's practice of episodic narrative, *Goya* catches its eponymous hero at the age of seventy-seven, in the "twilight of old age where the great become history."[4] However, the drama leaps back and forth in time from 1823 to 1794 to 1801 to 1780 et cetera, taking as its justification Beissel's adherence to "the essential facts of history" not so much as "an attempt to recreate the life and times of Goya" but as "an exploration of the creative imagination." (Preface, n.p.) While the cross-cutting technique does present tremendous practical problems to the lead actor (who has to drop or add years in a trice), it does have a filmic rhythm and does ground the theatricality in new (for Beissel) metaphysics.

Goya is gestural without pushing in favour of games of language, mime and incident for their own sake. It sometimes has a boisterous, lubricious carnival spirit, much bawdry, and all the sensual appetites of man. It caricatures politics, religion and puritan society. It parodies art and linguistic communication. And it plays hopscotch with chronology in order to create a mosaic rather than a linear vision of the totality of its hero. It never pretends that theatre is pure—that is, without connections to literature, painting, music, dance or allegory. However, it does share with the Absurdists a belief in tragicomedy, for implicit in its vision is the impulse to take nothing entirely seriously or entirely lightly. The comic and tragic co-exist, repulse each other and constitute a dynamic tension or balance.

Goya's struggle to create a final self-portrait is the act at the core of the play, and to compound this struggle and make it wholly credible in context, Beissel provides a vivid set of characters who bring history to life. At the outset the situation is stark: Goya, the prolific artist with a taste for the fast life, is in virtual retirement at his house, the Quinta del Sordo. His only companion is his mistress Leocadia. Sick, deaf and solitary, he has dark, nightmarish visions, filled with images of death, idiocy and vicious agitations of the soul. His paintings are attacked by the Church for being "without faith, black and barren." (5) Canon Juan de Llorente, Secretary to the Holy Office of the Inquisition, arrives on King Fernando's business to subjugate Goya. This sets the political code, for the Carnival outside the Gates of Madrid in the very next scene is a parody of the spirit of festivity that once thrived under the previous regime whose favour Goya enjoyed in a climate of liberalism. The spirit of Carnival—by which the high and low, the sacred and profane inter-mingle and even exchange roles as part of a masquerade—underscores the artist's connection with all classes, and establishes him as "a full-blooded man," (11) anti-authoritarian and an un-inhabited critic of the political and social order. Inspired, no doubt, by Goya's own penchant for satire (as in "Los Caprichos"), Beissel mocks the royal family (in Scene 7) whose frivolousness and distractions resulted in Spain's capitulation to Bonaparte and then in the tyranny of Fernando. At their portrait sitting, King Carlos IV, an essentially good but superficial man, is seen to be more preoccupied with clocks, violins and hunting than with important political matters; Queen Luisa is revealed to be lascivious (she falls in love with the thighs of General Godoy, who is rumoured to ride her as masterfully as he does his horse); and Prince Fernando, the future despot, is already a mean, petulant, imperious little villain. It is a scene of rather sour comedy, for it contains in its own exaggerations portents of grim tyranny and oppression.

Where the two native plays, *Inook* and *Under Coyote's Eye*, often pit man against his gods, *Goya* shows the terrors of those men who think they are gods. The Catholic Church is satirized mercilessly for its antagonism to the secular creative spirit, and for its pernicious dogmatism that tries to silence whatever is contrary to its assumptions of Divine Revelation and infallibility. Goya, who insists that "Faith doesn't make an artist, craftsmanship does," (55) goes counter to the injunctions of Llorente ("that scorpion in purple," 63) who decrees only sacred art "for the greater glory of God," but who fails to see that Goya's paintings are "the landscape of the soul." (55) Llorente mixes religion with politics, for as Fernando's functionary, he tries to force Goya to forswear the old Constitution. By 1823, Spanish liberals are rounded up and executed without trial—the inflammatory cause for Goya's "The Third of May."

Goya's problems, however, are not caused only by external forces; they have a substantial impetus from his own inner demons. A man of immense appetites, he is rampant with carnality. He fathers eighteen children by Josefa—of which only his son Javier survives—and a daughter by his mistress Leocadia. He lusts after the Duchess of Alba, and kills a drunken *hidalgo* in a tavern after this man has spread calumny against him and has tried to have his way with Alba. He is unable to be gentle with the world or with himself, for he is an opportunist who allows nothing to stand in his way as a man or artist. He admits to having married Josefa chiefly to advance his ambition, knowing that her brother is First Painter to the Court and Secretary of the Academy. He ends up hating her because he needs her. "I'm tied to you by my weaknesses and my failures. We're chained to each other and I want to be free!" he laments. (35)

But he is not always a victim of spontaneous passion. Sometimes he can be coolly calculating. The Majo accuses him of playing "all sides against the middle," (74) and Godoy charges him with having made a present to Carlos of the banned "Caprichos" in exchange for an annuity for Javier. Godoy also knows that Goya painted flattering portraits of French enemies under Napoleon's reign, while giving money to the Spanish army to fight and kill them. "You're as cunning as any courtier," Godoy remarks. (25) Goya replies in defence: "I tried to serve both Spain and my craft." (26) He is filled with self-recrimination for having sold himself to those in power. (66)

Yet there can be no doubt about his dedication to craft. "I submit to nothing but what I see," he proclaims boldly to Bayeu, his brother-in-law, when the latter appeals to him to satisfy the building committee for the Basilica of Santa Maria del Pilar. (29) The passion with which he leads his life, however erratically, is also the passion with which he paints his visions. Seeing corruption everywhere—even in love—he challenges "the power of darkness," (36) and seems to be possessed by either a demon or an angel who drives him, "day and night, who demands the impossible," who forces him "to paint everything, to say yes to everything." (36) This obsessive perennial "yea" to the world, is like some mad wound, and he is a bull maddened by "the fierce *pica*." (36)

Accused by Llorente of exaggerated notions of his craft, (55) Goya persists with his "solitary struggle that permits no compromises" in making visible the invisible. His etchings are "attacks on all forms of abuse and persuasion," (73) and he will not moderate the intensity, for to do so would be to hide from all the evils around and inside man. He sometimes cries out in his dreams as though hell's furies were tormenting him, (73) but he will not submit his vocation to his enemies. The exile he chooses at the end (in a scene that is strangely flat and anti-climactic) is not an evasion or disgrace, but an option of artistic freedom. (76-77) He will die, as Leocadia has anticipated at the beginning of the play, with a brush in his hand. (5) All his anomalies and defects are pieces of the self that he struggles to compose into an apocalyptic self-portrait. He confesses to folly, lust and optimism, but he will not be buried under his shame, nor under society's taboos and prescriptions.

The unifying metaphors of the play are those of blank canvas and deafness. An open stage bears nothing in the way of décor, but an easel, a small table, a mirror, a large old-fashioned chest and austere frames of different shapes and sizes, "large enough to allow live actors to act within and through them." (Stage directions, n.p.) The frames are filled with blank canvas on which slide projections are cast of some of Goya's most famous paintings, but their most fascinating use is as filmy screens for the "dramatization" and "tableaux" of such paintings as "The Burial of the Sardine," "Portrait of Godoy," "Family of Carlos IV," "La Maja

Desnuda," "La Maja Vestida," "The Third of May," "Yard With Lunatics," and "The Pilgrimage of San Isidro." At significant moments, the actors compose themselves into these pictures—sometimes under Goya's silent orchestration of movement, position and line—so that we obtain a sense of the process of artistic creation. Because such "dramatizations" and "tableaux" grow organically out of the narrative action, they provide a sense of the ways in which Goya found in reality the sources of his art. The variety of characters, incidents and tonal effects shows that Goya painted everything with the aim of achieving mastery of genres and media. In sum, he saw his life as a stretched canvas on which he placed the genius of his imagination.

The second controlling metaphor is that of deafness. There are numerous instances in the play where characters mime conversation to dramatize Goya's deafness—an affliction of old age and, perhaps, of syphilis. "The effect is that which you get in a movie when the sound is silently cut," and helps the audience experience "some of the disorientation, bewilderment and frustration that is the lot of every deaf person." (12) Goya, however, lip-reads this "inaudible" speech, and shows us by this that his eyes take in far more of the world than is normal. The deafness lies in counterpoint to the breathing sounds and overlapping voices in Scene 4, where through the quick vocal rhythm of his patrons and clients, Goya "hears" various demands made on his talent. The characters strain and stutter to articulate their exhaustive demands. Carlos wants a portrait for posterity; Luisa wishes to be immortalized; the Duchess wants romanticization; Llorente demands religious iconography; the Majo asks for social truth; Josefa seeks a fellowship of love. (17-21) To Goya (who is seventy-seven in this scene and has endured thirty years of human "silence") this is a hallucinatory experience, as the "shadowy figures from his paintings appear around him and vanish as he approaches them." Are they "ghosts from the past" he wonders. They are a "jumble of lines and colours," (22) and yet out of the confusion they become speaking masks, as it were, of his own nightmares and powers.

His deafness becomes a mask in a second sense. It enables him to keep out the voices of those who would pry into his soul or personal affairs. Because of his deafness, Goya can indulge in monologues with himself. Some people—even Leocadia—think him mad when he talks to himself, but his act is a rehearsal of his innermost preoccupations. Deafness intensifies his solitude as an artist, and is an undeniable part of his reality—along with his women, brandy, enemies, property and shame—and it compels him to "hear" with his eyes. When, in the sixteenth and final scene, he completes his conception of "The Pilgrimage of San Isidro" by picking up a guitar and taking the place of a missing character, (77) the mime of song and speech locks in place the image of an artist for whom all life is an earthly pilgrimage of lust, greed, cruelty and idiocy. By stepping silently into his own "picture," Goya seals the suggestion of an artist's soundless creative imagination. Ironically, it is we in the audience who are now "deaf," as it were, unable to hear the internalization of genius.

From the historical point of view, Beissel is very much of his time, addressing for his adoptive country moral and cultural themes that its population is not eager to probe. His aboriginal plays fit into the significant body of dramatic works (fashioned by the likes of Hershel Hardin, Carol Bolt, the late George Ryga, Sharon Pollock and Tomson Highway) that force Canadians to take stock of that part of history which they would rather forget or ignore. And *Goya*, despite its European content and technique, provides an effective reference for any Canadian artist who struggles with his burden in a philistine society. Beissel's plays seem to affirm that human existence is a process by which man brings into being the values and goals that he professes. By standing on tragicomic ground, Beissel charges his plays with irony and makes theatre serve as an aesthetic focus for human experience.

NOTES

[1] All dates refer to first production. Publication dates are provided in the following notes.

[2] Henry Beissel, *Inook and the Sun*, Toronto: Playwrights Co-op, 1974, 9. All subsequent references are to this edition. (Reprinted by Gage, Toronto, 1989.)

[3] Henry Beissel, *Under Coyote's Eye*, Toronto: Playwrights Canada, 1979, Author's note, unpaginated. All subsequent references are to this edition. (Reprinted by Quadrant Editions, Dunvegan, 1981.)

[4] Henry Beissel, *Goya*, Toronto: Playwrights Co-op, 1978, Preface, unpaginated. All subsequent references are to this edition.

Richard Perkyns

Michael Cook's *Jacob's Wake* and the European Tradition[1]

Michael Cook found his inspiration as a playwright in the harsh, bleak, remote landscape of Newfoundland and its equally rugged people. His writing, however, betrays a sense of tradition rooted in European theatre movements. On one hand is his urge to portray the panoramic scene through the Brechtian style of epic theatre with its timeless sweep of action, as in his first full-length stage play *Colour the Flesh the Colour of Dust*, or in the later historical sagas *On The Rim of the Curve* or *The Gayden Chronicles*. Conversely is the tendency to explore the existential-ist-absurdist world of Samuel Beckett in *Tiln* or *The Head, Guts and Soundbone Dance*, as well as the additional, more naturalistic exercises in monologue portraying Newfoundland characters, *Quiller* and *Therese's Creed*. Between the extremes falls a work which surprisingly takes us back almost to the *pièce bien faite: Jacob's Wake*.

While Cook was rightly sceptical about what critics may say concerning the influences upon his style, he was quick to acknowledge the importance of tradition to the writer:

> One of the nicest things about being a writer, or any artist, is learning from your companions, whether they've been gone a thousand years or are your peers. We have, as a community, a sense of tradition stronger than race, place or time, and struggle to give something tangible to each other.[2]

As T.S. Eliot has shown, acknowledgement of tradition in literature need not preclude a writer's originality; it may, rather, encourage the artist to draw on his appreciation of past masters as a stimulant in defining and establishing his own individual technique. Dryden acknowledged his debt to his master Shakespeare when he revised *Antony and Cleopatra* according to neo-classical principles in *All for Love*. Bernard Shaw unashamedly drew on his master Anton Chekhov in writing

Heartbreak House as "a fantasia in the Russian manner on English themes." Though Cook would have thrown up his hands in horror at the comparison with Shaw,[3] it can nevertheless be instructive for a broad interpretation of *Jacob's Wake* to seek first the world of Shaw and even trace that back to Chekhov. It would be facile to suggest that Cook was consciously influenced by Shaw. The styles of the two dramatists are in many respects poles apart. In *Jacob's Wake* Cook is much closer to the poetic naturalism of Chekhov than to the dialectics of Shaw. Yet the play implies an absorption, if unconscious, of a dramatic notion which informs *Heartbreak House* on several levels.

The metaphor of the house as a ship ruled by an eccentric and fiendish captain is central to both plays. Yet Cook's maritime setting gives the image a stronger relevance and consistency than could be argued for Shaw's play. Coming to Newfoundland as recently as 1965, Cook found he could write about the island and its people with a detachment that a native could not feel. In response to Rota Lister's questions about the artist's vision, Cook pragmatically denied that he had a vision, but asserted rather that Newfoundland gave him the "focal identity" that he needed: "and it was the sea and the sea's response to the land and people's response to the sea and the land and it was really like someone opening the shutters."[4]

Like Heartbreak House, the house/ship of *Jacob's Wake* symbolizes a disintegrating society. As Chekhov had done before him, Shaw took a group of people loosely based on the family unit as a microcosm of a world order in decay. Chekhov anticipated the fall of the aristocracy in the Russian Revolution; Shaw foresaw an idle society of wealth and privilege being swept away by World War I. In both *The Head, Guts and Soundbone Dance* and *Jacob's Wake* Cook is describing "a way of life in which individuals struggle with timeless questions of worth and identity against an environment which would kill them if it could."[5] The themes of failure and survival are implicit in the works of all three dramatists, but in Cook's drama human behaviour is more closely related to, and motivated by, a hostile environment.

Both Shaw's Captain Shotover and Cook's Skipper Eli view life in terms of a voyage, in which the present and future are bleak in comparison with the dangerous glories of the past. The speech of both is suffused with sea imagery, which becomes more pertinent to the world of *Jacob's Wake* as its atmosphere is increasingly dominated by the sea and the storm raging outside. Shotover tells Ellie Dunn, "I see my daughters and their men living foolish lives of romance and sentiment and snobbery. I see you, the younger generation, turning from their romance and sentiment and snobbery to money and comfort and hard common sense. I was ten times happier on the bridge in the typhoon, or frozen into Arctic ice for months in darkness, than you or they have ever been."[6] Unlike Shotover, Elijah does not exonerate the younger generation, but he finds all alike, children and grandchildren, incapable of steering the ship on a straight course. For this reason the ghost of the skipper returns after his death to take command once again and to order his son Winston to take the wheel, "Forty years, waiting to see if any o' ye could steer this ship." (136)[7] Both captains show flashes of wisdom even as their minds wander: they are commentators to oversee and lament the direction in which some if not all of the younger generation are moving. Yet where Shotover is central to the action of *Heartbreak House*, Blackburn at first seems peripheral to the action of *Jacob's Wake*. Although he is physically removed from the central scene, however, his spiritual presence becomes increasingly dominant until once again it commands the ship in the final moments.

The Skipper's return to the seal hunt in the "nightmare of the past" (42) is seen in counterpoint to the harsh realities of the present. Elijah has taken blame for the death of his son Jacob, when the old man took the boat out in a storm which "wor like the Divil had the ship in his hand." (58) As his mind travels between present and past he finds it hard to accept the death of Jacob, whose virtues he extols in comparison to the uselessness of his grandchildren: "Ye've no God," he declares. "And ye've no guts. Ye're nothin', the lot of ye." (76) Jacob's prime of life has been in the age of traditional Newfoundland values, the triumph of the sea and the fishing life; his wake, so many years after his death, is symbolized by a worthless, divided family, foundering in the house that the Skipper still sees as his ship. But it is also the foundering of a society and a way of life, the disintegration of the order of the old fishing life, taken a stage further than it is in *The Head, Guts and Soundbone Dance*. In the earlier play, even if Skipper Pete defies the changing order and dwells in the past, Uncle John finally accepts the changes; there remains an ambiguity at the end of *Jacob's Wake*, for although Winston symbolically takes the tiller, perhaps for the first time in his life, the storm dominates the closing moments in its fury, seeming to deny the Skipper's final affirmation: "Newfoundland is alive and well and roaring down the ice pack." (138)

The ambivalence of both skippers is due to a tension between a stubborn clinging to the past and an attempt to cover fear from the consequences of that stubbornness. Skipper Pete's connivance at the drowning of a child strains his determined will to breaking point; Skipper Eli's firm stance against his family is at odds with his dependence on them. In *Jacob's Wake* Cook has split his family unit fairly equally down the middle: on the one hand are the Skipper's relatively unlearned, rough-hewn son Winston and daughter-in-law Rosie, and his coarse but amiable grandson Alonzo; on the other are three who have pretensions to education and religion—Winston's sister Mary, and the other grandsons Wayne and Brad. The pivotal character in each group is the woman. The would-be patriarch is bedridden and fails to dominate the family. But as Cook asserted, Newfoundland is a matriarchal society.[8] Once again it was appropriate for him to follow the tradition set by Shaw and Ibsen before him, in which the woman's role is frequently dominant, and in which the males become correspondingly weak or subservient.

The roles of Mary and Rosie are hardly comparable with those of Captain Shotover's daughters in *Heartbreak House*. The mysticism of Shotover passes on to Hesione and Ariadne, whose feminine powers reduce the men in their lives to foolish ineffectiveness, and even inspire Ellie Dunn to exert her own will, first over Mangan and then over Shotover himself. While Cook may give Eli a certain mystical aura, there is nothing of the enchantress in either Rosie or Mary. The strength of Rosie lies in her genial acceptance of the divisions that split the family and in her conviction of her own rightness in anchoring the household as it drifts into helplessness. Like Mary Mercer in David French's plays *Leaving Home* and *Of the Fields, Lately*, or in the Irish tradition of Sean O'Casey, she is the quiet yet firm peacemaker when strife tears the family apart. To Winston she is "fat and comfortable and mindin' her own business" and "warm on a cold night" in contrast to the "frozen wharf junk" of Mary. (47) As with Jacob and Mary Mercer, the warmth of the love shared by Winston and Rosie, despite their bickering, can overcome the harsher realities of their lives: Act One ends on a note of tenderness as they recall their long-dead child Sarah, a loss they have never accepted; at the end of the play, when an unusually calm Winston declares that they shouldn't complain about what life has done to them, Rosie says softly, "I nivir complained, Winston." (132) To Brad she is the only "real person" in the family. (65) When Mary accuses her of over-generosity to her sons, she states with satisfaction, "Old habits dies 'ard." (49) She sees Alonzo's merciless baiting of Brad as "a bit of fun" (21) and it is she to whom the Skipper turns when he needs comfort. (61)

If Rosie is a matriarch by dint of a quiet presence, by the example of a traditional way of life rather than by an assertion of authority, Winston never measures up to the patriarchal role. At first he is an unsympathetic character, living on welfare and drinking hard, without the endearing roguishness which slightly exonerates the otherwise worthless "Paycock" of O'Casey, Captain Boyle. Winston's heavy drinking leads to bouts of violence: his conflict with "the old maid," his sister, culminates in the tearing of a student's exercise book she is marking; an unrepentant Winston is condemned by Mary as being "always destructive of anything he couldn't understand." (46) Later he baits the prim Mary by justifying the crudeness of his speech and behaviour because it amuses him to see her outrage. Mary's gibe about his "moral ignorance" makes him hurl a bottle across the room (124) and he takes a gun to the family when he finds his signature forged on the document to have the Skipper committed to a mental home. The anger which breaks out at such moments betrays a pent-up frustration at his failure and ineffectiveness as head of the household. When finally he seeks reconciliation with the family, Mary turns on him and throws the liquor in his face. Our sympathies turn more to Winston when we realize that it is on his shoulders that the burden of change has fallen: he cannot fulfill his father's expectations of him; he cannot become another Jacob, because almost alone he represents the disintegration of the life of Newfoundland fishing families after resettlement,[9] with its ensuing unemployment and inability of its victims to settle in a more urbanized way of life. Cook makes us feel Winston's frustration because he is incapable of preventing the disintegration of the family unit, the microcosm of a society in chaos symbolized by the storm. His final symbolic taking of the tiller seems contradictory, but Cook may be suggesting that human will could, if given the opportunity, overcome the seemingly insurmountable obstacles and once again give society a sense of direction.

One direction society can take is to seek a faith which will give it spiritual strength. The play is suffused with religious imagery which frequently suggests a battle between true and false gods. Brian Parker has commented on the names: Elijah, the prophet of doom; Jacob, the favoured son; and Winston as an Esau figure, the son who fails his father.[10] Only Rosie demonstrates true Christian virtues. When she and Winston lament the death of Sarah, Rosie puts their fate down to the will of the "Good Lord," but Winston denies her God: "They's nothin', Rosie. Nothin'. They's madness and they's death and they's some who work at it and some who wait for it." (80)

In an uneasy alliance with his father is Alonzo, cast in the role of an anti-Christ or Devil who tempts in turn the members of the family aligned on the opposite side, until it is his turn to be tempted by Wayne, in an exchange for a business deal, to forge a signature on the form which will have the Skipper committed. Alonzo glories in his immorality as the proprietor of a strip club. His temptations began before the play opens, with his inciting Brad into an affair with Mildred Tobin which had disastrous consequences for Mildred and which drove Brad into a religious fanaticism that is to become his undoing. When Brad returns to the family he casts Alonzo in the role of the Devil. (53) Alonzo's temptation takes the form of teasing, as he dances in the kitchen in Brad's dogcollar, or tries to force beer into Brad's mouth. In the third scene of Act One Alonzo taunts Brad by throwing his Bible on the floor and mocking his attempt to "learn to love" his brother. (67) Like his father, Alonzo teases Mary, by calling her "as ravishing as ever" (103) and suggesting that she derives a perverse enjoyment from being goaded.

Brad also sees Wayne in the role of a "Devil," as well as a "Judas" who betrayed him because he was ultimately responsible for Brad's being hounded from his parish. If Alonzo is an open, gleeful villain, Wayne is a smooth, underhand opportunist, hating Alonzo but willing to cross the line that divides the family to strike an unholy alliance. In the end he is able to persuade Alonzo to forge his father's signature in return for a motel contract, but it is Alonzo who openly admits their unscrupulousness: "What a bunch of rats we are." (72)[11] It is Mary whose influence has most affected Wayne since his childhood, and the bond between them is clearly established; though Mary warns Wayne about Alonzo's lack of scruples, Wayne has used Alonzo as a political party organizer and sees the advantage of striking a deal with him now. When Winston discovers the forgery, it is to Mary he first turns to blame her for her complicity, though she denies she ever wanted it that way. Mary persuades Wayne to take her to church in his car, but does so in order that the church can be "honoured by the presence of its most famous son," not because of religious conviction. (94)

Mary's influence is strong on both Wayne and Brad. Although she condemns Brad as an "emotional cripple," (16) who was bound to fail in his religious quest, it is to Mary he turns for help. But Mary remains unsympathetic. She is constantly being called "frigid" and "dried up." The Skipper contrasts the coldness of his own daughter with the warmth of his daughter-in-law. Mary remains throughout in her ice-cold tower: she condemns her father, brother and Alonzo for their lack of reverence, especially at the Easter weekend. She immerses herself in her schoolbooks in this "house of useless men." (43) She has to be seen to be going to church, unlike Rosie hypocritically contradicting Christian behaviour in her own life, to the end failing to be reconciled with Winston. Her bitterness is born of frustration, but unlike Winston's, which relieves itself in drink, hers becomes withdrawn into a carping and sanctimonious vindictiveness. Yet she stays in the house, not wanting Brad to cause disruption, but not admitting that she is one of its principal instigators.

Brad likewise is drawn back to this house of hate[12] when it is love he is seeking, only to suffer the mockery of all the family members except his mother. Perhaps it is more than coincidence that at Easter he sees himself as a Christ figure, despised and rejected of man, both in the parish from which he has been ejected and in his own family. His misguided religious fanaticism is turned against his family; he is accusing them at the same time as he is seeking their acceptance. In its way his religion is as false as Mary's. It is the product of mental delusion derived from his own insecurity, from his need to seek salvation in his retreat from a world which has treated him cruelly. The more he tries to convert his family, the more the scorn that is poured upon him. Brad's nightmare is of the souls of the damned, including Winston and Alonzo, burning in flames which reach to heaven. (50) His religious fervour later drives him to pray for a family condemned to hell, asking the Lord to spare his mother, the "one yet who is pure in heart, whose sins are of omission only." (111) Winston's fury at his upsetting of Rosie leads him to remind Brad of Mildred's bastard that Brad has fathered. When Winston orders him out of the house, Brad, like a small child, pathetically appeals to his mother, "I've nowhere to go." Told by his father to go to Hell, he walks out into the storm for the last time. (112-115)

While the complex family relationships are realistically depicted, the ending can only be fully appreciated if we also view the play as allegory. Brad may be a false messiah in the eyes of the family, but his "crucifixion" is consistent with the religious symbolism throughout the play. While much of the action and interplay of character can be seen in an Ibsen-Chekhov-Shaw tradition, the Easter setting has much in common with that of Strindberg's *Easter*, which likewise begins on Maundy Thursday and follows the family's misfortunes through guilt and suffering to final redemption at Easter. Cook takes us through the storm of family despair with its symbolic crucifixion of one member to the hope of reconciliation in the Easter resurrection. The death and resurrection of the Skipper give the play its much-criticized apocalyptic ending, but the apparition is acceptable only in terms of the play's constant symbolic dimension.

The total impact of the symbolism can be fully realized only in stage production. Cook suggests alternative sets, one with a detailed, Shavian realism, the other "stark" and "skeletonized." He indicates that in the first it is "minute attention to realistic detail that heightens the progression towards symbolism and abstraction in the action of the play." (9) He also visualizes the storm almost as an antagonist, "a living thing, a character whose presence is always felt." (139) It is important that as in Ibsen and Chekhov realism and symbolism co-exist. The voice of the Announcer, which progressively reiterates the impending storm and doom, is perhaps an unconscious echo of the Broadcast Official heralding the storm while the Fortune Teller urges Antrobus to save the family in Thornton Wilder's *The Skin of Our Teeth*. Here too is a microcosmic family, at this point in the play equated with Noah and the saving of mankind in the ark. Wilder's technique is much more in the tradition of German Expressionism, so that symbolism and allegory are essential devices of the play, whereas Cook gradually increases the significance of the storm in a principally realistic setting; while it is totally consistent with the Skipper's world, it is not until Mary and Wayne survive the storm in which Brad is lost that its full impact is made apparent. Cook is asking much of his stage director to bring the storm into the foreground of the play and give it the relevance the author requires.

The most controversial aspect of the play is its supernatural ending. Once again the full impact can be achieved only in stage presentation. We are prepared for the change by lighting effects which illuminate the Skipper's Death Mask, while the actor leaves the bedroom during a blackout to reappear as the ghost. The device is not as unacceptable as some critics would claim. It can be justified symbolically by the resurrection theme which is central to Cook's purpose in the play. The chief problem lies in the inconsistency of a primarily naturalistic technique turning into the full-blown melodrama of a ghost scene. Again we may turn to tradition. Ghosts have been accepted in tragic drama as far back as Seneca. Shakespeare's *Richard III*, Webster's *The Duchess of Malfi* and Otway's *Venice Preserv'd* are only three examples of plays in which ghosts are introduced, but not until the climax of the action. While it may be argued that Renaissance or neo-classical stage convention would allow for more inconsistency of dramatic style than modern drama, Cook's play is in the spirit and tradition of great dramas of the past: he has acknowledged Shakespeare, Webster, Ibsen, Strindberg, O'Neill, Beckett and Arden among his favourites.[13] There are echoes of all these playwrights in Cook's work, and a fuller combination in *Jacob's Wake* than in any other of his plays. Yeats rejected for the Abbey Theatre O'Casey's *The Silver Tassie,* with its symbolic second act between three realistic acts, because he considered it stylistically inconsistent, thus unleashing a famous literary controversy. Among those who defended O'Casey was Bernard Shaw, who a few years previously had written his own apocalyptic ending for *Heartbreak House*. Shaw gives us even less preparation earlier in the play for his ending than Cook does in *Jacob's Wake*; only in the closing moments is there suggestion of warfare with the Zeppelin raid, which releases Shotover's dynamite supply, destroying the two "burglars" and "men of business," and which is welcomed by Hesione and Ellie. Here too is a distinctly symbolic ending depicting the destruction of a society and of a way of life.

Michael Cook's regard for tradition makes him one of the widest ranging and most knowledgeable of Canada's playwrights. *Jacob's Wake* is exceptional in that it draws more extensively on those styles and qualities which enrich Cook's own observation of the distinctive life of Newfoundland. Many of these devices have been unconsciously absorbed over a lifetime's experience, while a few are consciously borrowed directly from other writers, in the same way that Cook establishes authenticity by using actual words and phrases spoken by people he has met in the province. In *Tiln*, for example, the relationship between Tiln and Fern, the style of dialogue, even the names of the characters suggest close affinities with Beckett's *Endgame*; or the almost maniacal defiance of William Gayden against naval injustice in *The Gayden Chronicles* strongly recalls Black Jack Musgrave in John Arden's *Serjeant Musgrave's Dance*. There is even a touch of *Endgame* in *Jacob's Wake* when Winston goes through the ritual of looking through the telescope to inform Elijah of the state of the sea. (60-61) This play is, on the other hand, a compendium of so many styles that no single influence emerges clearly; more often than not it is rooted in a realistic tradition reinforced with moments of poetic imagery and symbolism. Above all *Jacob's Wake* is marked by a strongly individual dramatic power, which gives us an often profound insight into the lives of the people in a province beset with multiple social, economic and personal problems. Through his art, Cook has universalized these experiences.

NOTES

[1] This article, with only minor differences, first appeared in English in *Canadian Drama/L'Art dramatique canadien*, Vol. 15, No. 2, 1989.

[2] Geraldine Anthony (ed.), *Stage Voices,* Toronto: Doubleday Canada Ltd., 1978, 219.

[3] Ibid.

[4] Rota Lister, "Interview with Michael Cook," *Canadian Drama/L'art dramatique canadien*, Vol. 2, No. 2, Fall 1976, 177.

[5] Quoted in Brian Parker, "On the Edge: Michael Cook's Newfoundland Trilogy," *Canadian Literature*, 85, Summer 1980, 23.

[6] G.B. Shaw, *Heartbreak House*, in W.S. Smith (ed.), *Bernard Shaw's Plays*, New York: Norton Critical Editions, 1970, 128.

[7] Page references for this and subsequent quotations from *Jacob's Wake* are taken from the Talonbooks edition, Vancouver 1975.

[8] In conversation with the author. See Richard Perkyns (ed.), *Major Plays of the Canadian Theatre 1934-1984*, Toronto: Irwin Publishing Inc., 1984, 447.

[9] Ibid., 444.

[10] Parker, "On the Edge," 37, 39. Could some devil also have hinted to Cook the irony of the name "Winston," suggestive of a leader so long in the political wilderness taking the helm of a floundering people in 1940?

[11] Winston later uses the same metaphor in a different context to describe their total situation: "Like rats in a trap, with the Welfare as bait." (125) The metaphor is also appropriate to the image of a sinking ship.

[12] This household can be compared with the Stone family in Percy Janes's Newfoundland novel *House of Hate*, Toronto: McClelland & Stewart, 1970, though the family in the novel is dominated by a stern patriarch.

[13] Anthony, *Stage Voices*, 219.

Klaus Peter Müller

Robertson Davies:
The Concept of History and Myth[*]

In 1949 director Tyrone Guthrie wrote about his friend and colleague Robertson Davies: "[He was] one of the pioneers of the still imaginary Canadian Theatre."[1] Today, however, many critics and readers believe that Davies is most successful as a writer of novels.[2] Still, Guthrie is right: without Davies, a history of Canadian drama would be incomplete, and Davies' achievement as a dramatist certainly deserves our recognition.

Robertson Davies, of Welsh and Scottish ancestry, was born on August 28, 1913, in Thamesville, Ontario. He took up studying at Queen's University in Kingston, Ontario, and later attended Balliol College, Oxford. He completed his study of English literature with a thesis on *Shakespeare's Boy Actors* and was awarded a B.A. Afterwards, he turned to acting, performing, for example, at the London Old Vic. Here he met Brenda Mathews, who became his wife in 1940 and, in the same year, returned with him to Canada. Davies worked as a journalist, became first editor-in-chief, and then, in 1955, publisher of the Peterborough *Examiner*, and still found enough time to devote to his work as creative writer and director. In 1948, his first play, *Eros at Breakfast*, a one-act play, earned him a "Dominion Drama Festival Award" for best Canadian play. The following year, Davies received another award for *Fortune, My Foe* and, in 1950, published one of his best-known plays, *At My Heart's Core*.

In the 1950s, Davies was one of the founders and promoters of the Stratford (Ontario) Shakespeare Festival, and it was during this period that he also started publishing his first novels: *Tempest-Tost* (1951), *Leaven of Malice* (1954) and *A Mixture of Frailties* (1958), which together form the "Salterton Trilogy." In 1960, Davies began his career as a professor at Trinity College, University of Toronto, where he taught until 1981. His interests are diverse, and he has made them the subject of many essays which are as witty as they are instructive. Davies is one of Canada's prime essayists. His second trilogy of novels, the "Deptford Trilogy," appeared in the 1970s.[3]

Davies' novels are distinguished by his erudition, his insight into human nature, a wealth of personal experience, and a sense of humour and satire as well as mysticism and religion; the quality of the language captivates the reader as much as the content and theme. The same distinctive attributes characterize Davies' plays, which are neither of interest to the literary historian only, nor are they merely a national matter—even if Guthrie says of some of them that "they could be occurring nowhere but in Canada."[4] Guthrie is thinking of *The Voice of the People* (1949) and, in particular, *Overlaid* (1948), which presents the underdeveloped countryside as a spiritual and intellectual waste land, not least (as Guthrie believes) with reference to rural Canada.

The protagonist of *The Voice*, Shorty Morton, has a very high opinion of himself, although he is, in fact, ignorant, prejudiced and intolerant. This short one-act play so expertly exemplifies wide-spread narrow-mindedness and bigotry that it was published in a school edition in 1968.[5] The characters in *Overlaid*, Davies' most famous one-act play, also stand for universal traits. Pop, an old farmer, is a lover of art in his own modest way. He is presented as an outsider who enjoys life, is wise and generous, but whom the people around him perceive as licentious, mad, egoistic, unsocial and irresponsible. His daughter Ethel, on the other hand, sees her purpose in life in the performing of her duties, as this guarantees social recognition. This attitude, however, has made her a grim and frustrated woman. Her one aim in life is epitomized in the only wish this woman is still capable of nourishing—a respectable tombstone for the family vault. Ethel is one of the many 'living dead' in world literature.

One may challenge, then, Guthrie's opinion that Davies' plays could be set nowhere but in Canada. They start out from situations which Davies himself deems, in part, 'typically Canadian', but then he always raises them into the sphere of the universal, which is influenced by his culture and set of values. This interplay results in a structure which this essay aims to investigate in greater detail, focussing on the notions of 'history' and 'myth'. It is a 'play' indeed, and Davies, who is in no way a post-structuralist, is more aware of the interchange of history and myth than are many of the critics who accuse him of ideological narrow-mindedness. However, in his opinion, his works express not only the play of art, but also the play of life. This results in an attention to values which far exceeds the arbitrariness of post-structuralism.[6]

Of Davies' eighteen plays, six—that is, a third—are given a precise and factual historical setting: *Hope Deferred* (one-act play, 1949) takes place in 1693, at the Chateau St. Louis in Quebec City, the seat of the Governor of New France. The conflict between civilization and art on the one hand and trade and religion on the other is represented in the historical figures of Count Frontenac (Governor from 1672 to 1682 and 1688 to 1698), and Bishop Laval, who became known for his Jansenist morals, his ascetic way of life and his assertion of church interests.[7] *At the Gates of the Righteous* (one-act play, 1949), is set in 1860, in rural Upper Canada. *At My Heart's Core*, a three-act play published in 1950, explicitly refers to the Mackenzie Rebellion of 1837. In *A Jig for the Gypsy* (three-act play, 1954), the gypsy woman, Benoni, lives in a remote house in Wales in 1885, a year in which parliamentary elections were heavily contested. Another three-act play, *General Confession* (1956), is based on the fact that Casanova served in later years as a librarian for Count "Waldstein und Wurtemberg von Dux;" (198) the action is set in the year 1797. *Pontiac and the Green Man* is based on a play of 1766, *Ponteach*, and a lawsuit in which the play's reputed author, Major Robert Rogers, was involved: in 1768, Rogers was accused of conspiring with the Indians. In the programme for a performance of *Pontiac* in 1977, Davies writes that he drew on historical material in order to point out "possibilities, rather than historical facts."[8] These possibilities consisted in Rogers' 'Vision of North America' and his heroic behaviour towards the Indians. Rogers succeeds in considering his private self, his public self and the country as parts of a whole. He recognizes the new spirit which the country may afford and which makes the new world better than the old one. This spiritual and intellectual idealism is at the core of Davies' conception of his character, while the historical Rogers was more strongly concerned with material pursuits like the search for the Northwest Passage.

Of Davies' other plays, seven are set in present-day Canada, yet they are by no means unhistoric: *Overlaid* (one-act play, 1948), *The Voice of the People* (one-act play, 1949) *Fortune, My Foe* (three-act play, 1949), *Hunting Stuart* (three-act play, 1955), *Leaven of Malice* (three-act play, 1960), *Brothers in the Black Art* (television play, 1974) and *Question Time* (two-act play, 1974). The perspectives in these plays are not restricted to our time. This is most obvious in *Hunting Stuart*, which accentuates each character's past and repeatedly emphasizes that each individual is also a product of his or her family and ancestors. Stuart, a minor official in contemporary Ottawa, is a descendant of Bonnie Prince Charlie and "the oldest living direct male descendant of the Royal House of Stuart."

(38) This idea is presented in an amusingly exaggerated manner, at the same time as being a romantic comedy and satire of Canadian middle-class pretentiousness. At the end of this play, Stuart sums up what may be considered Davies' credo: "In spite of environment and heredity and all that, I suppose what one is always remains very much a matter of choice." (100) For Davies, personal identity is indeed defined through the elements of environment, heredity and the individual freedom of choice left by the former two. The combination of these elements marks Davies as a classical modern.[9]

King Phoenix, a three-act play of 1948, is set in mythical prehistory, "a few hundred years before the Roman Conquest," "at Caercolvin in Albion." (106) Davies' starting point was the presentation of King Cole in Monmouth's *History of the Kings of Britain*: he was interested in why Cole is depicted as a "merry old soul."[10] Davies' answer, expressed through his play, is because Cole is not afraid of death and because he adapts to the natural cycle of life. This attitude towards life is also expressed in the play's title and an old folk song in an important passage at the end of Act II. The song tells the story of John Barleycorn and the three kings who attempt to kill him. (168f.) Its subject is the four seasons and their eternal cycle of return. The action of *A Masque of Aesop* (1952) reaches even further back into the past: the citizens of Delphi sentence Aesop to death because his teachings are unacceptable. However, Apollo, in his role as judge, acquits him. In this 'masque', entertainment and instruction make such a perfect blend that this play (which was originally written for a student performance at Davies' old "prep-school, Upper Canada College") also appeared in a school edition.[11]

Two unpublished 'Centennial' plays were also intended to connect Canadian history and myth. *Eros at Breakfast*, the one-act play of 1948, is a "psychosomatic interplay" which presents the interaction of the various psychic and physical elements in man. What is important in this early play is, again, the unity of life, which is the result of various and sometimes contradictory components.

The interaction of history and myth which is so characteristic of Davies' work, can be seen most clearly in his play *At My Heart's Core*. The play combines elements of national and political history ("the time 1837, when Canada was making one of its early revolts against the stifling, second-hand traditions of the Europe that gave it birth"[12]) with figures and ideas that play an important role in Canadian literary history. Davies himself describes *At My Heart's Core* as a play about the Canadian intellectual climate. This includes the present, because Canada, according to Davies, is still a country which is not living up to its people's full potential, and Canada has not yet left its pioneering days behind.[13] Davies' focus of interest, when studying historical materials for this play, was not only on the firm historical facts, but also on the attitudes and mores which people in real life often take for granted, the ideology of which they are frequently unconscious. Davies is aware of the fact that the unreflected transfer to a new country of accustomed ways of seeing and living may quickly result in misconception, a "falsification of the new land." This falsification is inseparable from what Davies calls "myth."[14]

The transfer of English middle-class ideology to Canada was particularly manifest during the first half of the 19th century, and it is no accident that Davies also chose its literary manifestations in order to present this situation. The play's three historical female figures, Catharine Parr Traill, Susanna Moodie and Frances Stewart were representatives of the educated English middle class who emigrated to Canada in the 19th century and rendered accounts of their situation in letters, tales and journals. They thus became important personalities in Canadian literary history.[15]

The Honourable Thomas Stewart, in whose house the play is set, is a member of Upper Canada's Legislative Council, an institution modelled on the British House of Lords, to which one was appointed, not elected as into the Legislative Assembly. He also acts as Justice of the Peace in the District of Douro. Stewart is as much a historical figure as Edmund Cantwell, whom Frances Stewart's letters mention as her neighbour in Canada and a friend of Lord Rossmore in Ireland and of Byron and Maria Edgeworth in England.[16]

The most significant historical reference in Davies' play, however, is the Mackenzie Rebellion of December, 1837. The action takes place during this very period, (3) and all the "gentlemen" have gone to York to defend the Royal government. "All the other men" have assembled at Peterborough, in order to defend the town in case of emergency. (26) The children, too, have been brought away to safety, so that only the women remain in their settlers' homes. The Stewarts' home reflects the family's financial affluence and middle-class taste: there are books, maps and some "good engravings." (3) Mrs. Stewart embodies "all the refinements of high cultivation." (4) For her house-keeping duties she has an Indian help, a woman of undefinable age, who is distinguished by a permanent smile and occasional, unmotivated giggling. (4f.)

A child has just been born, the daughter of Honour Brady, a young girl, and old Phelim Brady. Phelim and Honour are unmarried, as Phelim's wife has died only recently, and her body is still awaiting burial. The Protestant and the Catholic priest cannot agree on who is responsible, and Phelim refuses to co-operate. This is why Honour has sought refuge at Mrs. Stewart's. Quite obviously, Davies works in social and ethnic categories. Comic roles are assigned to the lower class and the ethnic minority, while the ruling class is presented in a more serious, but also more critical manner. In part, Davies makes use of stereotypical prejudices in order to make us aware of them, question or reconsider them. Sally, the smiling Indian, for example, is called a "heathen savage," (20) although she is much less 'savage' than the person who calls her thus. Phelim, who belongs to the group of poor Irish immigrants, at the same time wants to be distinguished from the Irish because he considers himself an artist, not a labourer. While in Ireland his art gained him recognition and consoled people in their misery, it is not appreciated in Canada, where people are preoccupied with work and have no time for thoughts about the mysteries and wonders of life. (27) Davies, then, not only picks up stereotypes, modifies or rejects them, but also creates new ones: Canada as a country adverse to art is a recurring topos in his writings.[17] Phelim, the artist and outsider who refuses to work like the others, to bury his wife and to marry his daughter's mother, represents a conception of art which Mrs. Moodie rejects vehemently: "there is a difference between the productions of an educated and disciplined taste and a rigmarole of memorized fairy tales!" Phelim agrees, but qualifies the difference in his own special way: "my poems and tales are rooted deep in a mighty past, and yours are the thin and bitter squeezings from the weary fancy of a heartsore woman." (24)

Davies' play characterizes Moodie's art as a glorification of patriotic feeling (for England, not Canada) of the ruling ideology, and as a moral bulwark against the rebels. Moodie recites her poem, "The Oath of the Canadian Volunteers," whose heroic phrases on death are met with distinct irony on the part of Mrs. Stewart. (10f.)[18] While Moodie's art is shaped by her political attitude and current history, Phelim ignores these aspects in his art—although he, too, is not unaffected by them. In *At My Heart's Core*, both views emerge as inadequate. Davies objects to both the stereotype of the politically and socially detached artist and the artistic attitude which uncritically supports the ruling system. Moodie's political conviction, expressed in her poem, that the rulers do right and are legitimized to enforce their ideas, is duplicated on the level of private relations when she fights with her sister for possession of the newborn child. Mrs. Traill protests against Moodie's "assumption of authority," (19) reminds her that one must not become dictatorial even with the best of intentions, advises her not to interfere (17) and assumes that it is Moodie's "peremptory manner" which provokes Phelim's resistance. (19) Through the quarrel about the newborn child and the question of responsibility for the baby, the play raises on the private level exactly those problems which are also important on the political level. The suggestion is, then, that the struggle "for possession of the child" (19) and the question of who is "responsible for the child," (17) are metaphors of the Canadian situation.

This connection between the private and political level is made directly in the text when Mrs. Traill voices her opinion that people like Phelim have to be told and shown what is good for them, even against their own will. Cantwell, a figure from the same social background as Moodie, Stewart and Traill, but an outsider, replies: "That is the simple principle of government, madam, which has given rise to the regrettable revolution, in suppressing which all your husbands are at present engaged." (30) When the members of this class sit down together for a meal and Phelim is excluded, the Irish immigrant again borrows terms from current politics in order to describe this private situation:

> B'God, it's the Family Compact sittin' down to their food! And where's the common people? Out in the cold, every time; out in the cold! Hurrah for Mackenzie and responsible government! (34f.)

This scene, with concepts from Canadian history that are highly political, forms the ending of Act I. In Canada, the term 'Family Compact', at the beginning of the 19th century, referred to the leading and politically influential men in administration. Many of them stemmed from the second generation of Loyalists and were educated, conservative, and, in part, influenced by aristocratic attitudes.

John Beverley Robinson, Christopher Hagerman, G. H. Markland, John Macauly and especially the Rev. John Strachan (first Anglican Bishop of Toronto, 1839, and named on page 65 of Davies' play) and William Allan were the most important members of this politically powerful group. They stood for a firm and comprehensive bond with England, the rejection of any democratic concept of the state, and the refusal to contemplate closer links with the United States, of whose republicanism and democracy they were afraid.

Since 1828, the Reform Movement had established itself against these positions and their enforcement, with men like Dr. W.W. Baldwin, Robert Baldwin, John Rolph and William Lyon Mackenzie. They demanded greater attention to the people's will (for example through plebiscite) and, above all, a "responsible government," i.e. a government (which had up until then been constituted by the Executive Council, a group of appointed advisors to the Governor, the representative of the English Crown) responsible to the elected representatives of the Assembly, who could, if necessary, also force the government to resign. The Legislative Council, too, was to be elected, comparable to the American Senate, but in more direct form. The name of William Lyon Mackenzie was, and is, closely associated with these and other ideas for greater openness and the democratization of government.[19] Historical background knowledge is of utmost importance for an understanding of the final scene of Act I and an evaluation of the play as a whole.

Apart from its political and historical elements and motifs, Act I also introduces another important motif which dominates the whole of Act II and appears to entirely superimpose the historical perspective. Act II is dominated by the apparently quite subjective 'temptation' of the three women by Edmund Cantwell. Cantwell feels unappreciated by the other families of his class, and because his wife suffers a lot from this situation and even turns deeply depressive, he attempts to get his revenge. From the very first, however, his stage appearance is also marked by a further dimension: again and again, Cantwell appears as the embodiment of temptation—he is a kind of devil figure.[20] In Act I, each of the three women has denied that there is any danger that she might be tempted. They claim that neither Cantwell nor the country of Canada could constitute such a threat. (33f.)

Act II proves them right—but in ways quite different from what they had imagined. The danger lies within themselves, and Cantwell so expertly succeeds in casting confusion on their own desires, self-images and ideals in life that their present situation appears highly undesirable. He deprives them of their peace of mind by confronting each woman with her heart's desires—that which is "at [her] heart's core" (80)—and comparing this image with a very different and negative reality. In Mrs. Stewart, he evokes memories of her former lover in Ireland, Lord Rossmore, with whom she could certainly have led an easier and more comfortable life than in Canada where her qualities and cultivated manners seem so very useless. (43f.) Mrs. Traill is made aware of her talents as a naturalist, which could enhance her reputation and be of greater use to her country than her tiring and unsatisfactory existence as a farmer's wife. (45f.) Mrs. Moodie is compared to the English writer Maria Edgeworth, whom she admires and whom she could equal—as Cantwell suggests—if only she had the leisure and peace of mind to write intensively. (52f.) Cantwell understands the women's secret, repressed and unspoken desires. What Cantwell tempts the women with is not gender-specific and only partly individual. It is their personal characteristics (Mrs. Stewart's romantic temperament, Mrs. Traill's rational, scientific interests and Mrs. Moodie's intellectual, literary ones) combined with unsatisfactory social conditions which lay them open to temptation. This constellation renders the figures susceptible to ideas which make a radical change in their momentary position seem desirable or even possible. In other words: they become susceptible to revolutionary ideas.

Act II, then, whilst appearing to deal with highly personal, subjective and individual problems, does not really abandon the play's historical basis. On the contrary, it leads us to the core of all problems, "the heart's core" as envisaged by Davies: the basis, reasons and motives behind historical as well as individual events—the myth itself. This basis is formed, on the one hand, by social, political and economic conditions (which are unsatisfactory in the play), and on the other hand by the individual situations, characteristics, desires, ideals and aims of the people concerned.

Both components combine, in Davies' play as in history, to form a constellation that is subversive, rebellious and anti-authoritarian. The three middle-class women's wish for radical change is checked by their sense of duty and their (Victorian) submission to a husband's dominance. Phelim, the Irish bard, rebels verbally, but also by refusing to co-operate. On the social-historical level, people's dissatisfaction with their social conditions finds an outlet in Mackenzie's Rebellion. Interestingly, historians, too, have emphasized the decisive influence Mackenzie's own character had on the planning, execution and effect of the rebellion. It is considered the enterprise of a man who acted in hot blood and emotionally: its organization chaotic, its performance amateurish. Its immediate effect was catastrophic, but in the long run, it effected changes in Canadian politics and history that were important and urgently necessary.[21]

At the end of Act II, Mr. Stewart returns to his home, only to find that something is wrong, that after the defeat of the rebels in the country, unrest has entered his own house. Most of Act III depicts Mr. Stewart's attempts to weigh up the evidence in this situation, and to form a conclusion on which action can later be taken.

Act III starts with a depiction of the concrete historical situation. The names of real historical figures are mentioned, such as Archdeacon John Strachan, the Governor and the military leader of the Loyalists, James Fitzgibbon. (65) Then Mr. Stewart compares the historical situation with the religious myth of the rebellion in Heaven and the banishment of Satan. (67) Stewart believes that this banishment has perpetuated evil rather than disposed of it, and he therefore rejects a similar procedure in the present situation. He admits that he has been forced to question a system in which he himself participates and concludes that "a grave suspicion assails me that what we have at York is order without law. And that is tyranny." (67)

Stewart is a traditionally-minded man, but also characterized by *joie de vivre* and a great sense of humour. He accepts that jurisdiction is no perfect instrument (71f.) and that judging the three women's situation is not really his responsibility. Cantwell and Mrs. Moodie refer to the situation as a "moral issue." (76f.) This it is indeed, because everything revolves around the questions of 'what is good?' and 'which kind of behaviour is right and appropriate?'. The women have to ask themselves whether it is right to stay in Canada and put their own personal interests last or even suppress them. The issue for Cantwell is whether the class who sets the tone in the country has welcomed the new settlers and treated them sensitively enough. He accuses this class of failure in this respect, as a result of which his wife has fallen ill. (78f.) His accusation against the Stewarts, Traills and Moodies is an individual variation of society's accusation against the Family Compact. The behaviour of the Compact, too, satisfies neither universal notions of morality nor the conditions of social reality. Cantwell himself extends his reproach to Canada's entire ruling class:

> what a tight, snug, unapproachable little society you have here in Upper Canada. I am not surprised that you have brought a rebellion upon yourselves. (79)

Just as the social situation has not been settled by the rebels' defeat (66: "the bitterest part has just begun"), the women cannot find their peace of mind by trying to forget or suppress the ideas which alarm them. (79) Falling back on their sense of duty is also insufficient. In Act III of his play, Davies points out that ideas of rebellion must be dealt with on a conscious level, in both the private and public sphere. Only then may one realize whether revolutionary ideas contain meaningful and desirable elements and how these can be put into practice. This will take time anyway, as the actual situation in which one is caught up, and its attendant demands, slow the process down.

This insight is accompanied by a sense of duty towards other people. Both elements combine to prevent the greatest temptation to which the three women in the play and humanity in general are exposed: "the temptation of discontent" which deprives people of their "peace of mind." (80) But insight into the actual situation and a sense of duty do not suffice to resist temptation. One needs two other properties as well, which Cantwell names explicitly and which are born out by the play: "humility" and "charity." (80) Only these four elements together will prevent doubts about oneself, one's status and one's identity from gnawing away at, and finally destroying a person's life. (80) Only such a combination of elements will lead to maturity and help a person move from regressive, unformed and childlike ideals to more progressive and dynamic adult actions.[22]

Davies thus combines elements of enlightenment (awareness of one's own personal and social situation as well as practical action) with the postulate of duty and responsibility towards others and the (amongst other things Christian) attitude of modesty and charity to form his basic concept of a satisfactory and meaningful life. This ideology is characteristic of Davies' oeuvre, and these are the basic components of his myth of a 'humane' life. It becomes obvious that he is much more an 'aristocratic reformer' than a 'proletarian revolutionary'.[23] But his sympathies lie with the rebels, and he prefers Phelim's idea of art, which does not seek to pacify any sector of society but deals everybody equally an awakening blow, to Susanna Moodie's reactionary concept of art which uncritically supports the rulers. (40)

Davies is a concerned writer. He is not in favour of postmodern 'playing', which so often seems indifferent and non-committal. He believes too much in the meaning of life (if not necessarily a meaning that is specific or predetermined) and the fact that each individual must accept the responsibility of *making* his or her life meaningful. For Davies, 'history' is that part of human attempts to render life meaningful which is reflected in external facts, perceivable events. 'Myth' is the part which underlies the external, which encompasses the motives and aims of the individual or of groups which share a common aim. Myth is "at the heart's core," it is essential. Davies once ironically put this concept into one of his characters' mouth:

> The bee in his bonnet was that history and myth are two aspects of a kind of grand pattern in human destiny: history is the mass of observable or recorded fact, but myth is the abstract or essence of it.[24]

Robertson Davies is not a historiographer; he compares plays not to photographs, but to paintings.[25] His oeuvre is not concerned with historical documentation or realism. Rather, he wants to point out and evoke what he considers the essential in life: its boundless diversity, its unexplored miracle of creation and decay, its endless but by no means arbitrary attempts to render life meaningful—in short, myth is at the core of his works. This is why the human psyche is as important in his work as are mysticism and religion. While some of his critics consider this old-fashioned and think that Davies has little appeal for the contemporary reader, others claim the opposite. Davies' commercial success suggests that a growing number of readers are (again) willing to contemplate his questions and perspectives. Basically, his myths are as old as humanity itself, perennial as the eternal problems of life, and Davies' modes of presentation are as far from revolutionary as is his ideology.[26] However, his works as well as his myths may help to reveal the discontents, emptiness and frustrations of life both past and present, and pave the way for hope and change.

In the course of his life and literary work Davies has paid less and less attention to external history, while his interest in myth has steadily increased. The human psyche has become a focus of his attention, and the criticism that he is losing sight of the necessary dialectic interplay of 'objective conditions' (like history, politics and economy) and 'subjective consciousness', is becoming more important.[27] *Question Time*, one of his latest plays, treats of the self-discovery of the leading Canadian, the 'son of Adam', Prime Minister Peter Macadam. The sole survivor of a plane crash, Macadam wrestles with death in the Canadian Arctic, which is less a geographical site than Macadam's 'personal Arctic," his "Terra Incognita." (8) Macadam is the prototype of man determined by external forces, who does not live according to his own values and convictions, but 'operates' according to what others expect of him. It is this lack of individual human qualities which Davies regrets again and again.[28] In *Question Time*, Macadam's wife Sarah voices the author's opinion:

> What is a man that other men should exalt him if he is not someone whose life on the personal level—on the deepest bedrock of the personal level—is of worth, and colour and substance and splendour that makes him a man in whom other men see something of what is best in themselves? (64)

This attitude does not express a dangerous subjectivism which ignores reality, but is based on Davies' concept of self-knowledge, which imposes on each individual the responsibility towards him/herself and his or her behaviour towards others. Here, Davies largely goes back to the theory of C.G. Jung, whom he quotes in a review:

> no state is better than the individuals who compose it, and the resignation of individual responsibility to the state is an abdication of man's most serious duty—his duty to develop and integrate his whole being to the uttermost.[29]

This kind of knowledge is part of Davies' myth as it has been described above. It serves to prevent egocentrism as well as aggression and hostility towards others. Only this, Davies claims with Jung, could have prevented the historical horrors of the Third Reich and Stalinism. And only this, we many continue, will prevent the repetition of Auschwitz and other inhuman facts of history.[30]

Another concern of Davies is to underline the mythical unity of the quite varied elements of which human life is made up. *Question Time* mentions, for example, the necessary connection between the civilized world and the primitive, the social and individual, (17) between intelligence and feeling, (19) between the external and the internal, (24) and demands a "free trade between the world of fantasy and the world of reality." (25) The connection between the real and the ideal, between history and myth is also apparent in Davies' description of *Question*

Time as a play "about the relationship of the Canadian people to their soil, and about the relationship of man to his soul. We neglect both at our peril." (xiii)

Davies could be accused of tending to neglect the concrete historical and realistic aspect in his works as a whole. Davies himself sees reasons for this in his own history and origin. He stems from the middle class and has little personal experience in other circles and social backgrounds.[31] Still he wants a "theatre of wholeness," which is also important as an "agent of social change, and particularly of psychological change."[32] When it comes to forming and reshaping human history, Davies even agrees with Marx: "Men make their own history, but they do not know that they are making it."[33] But Davies has his own opinion about the involuntary, partly unconscious, ideological and mythical forces which make up history. This opinion is neither revolutionary nor reactionary, but worth considering and highly topical , because history is by no means ignored and replaced by a purely subjective internal world. Davies wants to have the Jungian archetypes, which are essentially a-historic, recognized as a-historic and compared with actual concrete reality, so that people can live and act adequately in reality, i.e. in a conscious and humane manner: "Our great task is to see people as people and not clouded by archetypes we carry about with us, looking for a peg to hang them on."[34] Such an attitude encompasses the recognition of the historical, political, economic and other influences external to oneself as well as the attempt to discover the mythical forces behind them and compare them with one's own myths. Davies writes about man's inalienable right to a humane life. The fact that he focusses more on the individual and self-knowledge than on sociopolitical instruction has understandable historical reasons for which he cannot really be blamed.

*PLAYS BY ROBERTSON DAVIES

Eros at Breakfast and other plays, Toronto: Clarke & Irwin, 1949 (*Eros at Breakfast*, a psychosomatic interlude; *The Voice of the People*; *Hope Deferred*; *Overlaid*; *At the Gates of the Righteous*).

Fortune, My Foe, Toronto: Clarke & Irwin, 1949.

A Masque of Aesop, Toronto: Clarke & Irwin, 1952.

A Jig for the Gipsy, Toronto: Clarke & Irwin, 1954.

A Masque of Mr. Punch, Toronto: Oxford University Press,1963.

At My Heart's Core & Overlaid, Toronto: Clarke & Irwin, 1966 (First editions: Toronto: Clarke & Irwin, 1950 resp. Toronto: French 1948).

Centennial Play, Ottawa: Centennial Commission 1967 (In collaboration with Arthur Murphy, Ives Thériault, W.O. Mitchell and Eric Nicol).

Hunting Stuart and other plays, Toronto: New Press, 1972 (*Hunting Stuart* (written in 1955); *King Phoenix* (written in 1948); *General Confession* (written in 1956)).

Question Time, Toronto: Macmillan, 1975.

Pontiac and the Green Man (1977; Robertson Davies kindly provided me with a manuscript of the play).

NOTES

[1] Guthrie, "Introduction," in Davies, *Eros at Breakfast & Other Plays*, Toronto: Clarke & Irwin 1949, ix-xiv, here x. For Davies' own assessment of Canadian theatre at this time cf. his dialogue about "The State of Theatre in Canada," written for the Massey Commission in 1959 and reprinted in *Canadian Theatre Review*, 5, 1975, 16-36.

[2] Cf. the entries on Davies in *The Canadian Encyclopedia*, Edmonton: Hurtig, 1983; James Vinson (ed.), *Contemporary Dramatists*, London/New York: St. James Press, 1973. Also cf. Frederick Radford, "Padre Blazon or Old King Cole—Robertson Davies: Novelist or Playwright?," in *Canadian Drama*, 7, 2, 1981, 13-25; Michael Peterman, "Bewitchments of Simplification," ibid., 94-109; Geraldine Anthony (ed.), *Stage Voices. Twelve Canadian Playwrights Talk about Their Lives and Work*, Toronto: Doubleday, 1978, 57f; Susan Stone-Blackburn, *Robertson Davies, Playwright. A Search for the Self on the Canadian Stage*, Vancouver: University of British Columbia Press, 1985, 220. Carl F. Klinck (ed.), *Literary History of Canada. Canadian Literature in English*, vol. III, Toronto: University of Toronto Press, [2]1976, largely ignores Davies' dramatic work, as does William H. New, *A History of Canadian Literature*, London: Macmillan 1989. For a more balanced presentation of Davies' plays and fiction cf. W. J. Keith, *Canadian Literature in English*, London: Longman 1985. Keith calls Davies and Reaney "our most substantial playwrights to date." (190)

[3] *Fifth Business* (1970), *The Manticore* (1972) and *World of Wonders* (1975) (all Toronto: Macmillan). The following quotations are given from the edition Harmondsworth: Penguin, 1983. The "Salterton Trilogy" first appeared with Clarke & Irwin, Toronto; for a one-volume edition cf. Harmondsworth: Penguin, 1986.

[4] Guthrie, xii.

[5] Agincourt, Ont.: Book Society of Canada. (Searchlight, No. 304)

[6] For a discussion of values in post-structuralism cf., for example, Manfred Frank, *Was ist Neostrukturalismus?*, Frankfurt: Suhrkamp 1984, whose critical attitude towards post- and neo-structuralism I largely share. For other positions cf. Philippe Forget (ed.), *Text und Interpretation. Deutsch-französische Debatte mit Beiträgen von J. Derrida, Ph. Forget, M. Frank, H. -G. Gadamer, J. Greisch und F. Laruelle*, München: Fink 1984. On the notion of 'myth' cf. Hans Blumenberg, "Wirklichkeitsbegriff und Wirkungspotential des Mythos," in Manfred Fuhrmann (ed.), *Terror und Spiel. Probleme der Mythenrezeption*, München: Fink, 1971 (Poetik und Hermeneutik 4), 11-66, and note 24. For a discussion of the notion of 'history' cf. A.C. Danto, *Analytical Philosophy of History*, Cambridge: University Press, 1965 and F. Fellmann, "Das Ende des Laplaceschen Dämons," in Reinhart Koselleck/Wolf-Dieter Stempel (eds.), *Geschichte—Ereignis und Erzählung*, München: Fink 1973 (Poetik und Hermeneutik 5), 115-138. On 'play' in post-structuralism cf. Jacques Derrida, "Die Struktur, das Zeichen und das Spiel im Diskurs der Wissenschaften vom Menschen," in Derrida, *Die Schrift und die Differenz*, Frankfurt: Suhrkamp 1976, 422-442; on the 'teleological or eschatological horizon' of history, which ought to be *deconstructed* just as the metaphysics and identity connected with it, cf. ibid., 121-235 ("Gewalt und Metaphysik. Essay über

das Denken Emmanuel Levinas," reference to 227) and "Die Différance" and "Fines Hominis" in Derrida, *Randgänge der Philosophie*, Frankfurt: Ullstein, 1976, 6-37 and 88-123. On the history of the postmodern cf. Gérard Raulet, "Zur Dialektik der Postmoderne," in A. Huyssen/K.R. Scherpe (eds.), *Postmoderne. Zeichen eines kulturellen Wandels*, Reinbek: Rowohlt, 1986, 128-150. For negative evaluations of Davies' ideology see Stephen Bonnycastle, "Robertson Davies and the Ethics of Monologue," in *Journal of Canadian Studies*, 12, 1, 1977, 20-40; Norman Snider, "Robertson Davies: The View from High Table," in John Metcalf (ed.), *The Bumper Book*, Toronto: ECW, 1986, 69-77; Sam Solecki, "The Other Half of Robertson Davies," in *Canadian Forum* (Dec./Jan. 1981), 30f., 47. For important objections cf. the recommendable article by Larry MacDonald, "Psychologism and the Psychology of Progress: The Recent Fiction of MacLennan, Davies and Atwood," in *Studies in Canadian Literature,* 9, 2, 1984, 121-143.

[7] Bibliographical references for Davies' plays are given in the bibliography at the end of this essay. Page numbers in parentheses refer to the editions listed there. John Ryrie, *Robertson Davies, an Annotated Bibliography*, Toronto: ECW, 1981, mentions a number of manuscripts apart from the 18 plays which cannot and need not be considered here. On the historical context see, for example, Kenneth McNaught, *The Pelican History of Canada*, Harmondsworth: Penguin, 1983 (repr.), 29-35.

[8] Davies quoted in Stone-Blackburn, 208; 207 lists a number of other sources used by Davies.

[9] Also cf. his novel *What's Bred in the Bone*, Harmondsworth: Penguin, 1987, as well as the following. Cf. the excellent essay by Paul Davy, "The Structure of Davies' Deptford Trilogy," in *Essays on Canadian Writing*, 9, 1977-78, 123-133, in particular the passages on 'art' as a sphere of 'choice'. (129) Judith Skelton Grant, in *Robertson Davies*, Toronto: McClelland & Stewart, 1978, describes the choice between God and the Devil which characters in the "Deptford Trilogy" are given. It is not a choice made once only, for "in Davies' world, individuals continue to make meaningful choices." (48) Davies himself has expressed his view of 'choice' in connection with melodrama, a genre for which he has a particular liking; cf. Anthony, *Stage Voices*, 63.

[10] Cf. Davies' preface, 105. However, nowhere in the standard Monmouth editions is the Duke of Kaelcolim (Colchester), named Coel (!), characterized as a "merry old soul." Cf. Acton Griscom (ed.), *The Historia Regum Britanniae of Geoffrey of Monmouth*, Geneva: Slatkine Reprints 1977 (2 vols.); Jacob Hammer (ed.), *Geoffrey of Monmouth, Historia Regum Britanniae. A Variant Version*, Cambridge, Mass.: Medieval Academy of America, 1951; J.S.P. Tatlock, *The Legendary History of Britain. Geoffrey of Monmouth's Historia Regum Britanniae And Its Early Vernacular Versions*, Berkeley: University of California Press, 1950.

[11] Toronto: Clarke & Irwin, 1955.

[12] Davies in Anthony, *Stage Voices*, 76.

[13] Cf. ibid., 77, and note 14.

[14] Davies, "Epilogue," in Davies (1966), 112; also cf. 1-115, and Davies, "The Canada of Myth and Reality," in Davies, *One Half of Robertson Davies*, New York: Viking, 1978, 271-286: "What do I mean when I speak of myth? In national terms I mean the sort of attitude which most people take for granted, the belief that nobody questions because nobody troubles to put it in concrete terms." On page 275 of this essay, Davies refers to myth, with a term coined by Joseph Campbell, as "'life-supporting illusions'" and describes their importance in his literary work and for the writer in Canada, "to show Canada to itself." (281)

[15] The letters of Frances Stewart (1794-1872) were first published in 1889 as *Our Forest Home* (cf. the second edition Montreal: Gazette 1902). Susanna Moodie (1803-1885) is the author of *Roughing It in the Bush*, London 1852 (cf. Toronto: McClelland & Stewart, 1962) and *Life in the Clearings*, London, 1853. Catharine Parr Traill (1802-1899) wrote, for example, *The Backwoods of Canada* (London, 1836), *The Canadian Crusoes* (London, 1852), *The Female Emigrant's Guide* (Toronto, 1854), *Canadian Wild Flowers* (Montreal, 1868), and *Pearls and Pebbles* (Toronto, 1894). For information on Traill and Moodie cf. any literary history of Canada, but in particular New, 79f., where New speaks of "conventional attitude" and "conventional role-modelling" and comes to the conclusion that "their 'realities' remain fictitious." The fictive arises, in particular, from an ideology that is inadequate for the country and becomes a life-destroying myth.

[16] Cf. Stone-Blackburn, 75.

[17] For a detailed treatment cf. *Fortune, My Foe*; also cf. *Heart's Core* (26, 37, 41, 46, 79), *Hope Deferred* (68, 70f., 76) and the novels of the "Salterton Trilogy" as well as the satirical essays in *The Diary of Samuel Marchbanks*, Toronto: Clarke & Irwin 1947, and *The Tabletalks of Samuel Marchbanks*, Toronto: Clarke & Irwin 1949.

[18] Davies quotes two of the three stanzas which are contained in Moodie's *Roughing It In The Bush*, London: Virago, 1986, 416f. Also cf. Moodie, *Letters of a Lifetime*, Toronto: Toronto University Press, 1985, 77. Rick Salutin's play *1837: The Farmers' Revolt* also shows Moodie and the world-view for which she stands in a negative light. Cf. Jerry Wasserman (ed.), *Modern Canadian Plays*, Vancouver: Talonbooks 1985, 113-137. Here, Moodie is named "Lady Backwash" and wants to give her female friends a lecture on her adventures in Upper Canada, entitled "Roughing It In The Bush" (119). Salutin's preface emphasizes his political intention: "it was to be an anti-imperialist piece" (103-113, here 104).

[19] Cf. Gerald M. Craig, *Upper Canada. The Formative Years 1784 - 1841*, Toronto: McClelland & Stewart, 1972; David Flint, *William Lyon Mackenzie: Rebel against Authority*, Toronto: Oxford University Press, 1971; William Kilbourn, *The Firebrand: William Lyon Mackenzie and the Rebellion in Upper Canada*, Toronto: Clarke & Irwin, 1956. Craig, 206, points out the importance of the Justice of the Peace and gives a historical sketch of this position, which in Davies' play is taken by Mr. Stewart.

[20] Cf. 24, 32f., 48, 79, 82, and Davies' own view in Anthony, *Stage Voices*, 77. Also see Patricia Morley, *Robertson Davies*, n. p.: Gage, 1977, 23, and Stone-Blackburn, 74-77.

[21] Cf. the studies mentioned in notes 7 and 19 and J.L. Finlay/D.N. Sprague, *The Structure of Canadian History*, Scarborough, ON: Prentice-Hall, [2]1989, 124-127. *Heart's Core* itself contains the following sentence: "this rebellion is being conducted in an uncommonly slipshod fashion" (65).

[22] Cf. Mrs. Stewart's confession: "when I think of him now, which is rarely, I think of him as he was then, and I see him, sometimes, with the eyes of a girl. But if we were to meet again I am sure that the whole thing would dissolve." (85) On the great importance of "humility" also see the "Deptford Trilogy," 512. The scope of the perspective chosen here, which considers 'history' and 'myth' as a unity, is particularly obvious in the unity of historical and private elements in the play. This view transcends evaluations and interpretations which claim that *"At My Heart's Core* is a romantic comedy of great charm, marred by ambiguity as to its central intent" (Morley, *Davies* 24). Little understanding of the play's content is also reflected in reviews of its performances and published version, reprinted in Ryrie, *Bibliography* 236-238, 261-264. The ambiguity of meaning noted here had no effect on the play's widely positive reception, "which many hailed as the finest to date" (Stone-Blackburn, 91).

[23] The chapter in McNaught's *History of Canada* on the years following the rebellions in Upper and Lower Canada is entitled, "Aristocrats of Reform." In my understanding, this expression is aptly suited to justify a qualification or rejection of attacks on Davies' ideology (cf. note 6). Also cf. Rod Willmot, "If Hearts are Trump: The National History Play," in *Canadian Drama*, 7, 2, 1981, 50-61. Davies also says on his concept of a 'good' life: "it's the fully realized human life, the fulfilling of one's potential. The person who lives that way can't help but be enormously valuable to an awful lot of people. And he's not going to do harm, because he knows himself." (Davies, "A Talk with Tom Harpur," *Toronto Daily Star* (February 16, 1974), quoted from Judith Skelton Grant (ed.), *The Enthusiasms of Robertson Davies*, Toronto: Macmillan, 1979, 315-320, here 319).

[24] Davies, *The Deptford Trilogy*, 377 (in *The Manticore*). Also cf. 18ff., 50, 75, 114, 180f., 212 (Hitler's myth), 230 (poetry and myth), 265 (the personal myths of the protagonists) (in *Fifth Business*), 429 (myths as objectivations of basic truths), 456 (myth as a "pattern in the spirit" which shapes reality and history) (in *The Manticore*); 567ff. (in *World of Wonders*) and elsewhere on the connection of 'history' and 'myth', which may be considered the base structure of the whole trilogy. Davies' concept bears great similarity to the definitions of history and myth of Claude Lévi-Strauss. Cf. his *Structural Anthropology*, Harmondsworth: Penguin (Peregrine), 1971, 12ff., 17f., 23f., 209ff. Mythology, in Lévi-Strauss, is defined, as in Davies, by the connection of opposites and the transition from the explicit to the implicit, from the particular to the universal and from the conscious to the unconscious. Cf. ibid., 218f., 224ff. Where Davies neglects the concrete historical component, he is thus also affected by the criticism of Lévi-Strauss made by Alan Jenkins, *The Social Theory of Claude Lévi-Strauss*, London: Macmillan, 1979, in particular 89ff. and ch. III: "Ideology and Mythic Thought," 94-155. On the history of mythological thinking (as manifested in Davies) and relevant predecessors (Schelling, Cassirer, Durkheim) see Marcel Detienne, "Mythologie ohne Illusion," in C. Lévi-Strauss et al. *Mythos*

ohne Illusion, Frankfurt: Suhrkamp, 1984, 12-46 and Manfred Frank, *Der kommende Gott. Vorlesungen über die Neue Mythologie*, Frankfurt: Suhrkamp, 1982.

[25] Davies, "A Preface in the Form of an Examination," in Davies (1975), viii: "A playwright is a painter, not a photographer."

[26] Davies might be accused of a certain lack of modernity in his modes of presentation and the situations he chooses to write about. However, the problems, themes and questions treated remain valid. Also cf. Lévi-Strauss, *Structural Anthropology*, 208 and 21: "these forms [which the unconscious activity of the mind insists in imposing upon content and which anthropology (and mythology) strives to discover] are fundamentally the same for all minds—ancient and modern, primitive and civilized." The search for the 'forms' entails the search for 'meaning': "In mythology, as in linguistics, formal analysis immediately raises the question of *meaning*." (ibid., 241, similar in Lévi-Strauss, *Myth and Meaning*, New York: Schocken Books 1979, 17.) Davies says about himself: "As a playwright, I am old-fashioned." (Ann Saddlemyer, "A Conversation with Robertson Davies," in *Canadian Drama*, 7, 2, 1981, 110-116, here 114.)

[27] MacDonald, 137.

[28] Cf. Davies (1975), 9, 12 and David Riesman, *The Lonely Crowd. A Study of the Changing American Character*, New Haven: Yale University Press, 1950. Also cf. Davies' comment on this book: "Do the Other-directed Enjoy It?," in Davies, *A Voice from the Attic*, New York: Viking 1960, 289-291. Macadam experiences, concretely and symbolically, what Davies describes as a characteristic of the Canadian identity, in which the responsibility of all people manifests itself most obviously. Davies sees the answer to the question of a Canadian identity expressed in Douglas LePan's poem, "Coureurs de bois": "The Canadian is the *coureur de bois* who must understand—understand, not tame—the savage land. [...] this is a metaphor for that equally savage land of the spirit. The Canadian voyage, I truly believe, is this perilous voyage into the dark interior of which the poet speaks. [...] it is the heroic voyage of our time." According to Davies, Canadians are particularly fit for this task because they are less burdened than others with a national heritage and thus freer to encounter themselves (Davies, "The Canada of Myth and Reality," 284-287.)

[29] Davies, "The Undiscovered Self," in *Saturday Night* (May 24, 1958), quoted from *The Enthusiasms*, 174-177, here 174.

[30] Cf. ibid., 174f.: "By the development and integration of personality Dr. Jung does not mean rampant egotism or 'personality' as salesmen or show-people use the word; he means self-knowledge, particularly of those parts of the mind which we usually seek to ignore, and those parts of the personality which seek their gratification in aggressive and hostile attitudes and actions towards others. Such self-knowledge is a curb on egotism, not an encouragement to it. [...] Jung writes: 'Ultimately everything depends on the quality of the individual, but the fatally short-sighted habit of our age is to think only in terms of large numbers and mass organizations, though one would think that the world had seen more than enough of what a well-disciplined mob can do in the hands of a single madman....'" Also cf. Davies' myth of a 'good' life (note 23).

[31] Cf. Davies in Anthony, *Stage Voices*, 73: "Underprivileged groups and the fringes of society do not occur to me as material for plays because I do not know enough about them to reach far into their psychology, yet I am too much aware of the pain and wretchedness of their situation to risk falsifying it." The criticism of an a-historic perspective (and thus a lack of liveliness and attractiveness of his characters and situations) has also been made for Davies' recent novel. See Phyllis Rose, "King Arthur in Toronto," in *New York Times Book Review* (January 8, 1989), 7, on *The Lyre of Orpheus*, New York: Viking, 1988, which forms the final part of the trilogy begun with *The Rebel Angels* (1981, Harmondsworth: Penguin, 1983) and *What's Bred in the Bone* (1985).

[32] Ibid., 79, and Davies, *The Mirror of Nature. The Alexander Lectures 1982*, Toronto: University of Toronto Press, 1983, 11. Here also cf. the definition of "nature," 6f.

[33] Marx quoted from Lévi-Strauss, *Structural Anthropology*, 23.

[34] *The Manticore*, 479.

Malcolm Page

David Fennario's *Balconville*:
Document and Message

David Fennario is a proletarian writer, by birth and in his chosen subject. This is rarer in North America than in Europe, and rarer in the 1970s than in the 1930s. His first play, *On the Job* (1975) was set in the workplace, the warehouse of a dress factory, and his second, *Nothing to Lose* (1976) in a tavern. After the failure of his third play, *Toronto* (1978), he returned to the Montreal working class in *Balconville*, which premiered in January 1979. He says in his *Blue Mondays* essays that he writes of the "the unemployable poor that have no choice but to stay in the Montreal of the eighties in a Quebec that doesn't officially recognize that there ever was an Anglo working class in this city."[1]

Fennario documents working-class life, men and women, teenagers and their parents. There are eight characters: seven people from three families, and a delivery man. These severally go to work, in a factory and in a café as a waitress or wait for unemployment payments to arrive. They smoke, drink a lot of beer, and grumble. Summer holidays will be spent on their tenement balconies, hence the title. The play covers a few hot weeks one summer.

Other dramatists of the working-class have shown audiences Dublin (Sean O'Casey), New York (Clifford Odets) and the East End of London (Arnold Wesker). Michel Tremblay in such plays as *Les Belles Soeurs* and *En Pièces Détachées* has presented francophone Montreal.[2] Fennario writes of an unusual area, Point St. Charles, an English-speaking working-class enclave in Montreal, settled by Irish and Scots as long ago as the 1840s. He was born there in 1947, and has lived there, and in adjoining Verdun, almost all his life.

The second act of *Balconville* opens with men singing drunkenly "We don't care for all the rest of Canada/We're from Point St. Charles,"[3] heard also in *On the Job*. *The Point*, an excellent National Film Board production, catches the spirit of this poor, tough community. Robert Duncan, director of the film, explained:

> I wanted to make a film that showed that not all the English in Montreal live on the hills of Westmount or in the suburbs of the West Island. The guy who cut the sound for the film, he's French, he's lived in Montreal all his life and he didn't know there *was* a poor English community. There are 600,000 English-speaking people in Montreal. I say that to people in Vancouver and their jaws drop.[4]

The Point shows empty warehouses, boarded-up slums, an unused canal, dependence on welfare cheques—and the rowdy high spirits of lighting Victoria Day bonfires in all the back alleys.

Fennario is more adventurous in *Balconville* than in his previous plays, as one of the three families is French. Remarkably, this seems to be Canada's first bilingual play.[5] Nearly one-third is in French, in the distinctive *joual* of Quebec. The French in fact came from Guy Sprung, director of the first production, and the four francophone members of the cast, for Fennario does not speak the language.[6] The francophone characters are bilingual, switching into English to speak to the anglophones. The languages, as often in Quebec, are sometimes mixed, e.g. "Ils ont toujours besoin de waitress cute," (305; 105) The tentative hope in the later part of the drama includes Johnny making his first fumbling effort to reach his neighbour, Claude Paquette, in French (307; 114).

Two moments present visually the two solitudes.[7] Johnny and Claude both sit on their balconies watching a Montreal Expos baseball game, with commentaries in different languages. Thibault, the simple-minded delivery-man, underlines this "Hey, hey, it's the same game! …They're losing in French too" (300; 86, 89). When the two men quarrel, Johnny nails up a Canadian flag on his door and Claude reacts by putting up the Quebec *fleur-du-lis*.

The set itself is distinctive, a two-storey tenement with two apartments up the outside staircase and another on the ground floor. The building is old, shabby and squalid, with dustbins and discarded car tires scattered round. Fennario remarked that "the setting is almost the star. It just sits there, and even when it's empty it freaks me out."[8] He sent the designer, Barbra Matis, to look at a particular building, which she photographed and then copied exactly.

Fennario's stagecraft has rarely been noted, because of the focus on content. He keeps his play on the move: dancing, drunken collisions, stumbles on the broken step, Muriel tipping spaghetti on her son's head

(288; 41) and much more. Three characters are carefully associated with music: young Diane through her record "Hot Child in the City;" Tom trying to play "Mona" on his guitar; Johnny the one-time Elvis Presley imitator. Johnny is furious that the politician's van plays Elvis' music—yet admiring Elvis, an American, is one of the few opinions shared by the French and the English. Johnny, however, progresses, coming to terms with the present, when he finally insists, in the second act, that "Elvis is dead" (296; 73).

This rough comedy of eight people forced to live too close to each other risks becoming a soap opera or situation comedy. Indeed, the performers suggested that it might become a television comedy series.[9] The first three scenes establish the typical way of life (late night; leaving for work in the morning; returning from work in the late afternoon) and the plot starts to move forward only in the fourth scene. Mark Bland-ford, who directed the good, though substantially abridged, television version,[10] comments:

> At one moment it's high drama—and then at other moments it goes into broad comedy, almost farce. And one of the things I've been aware of is having to walk that line between the two. You don't want to go too far on one side and lose the fun of the play, and you don't want to go too far on the other end and lose the dramatic impact. So much working-class drama either betrays what's going on by going too far into comedy, so that basically the social comment just vanishes and it becomes just a trite set of laughs; or it goes so heavy on the liberal, what-are-we-going-to-do-with-the-working-class crap that, while it's message may be terrific, it's dramatically uninteresting, and you're not allowing the audience to have a good laugh and then go on to the next message.[11]

Fennario effectively juxtaposes the serious, such as Claude losing his job, and the comic, as when Cécile waters her flowers and Muriel, standing below, gets wet.

In *Balconville* and his earlier work, Fennario writes conventional plays, performed for the largely middle-class audiences of such theatres as the Centaur, Montreal, which premièred all four pieces. Yet Fennario's purpose appears to be to prompt first self-recognition and then uniting for action in the working class. I discussed this contradiction with him in 1980, and he gave me several answers. First, that people from the Point who had never seen a play before had gone to see his at the Centaur, because they had heard his subject was the Point—and had liked the plays. He could identify spectators from the Point because they alone laughed at certain lines. Second, he defines the middle class as wage-slaves too, with no control over their working conditions, so the plays' messages are also for them. Third, as English-language theatre in Quebec lacks radicalism, he was starting to build contacts with

Left-wing people in French-language theatre.[12] Further, after one more play for the Centaur, *Moving* in 1983, he switched to working within the Point community at the Black Rock centre.[13]

Does *Balconville* merely show the unchanging realities of the existence of the masses of Point St. Charles, of beer and welfare, a life of noisy desperation? Or does it also urge change, show that communal effort can transform and revolutionize their way of life?

Fennario has often made his Marxism (which, curiously, he discovered by way of Erich Fromm's *The Art of Loving*) clear:

> I want to change the system as well as survive in it. I've got to move people and I won't stop until I do.... I'm still working for revolution but I don't turn people off by screaming at them.... The system has to be overthrown because ninety percent of the people who are the workers have no control of their lives, over where they work.[14]

He belonged first to the Socialist Labour Party and in 1982 joined the International Socialists, a Trotskyite group. Fennario's commitment is more easily understood in Quebec than in English Canada. As he says, "When I talk socialism in Quebec it seems to make sense; when I talk it anywhere else it seems like rhetoric."[15] His sense of class solidarity, too, is more European than North American. He demonstrated his beliefs when, in the *Balconville* revival of January 1980, he gave more relevance to the piece by adding a speech in support of the ushers and cloakroom attendants at the Place des Arts, who were then on strike.

Critics have sometimes minimized the importance of Fennario's political views. Maureen Peterson of the *Montreal Gazette*, for example: "Fennario is a closet humanist.... *Balconville*...has more heart than party line, more blessed doubt than dogma, and more humanism than a political platform could ever contain.... The escape route is sketched more as a matter of self-re-evaluation and personal change than as something that could be achieved through political channels. Is it socialism to say we must look into our own heart and mind to find the answer to our problems?"[16] This smacks of the capitalist press attempting to minimize what it finds awkward and disquieting. Further, one political working-class writer can be seen as an intriguing curiosity, and a chance to display tolerance; others might find it much more difficult to be heard.

Guy Sprung records that he advised Fennario to reduce the specific messages:

> Originally in *Balconville*, the young boy was a writer and there was also a character who was the political organizer, who came to the door to tell people the party line. In other words: David's old self and his new self. I convinced David to make the boy a musician so he wouldn't identify with him as much.... It's not good politics to have politics come over badly. I

always fight with David to give the audience some credit for being able to make judgements, to see and observe and make decisions on their own.[17]

Fennario understands this difficulty for himself. As early as in 1978 he was pointing out that "my socialist friends come and say: 'Where is the message?' It's there. It's got to come out through the characters. Otherwise they might as well have a message stamped on their foreheads."[18] In 1981 he maintains that his message is central: "Up until now, as far as I've been able to make it work on stage, I've been showing people that things can be changed."[19] Equally, Fennario knows he risks writing noisy and high-spirited comedy which would be merely an entertaining night out for the affluent.

Fennario presents his message in three ways, through speeches, characters and actions. Various lines express contempt for employers who are foreign: Thibault works for Kryshinsky and Claude for a multinational company which eventually shuts down the plant and moves to Taiwan. Claude's firm provides air-conditioning for the offices but not for the shop floor. When Thibault tells his boss that he was hit by a Cadillac, the response is "How's the bike?" (308; 116). His boss "est jamais content anyway" (282; 19). Thibault in fact is probably the most intriguing character, a wise fool in the tradition of Lear's Fool, a detached chorus figure. Typically, it is Thibault who observes: "It's funny, I watch it all change, but it's still the same thing" (285; 30).

As usual in Canadian and American literature, unions are unhelpful, indeed a joke: "Hey, the union. It's too hot to laugh," says Claude (284; 27). Doctors are rich: "There's this fat pig making $80,000 a year, living in Côte Saint-Luc, telling me not to be a nervous wreck," says Muriel (305; 107). Landlords are contemptible, for they would raise the rent if the stairs were mended and may be burning down houses to claim the insurance. The landlords are also self-interested politicians. The local Member of Parliament, campaigning for re-election, is heard several times from a loudspeaker van. Irene comments that "Bolduc is on *his* side," and Claude adds that "he was okay until he got the power. Then, that's it. He forgets us" (287; 37). When Bolduc appears in person, canvassing, he is rejected at all three households. Muriel tears down his posters and Johnny throws eggs at him. So no help can be expected from outside; organizing working-class solidarity is shown to be the only possible means to change.

Irene works for the Point Action Group: "We're going down to the City Hall to demand more stop signs on the streets. Kids are getting hurt" (285; 32). She urges her husband, "Why don't you come down to our Unemployment Committee meetings?" (286; 36) And later, "We're gonna march in front of the UIC [Unemployment Insurance Commission] building. Let them know we don't like the forty percent unem-ployment down here" (307; 112). Irene practises individual kindness, too, offering to accompany the frightened, sick Muriel to the doctor. She tells Muriel of the clinic in the Point where "the doctors treat ya like a human being" and it doesn't matter if they are "Commies" (305; 107).

Fennario confirms that the women are indeed the activists:

> In the community group I belong to, the women are much more active than the men.... The men are out drinking if they're not working, and if they're working they're too tired to do anything. The women are more active in getting the ceiling fixed or fighting the landlords and getting Stop signs up so the traffic'll slow down.... The guys...are not fighting back too well right now, but I hope they do.[20]

Brian Pocknell writes sociologically of the play that Fennario "uses [the employment question] to show how personal relationships and attitudes towards society are affected by changes in the employment status of his characters and by the socio-economic conditions of the period."[21] In human terms, family life is shown to be damaged both by the dead-end work of Irene and Claude and by the unemployment of Johnny and Tom. The men constantly swear and drink because they have been brainwashed, brutalized and almost destroyed by the system under which they live.

In the final scene Diane has to leave school to get work because her father has lost his job, unmistakably a setback for both. Tom has taken a boring job in a laundry: "I'm there twenty days and already going nuts" (306; 110). Perhaps he can save and then leave the Point. To offset these changes, Tom and Diane, English and French, start dating.

Three reconciliations occur near the end. Tom is reconciled with his mother, buying her a brooch with his first pay-cheque. She overcomes bitterness and indecision about her absent husband and begins to move his possessions out, Tom for the first time going willingly to help her. Muriel, no longer passive, is helping Irene to organize a demonstration and Diane will join them (307-308; 112-115), Johnny comes through his bout of drunkenness to a reconciliation with his wife. Whether or not he returns to making music, he can assert "I'm a survivor" (306; 109), a word Margaret Atwood has shown to be a key to the Canadian experi-ence. As important as the reunion between Johnny and Irene is his swallowing of pride to attempt the reconciliation with Claude, even though it forces him to try to speak French (307; 114).

Johnny's action in mending the step is a more convincing change. The missing step has provided laughs throughout the show, as charac-ters either fall through the gap or narrowly avoid doing so. Now it is Johnny who puts in a new step, and builds a closer relationship with

Irene as he does so. Metaphorically, as Jerry Wasserman puts it, "There are real signs of hope…. It can only happen one small step at a time."[22] However, moments later fire approaches the tenement, so, ironically, the step may be burned minutes after Johnny completes the repair.

The blaze provides a powerful close for *Balconville*, and an image of French/English co-operation. As fire comes close, all rush to save their most valued possessions. The men grab their television sets and cases of beer; Irene saves Johnny's guitar; Cécile carries a few plants downstairs and then sits down with her rosary. Johnny and Claude collide on the stairs, so Irene urges teamwork and the men carry out the couch together, with Claude once again using English, "Okay, allez, Johnny…. We go move ton sofa" (309; 120). Muriel looks at the approaching fire and says "Christ, we're next!," (309; 120) perhaps an echo of Hector Hushabye listening to the approaching bombs and shouting "Our turn next" at the end of Bernard Shaw's *Heartbreak House*.

Here, the two versions of the play diverge. In the earlier text, the fire is controlled and their building is safe. Johnny and Claude agree that their real enemy is the landlords, and Johnny closes with "You fuck 'em in French and I'll fuck 'em in English."

In the later version, used for the revival in the Autumn of 1979 and the one published, Johnny earlier uses a similar line "Together we can fuck Bolduc" (307; 114), but at this point the unhappy Claude will not listen. At the end of the later version, the fire is still coming nearer, and the irrelevant loudspeaker voice of Bolduc is heard again. The anglophones turn to the audience and ask in unison, "What are we going to do?" and the francophones echo "Qu'est-ce qu'on va faire?" (309; 121) On film, Bolduc's voice is cut and both last lines are spoken by Cécile alone.

Fennario explains the revised ending:

> I and a lot of other people like seeing the French and English sit down together for a change. But I felt, looking at it, that it was too much of a magic-wand number and that it was best to leave it as a question to the audience…. Maybe the other ending was more enjoyable but this one seems more true…. Something has already happened. They have been forced to work together and to organize to help themselves in that situation. That is a start.[23]

Later he commented:

> I'm still thinking about that second act. I'd like to show the workers coming together, but so far I haven't been able to make it work. I did like the idea of leaving the question to the audience, though. And I know that's going to remain.[24]

The revised ending is more tentative. The final question has still to be asked in both languages. Yet it is identifiably Lenin's famous "What is to be done?"[25] The exact impact of the ending is determined partly by whether the anglophones and francophones are now mixed, or standing as two separate groups—a director's decision. The "we" and "on" include the audience, making this the kind of play where the real ending is in the lives and actions of the audience in the days and weeks after seeing the play.

Fennario's message, about the need for English/French co-operation as the preliminary to change, is clear, though more illustrated than stated. As Mark Blandford puts it: "The beauty of the play is that if you concentrate on the human beings, the political message just comes out naturally, without seeming to hit the audience over the head."[26] Though Fennario has not written a propagandist drama, the thrust is unmistakable. The days of politicians and landlords are numbered. Change can and will come. Further, *Balconville* is a play English Canada has needed for many years, a hands-across-the-solitude bilingual drama.

NOTES

[1] David Fennario and Daniel Adams, *Blue Mondays*, Verdun, Quebec: Black Rock, 1984, 2. Fennario also writes about Montreal in *Without a Parachute*, Toronto: McClelland & Stewart, 1974.

[2] For the parallels and contrast with Tremblay, see Paulette Collet, "Fennario's *Balconville* and Tremblay's *En Pièces Détachées*," in *Canadian Drama/L'Art dramatique canadien*, 10, 1, 1984, 35-43.

[3] As *Balconville* is readily available in two editions, here and subsequently in the text, the first page reference is to *Modern Canadian Plays*, ed. by Jerry Wasserman, Vancouver: Talonbooks, 1985 and the second to the play separately published Vancouver: Talonbooks, 1980; here: 296; 71.

[4] Quoted by Wayne Grigsby, "Point Counter Point," in *Macleans*, August 6, 1979, 6. See also Grigsby, "Another David Triumph over Goliath," in *Macleans*, June 1, 1981, 16-18.

[5] A more recent bilingual play is Marie-Lynn Hammond's *Beautiful Deeds*, about her grandmothers, one Franco-Ontarian and one English-Canadian. Hammond's play actually includes passages such as these:

> quand Corinne était jeune she dreamed of love
> et toutes les belles chose that a girl thinks of
> but suddenly at sixteen la voilà mariée
> and one year later la mère d'un p'tit bébé.
> > (Excerpt in *Dandelion* [Calgary], 11.2, Fall-Winter 1984-85, 17-31).

Marianne Ackerman's *L'Affaire Tartuffe* (1990) is a later example.

[6] "Shaping the Word: Guy Sprung and Bill Glassco" [interview], in *Canadian Theatre Review*, 26 (Spring 1980), 32.

[7] This well-known phrase for the separation between French and English Canada comes from the title Hugh MacLennan gave to a novel he published in 1945; MacLennan took the phrase from Rilke.

[8] Quoted by Paul Milliken, "Portrait of the Artist as a Working-class Hero," in *Performing Arts in Canada*, 17 (Summer 1980), 22.

[9] Richard Horenblas, "David Fennario Burning Houses Down," in *Scene Changes*, March 1980, 27.

[10] The film was shown on the Pay-TV Superchannel in February and March 1984 and by CBC-TV later in the year.

[11] Quoted by Geoff Yates, "If you Can't Take the Heat," in *TV Guide*, February 25, 1984, 10-11.

[12] Unpublished interview with M. Page, February 21, 1980.

[13] On Fennario's work at Black Rock, see Michael Benazon, "Working-class Theatre in Montreal," in *Matrix*, 18 (Spring 1984), 60-61; Jim Deeson and Bruce K. Filson, "Where is David Fennario Now?," in *Canadian Theatre Review*, 46 (Spring 1986), 36-41; Cy Gonick, "David Fennario: a Revolutionary Playwright," in *Canadian Dimension*, April 1987, 22-25; and David Homel, "Class Acts," in *Books in Canada*, May 1984, 4-5. Fennario's work for Black Rock was *Joe Beef: a History of Pointe Saint Charles*, Vancouver: Talonbooks, 1991. A second play for Montreal amateurs is *Doctor Thomas Neill Cream (Mystery at McGill)*, Vancouver: Talonbooks, 1994. Fennario eventually returned to mainstream theatre, to the Centaur, Montreal, with two plays: *The Murder of Susan Parr* (1989) and *The Death of René Lévesque* (1991). In 1994 he performed a short monologue, *Banana Boots*, describing his experiences when *Balconville* played in Belfast.

[14] Quoted by David Pyette, "Fennario still Sees Red," in *Montreal Star*, February 11, 1978.

[15] Talk at Capilano College, North Vancouver, B.C., February 21, 1980.

[16] Peterson, "*Balconville* a Loveable Play," in *Montreal Gazette*, January 6, 1979; reprinted in a section on the play, in *Canadian Drama/L'Art dramatique canadien*, 11, 1, 1985, 160-168.

[17] "Shaping the Word," 32-33.

[18] Quoted by Bruce Kirkland, "This Street Punk is our Hottest Playwright," in *Toronto Star*, January 21, 1978.

[19] Quoted by Deirdre King, "The Drama of David Fennario," in *Canadian Forum*, February 1981, 15.

[20] Martin Bowman, "Interview with David Fennario," in *Cencrastus* [Edinburgh], 8, (Spring 1982), 8.

[21] Pocknell, "'Moe, tout c'que je veux, c't'une job': The Employment Question in Canadian Plays of the Seventies," in *Etudes Canadiennes*, 15, 1983, 61.

[22] Wasserman, *Modern Canadian Plays*, 276.

[23] *The Work: Conversations with English-Canadian Playwrights*, ed. by Robert Wallace and Cynthia Zimmerman, Toronto: Coach House, 1982, 299, 300-301; part of the interview is reprinted in *Canadian Drama/L'Art dramatique canadien* 11, 1, 1985, 166-168.

[24] Quoted by Paul Milliken, 24.

[25] Canadian theatregoers were reminded of the phrase, *What is to be done?*, when Mavis Gallant used it as the title of her play about the political education of two young women in the 1940s, staged in Toronto in 1982 and at the Centaur, Montreal, in 1984.

[26] Quoted by Geoff Yates, 13.

Sarah Gibson-Bray

"To Engage, to Inform and to Empower:" Dennis Foon's Child Advocacy Drama

Kids are short people with no rights. And as long as children don't have power, and are undervalued in a society, artists who work for children are going to be held in low esteem.[1]

— Dennis Foon, 1986

As one of English Canada's foremost playwrights specializing in plays for young people, Dennis Foon has devoted enormous energy to ameliorating the lives of children and teenagers, and to elevating the status of Theatre for Young Audiences, both nationally and internationally. In his nineteen years of working in professional theatre in Canada, Foon has played many roles, as dramatist, director, administrator, storyteller, advocate, social critic, anthropologist, reformer, mouthpiece, humourist, and iconoclast. His most significant contribution to the arts in English Canada has been as a pioneer playwright who has helped to forge a new, realistic, issue-oriented, dramatic and theatrical genre christened "child advocacy theatre." His six experiments in this new form, *New Canadian Kid* (1981), *Skin* (1984), *Invisible Kids* (1985), *Liars* (1986), *Mirror Game* (1988) and *Seesaw* (1993) have been enthusiastically received by over a million school children, as well as by teachers, parents and critics across Canada and around the world.

Foon's career as a playwright splits naturally into two discrete stylistic phases, "Phase One"—the early period between 1975 and 1979, and the more mature "Phase Two"—from 1980 to the present. Both phases reflect the evolution of Foon's own theatre company, Vancouver's Green Thumb Theatre for Young People, from a fledgling amateur troupe into a vibrant, innovative and financially successful professional touring company committed to the development and production of new Canadian plays for young people. From Green Thumb's frivolous inception in 1975 by Foon and four fellow graduate students in Creative Writing from the University of British Columbia, until 1988 when the playwright turned over its artistic directorship in order to devote more time to his writing, the theatre company provided Foon with a well-appointed dramatic and theatrical laboratory for playwriting, direction, and theatrical administration, and also with a stimulating, collegial environment which afforded him frequent contact with other artists working in Canadian theatre, and abroad.[2]

As a neophyte writer searching for his own distinctive dramatic voice, during Phase One Foon experimented at Green Thumb with a variety of traditional dramatic genres and theatrical forms. Revealing a keen interest in the art of storytelling, Foon's diverse early works include *The Last Days of Paul Bunyan* (1977)—a nonsensical puppet version of an American tall tale, *The Windigo* (1977)—a haunting Native Canadian Ojibway legend re-interpreted poetically for the stage, *Raft Baby* (1978)—a tragicomic British Columbian folk tale crafted into a theatrical folk ballad, and *Heracles* (1978), Foon's complex and highly spectacular version of the classical Greek myth.

The year 1979 marked the transition to Foon's second phase as a playwright for the young, spurred on by two innovative Green Thumb Theatre première productions: *Hilary's Birthday*—Joe Wiesenfeld's novel, naturalistic "kitchen-sink" drama about divorce seen through the eyes of a nine-year-old girl; and Campbell Smith's *Juve*, a pithy new "slice-of-life" play about (and performed by) teenagers, based on Smith's extensive interviews with a cross-section of Vancouver's youth. Through *Juve* Foon became involved in an improvisational theatre project for street kids and teenage prostitutes set up by Vancouver dramatist Tom Walmsley. His awakening to the dire long-term consequences of child abuse, through direct contact with these homeless youths in limbo, prompted Foon in 1980 to collaborate on the first child sexual abuse prevention programme to be produced by a professional theatre company in Canada. Entitled *Feeling Yes, Feeling No*, the extensively researched, collectively written Green Thumb "Theatre in Education" programme employed realistic theatrical scenarios involving children and abusers (all portrayed by three adult actors *cum* facilitators), music and audience participation as a means to equip children with the tools to protect themselves against potential abuse, and to inform past and present victims about the kinds of help available to the young. Following its highly successful première in 1982, the programme has continued to be produced elsewhere in Canada, and was also released by the National Film Board as a four-part film in 1985.

Feeling Yes, Feeling No sparked Foon's fascination with the themes of victimization and empowerment, and illuminated a new dramatic path which he would explore at length in his subsequent writings for the theatre. In these Phase Two child advocacy plays, Foon demonstrates a clear, threefold set of dramatic objectives: to engage, to inform and to empower his young viewers. "Create work that connects directly with your audience and you'll have a success,"[3] the playwright maintains. With an anthropologist's eye for detail, Foon recreates in his texts and on stage all the highly specific trappings of youth culture. Holding "a mirror up to nature," he crosses such external cultural manifestations as distinctive idiomatic language, currently popular forms of music like rock and roll, heavy-metal, rap or reggae, and contemporary youth fashion, with recognizable locales and everyday situations, in order to create a theatrical world with which his young audience can directly identify.

Foon bases his observations of youth culture primarily on oral history and documentary material which he gleans from extensive personal interviews with young people. He believes that topicality and contemporaneity play integral roles in generating and sustaining audience identification. As a result, in the notes to his playscripts Foon strongly encourages subsequent directors of his works to update and revise his texts to suit their particular audiences, as well as any anachronistic production elements which might undermine the play's credibility:

> Because the everyday situation of children changes so rapidly...every effort should be made to make the references as topical as possible, with the objectives of reflecting the realistic conditions, language and concerns of children in the area.[4]

Unlike more traditional children's plays, which combine elements of fantasy and fairy-tale with theatrical spectacle, and often place greater emphasis on light entertainment than on meaningful content, Foon's Phase Two plays deal explicitly with the child's or teenager's perspective of controversial and often taboo "real life"[5] social issues such as racism, sexual abuse, alcoholism, peer pressure, suicide, drug abuse, and domestic violence. Though each of Foon's child advocacy pieces stands on its own, the six plays fall naturally into two thematic trilogies: in *New Canadian Kid*, *Skin* and *Invisible Kids*, the playwright tackles racism in its many guises; in *Liars*, *Mirror Game* and *Seesaw*, he examines dysfunctional families, and psychological and physical abuse. "It can be difficult to write on a child's level," Foon acknowledges. "That's why the most important part of the company's work is the research."[6] Based on his many conversations with young people, as well as his consultations with numerous sociologists, psychologists and youth workers, Foon makes three assertions: first, that young people are acutely aware of these serious social issues, often through direct personal experience; secondly, that they badly want to discuss these experiences or related concerns; and thirdly, that young people desperately need to acquire the tools to cope with these problems for themselves. Foon reflects:

> A lot of people try to protect their children from the terrible things that they'll have to face as adults. They encourage them to enjoy themselves while they're growing up in the hope that when they get older things will automatically get easy for them. But there is a certain irresponsibility in that attitude. It ignores the fact that children are totally aware of what's going on in the world, and are uptight and concerned about even things they face in the schoolyard, to say nothing of the possibility of nuclear war, which they read about in newspapers and hear discussed on radio and television.[7]

All of Foon's plays for young audiences have a strong central narrative: "The greatest strength we have in drama is the story," he maintains. "When it's really working, the tale becomes part of the firsthand experience of the audience."[8] Like his Phase One works, Foon's child advocacy plays also tell a story, but in this case from a less conventional perspective. Whereas Foon's plays *The Windigo* and *Raft Baby* are fictional tales involving grown-up characters written by an adult for children, *New Canadian Kid, Skin, et al.* are the playwright's distillations of actual events and reflections recounted to him by the children themselves, which he in turn relates to his young audiences using child or teenage protagonists. As a playwright of child advocacy, Foon serves as a mouthpiece through which children can express their views and concerns to their peers, and to some adults. In part, his plays function as a young people's forum.

In Foon's Phase Two plays particularly, the playwright makes highly effective use of the dramatic device of juxtaposition. By putting two seemingly disparate characters together in the same dramatic world, as in *Liars* for example where studious, preppy Leonore encounters rough-cut "head-banger" Jace, the playwright reveals a hidden connection between the two young people through their common experience of parental alcoholism. At the same time Foon also implicitly assesses the efficacy of their two very different methods of coping with the resultant emotional and physical trauma. By juxtaposing the familiar (Canadian kids speaking English with a gibberish twist) and the foreign (Nick, the alien Everyman) in *New Canadian Kid*, Foon sheds light on the new immigrant's first experiences in Canada. In *Skin*, he intricately interweaves the personal accounts of three Canadian teenagers from different visible minorities (Black, Vietnamese and East

Indian) who contend with some form of racism in their daily lives. With this complex narrative tapestry, the playwright depicts the disturbingly wide range of racial discrimination occurring in Canada, presents a young audience with a catalogue of coping devices, and underlines the universality of human experience regardless of race, creed and colour. In *Invisible Kids,*[9] Foon draws a parallel between an eleven-year-old black girl and a celebrated South-African Olympic runner, which exposes the inconsistency of government immigration policies: young Georgie is excluded from a school trip to France because she lacks a British passport, though she has lived in England for nine years; Zola Budd, however, is granted British citizenship in less than a week, in order that she may side-step an international protest against apartheid and compete for Britain in the Olympics. Foon also juxtaposes young Vince's determined and effective scheme to possess a special BMX bicycle with his friend Georgie's uncertain quest for citizenship. In two later plays dealing with dysfunctional families, *Liars* and *Mirror Game*, the playwright dovetails and layers past and present conversations and events using voice-overs and flashbacks in order to show destructive histories repeating themselves between friends and across generations, and ultimately to suggest how such patterns can be broken. In all of his later plays (to varying degrees), grimly realistic moments of conflict are cushioned with timely outbursts of infectious verbal and physical comedy.

Though Foon's Phase Two plays present dramatic situations as seen from a child's-eye-view, they are written for a cast of young adult professional actors for three main reasons: first, because the plays were originally designed for extensive and lengthy school tours[10] by Foon's own Green Thumb Theatre company, a factor which also influenced the degree of complexity of the requisite staging elements;[11] secondly, since the staging needed to be kept simple, the strength of both the text and the actors had to carry the show; and most importantly, in order to ensure the mature and responsible treatment of complex subject matter,

> ...there is an enormous responsibility placed upon an actor working for young audiences. If they're doing a piece on a delicate issue like sexual abuse...it is crucial that the message of the piece be very clear to the kids. That can mean a lot of psychological pressure on the actor.... That's why an actor has to be included in the rehearsal process...why discussions and research are extremely important. They have to spend a lot of time discussing it, figuring out what the issue is all about...so that when they in turn are asked by a kid after the performance—'Did this happen to you?' —they have the ability, and the confidence to talk to that kid.[12]

In order to sustain his young viewers' willing suspension of disbelief in his child advocacy plays, Foon insists on a naturalistic acting style from his adult actors: "They [the audience] much more readily accept us as we are, playing young people their own age," he explains. "Fundamentally, it's the problems that we deal with that are of prime importance to them."[13] In order to reflect the cultural and ethnic diversity of his Canadian audiences inherent in his mature writing for the stage, Foon strongly advocates the employment of actors with varied backgrounds:

> You hardly ever get a chance to see a minority actor on stage, and so how do you expect the audience to relate to a predominantly white Caucasian cast, when they [the actors] themselves cannot relate to and experience the feelings of this silent majority?[14]

Whether dealing with child sexual abuse, social ostracization, racial prejudice in the school system or violence in teenage relationships with adults and with each other, all of Foon's issue-oriented plays explore the dynamics between bullies and their victims. Each piece presents the schoolyard bully, an archetypal figure recognizable to every child, in a different but equally intimidating guise. Whether he appears as an exploitative hockey coach, as in *Feeling Yes, Feeling No*, a tough-talking pre-teen as in *New Canadian Kid* and in *Seesaw*, a raging, drunken father as in *Liars*, a bigoted, reptilian, school teacher as in *Skin*, an insensitive eleven-year-old as in *Invisible Kids*, or a "cool," weight-lifting, high school senior as in *Mirror Game*, this antagonist imposes some form of tyranny on his scapegoat. Foon's objectives are first to present the bullying experience from the victim's perspective, as the molested child, the harassed newcomer, the intellectually-suppressed, visible-minority student or the battered girlfriend, and then to demonstrate a means whereby each victim can liberate herself/himself from this destructive role. In clearly illuminating the underdog's point of view, often through intimate revelations played directly to the audience, Foon also strives to shatter widely-held cultural and hierarchical stereotypes.

Each of Foon's child advocacy plays reinforces the need for young people to look to each other for help in combatting their antagonists, as well as to their parents, guidance counsellors, teachers and social agencies. As Foon's extensive research into the many profound social issues affecting young people has graphically revealed, parents themselves and other adults are often the source of rather than the solution to children's problems, as emotional and physical bullies. Through his candid portrayal of characters like Leonore's drunken mother in *Liars* (for whom Lenny covers during frequent alcoholic binges), Luke's manipulative brutish father in *Mirror Game* (who beat Luke as a small boy at the slightest provocation) and Josh's workaholic parents in *Seesaw* (who unwittingly neglect their only child for their work), the playwright tackles the myth of adult's infallibility, and graphically demonstrates for his young audience the capacity of adults to do wrong. Using his play *Liars* as an example, Foon explains,

> ...[In *Liars*] the whole issue for the kids is that they have to become independent. They have to separate themselves from their parents. Their parents aren't there for them. It's a sad, awful thing to discover.[15]

As Foon's primary interest lies in how children and teenagers are affected by such situations, he devotes little time to causal analyses of, or curative solutions for, the parents' difficulties. In fact, adults play an increasingly secondary role in his more recent plays like *Mirror Game*, in which five grown-up characters are reduced to voice-overs and shadowy projections on a scrim, or *Seesaw*, in which (with the help of ingenious puppetry) parents are transformed into cats and dogs, sportscars and briefcases. Though many of Foon's adult characters are in some way corrupt or emotionally unstable, in his plays *Invisible Kids* and *Skin* for example, the playwright balances this harsh portrayal by including admirable adults who clearly do have young people's interests at heart.

As iconoclast and provocateur, Foon consistently encourages his young viewers to take an active, rather than a passive, stance towards their human or institutional oppressors. Filled with analytical conversations, his Phase Two works are primarily discussion plays in which two or more young people pool their intellectual resources in order to solve a problem collectively: in *Feeling Yes, Feeling No*, for example, small children learn how to say no to exploitative grown-ups; in *Liars* two teenagers from different backgrounds confide to each other their common concerns about the forbidden subject of parental alcoholism, providing at least one with the courage to confront her family with the issue; in *Skin*, one young black girl challenges another to strive academically in spite of a teacher's bigoted put-downs; in *Invisible Kids* five elementary school children of different racial backgrounds peacefully protest what they perceive to be inegalitarian government immigration policy; in *Mirror Game* two high school students help a third extricate herself from a destructive romantic relationship. While Foon's plays present slices of real life without the rose-coloured tint characteristic of much conventional children's theatre, he tempers each work with a cautious optimism: with some blood, sweat and tears, Foon implies, change is possible.

Though Foon's child advocacy plays often address disturbing situations, they are neither excessively grim, nor oppressive, pieces of theatre. "I can talk all I want about my passion and anger," Foon reflects, "but the fact is that the best way for people to listen is using humour...if I can make them laugh, I can make them cry."[16] Foon tempers his weighty subject matter with a delightfully Rabelaisian sense of humour and abundant physical business. Episodes of emotional intensity and graphic violence are offset by comic relief. In *Liars* for example, Jace is knocked down by his father in an alcoholic rage, but later he and Lenny escape their troubled homelives to roughhouse affectionately like children in the park. In one scene in *Mirror Game*, Sara endures a black eye from her excessively jealous boyfriend Luke, while Bob and Maggie (a typical Foonian comic duo) commiserate about "zits" and "thunder-thighs" in another. "Of course you don't want to do everything for cheap laughs," Foon reflects, "but one of the most important messages is that this is theatre for them [young people]. This is their space, and it's liberating for them to see their kind of humour on the stage."[17] The playwright's texts are peppered with earthy references to teenage acne, "corny" puns on politician's names, spoofs on contemporary television commercials, and bewildering teenage colloquialisms, accompanied by outbursts of out-and-out horseplay, martial arts displays, gymnastics, and schoolyard games. Though Foon's deceptively simple unpoetic scripts may seem mundane on the page, they spring to life in performance. During one presentation of Foon's *Mirror Game* given by Toronto's Young People's Theatre in 1991 for example, I was struck by the playwright's sharp ear for the specialized dialect of teenagers, and by the verisimilitude of his young protagonists; the identification experienced by my vociferous adolescent co-auditors was almost tangible. Foon underscores each text with cleverly selected contemporary popular music, arguably the most potent and distinctive expression of youth culture; snatches of rock-and-roll, reggae and heavy-metal serve programmatically as a compelling musical counterpart to the action, as well as a stirringly dynamic underlying pulse. In *Invisible Kids* for instance, Foon uses black singer Chaka Kahn's song "I feel for You" to reflect Georgie's friends' empathetic support in petitioning the Prime Minister to grant her citizenship. At the play's end, the chorus from "One Love," reggae singer Bob Marley's anthem to solidarity and peaceful coexistence, aptly embodies the children's hope that their petition will succeed: "Let's get together and feel alright."

While Foon reproduces naturalistic language and everyday situations in his Phase Two plays, he also takes frequent liberties with the unities of time and place. Using flashbacks and overlapping scenes, he employs juxtaposition to reveal recurrent patterns of destructive behaviour. His characters often disregard the "fourth wall" and deliver their monologues and asides directly to the audience. Foon first employed this presentational device very engagingly in *New Canadian Kid*. Nick, the young foreign protagonist in the piece, shares the pitfalls of being a recent immigrant with the audience in his Homelander dialect (which sounds like plain English); his Canadian schoolmates speak in their unintelligible "native" tongue, a ridiculous, nonsensical form of gibberish. The playwright uses similar narrative techniques to more serious effect in plays like *Skin* and *Mirror Game*.

Foon's later plays are comprised of a series of short, fast-paced scenes tailored to fit either into a fifty-minute school period, or in some cases, a seventy-minute show. Writing for an ensemble of four or five actors, Foon skilfully maximizes his small casts through the doubling and tripling of roles, and the innovative use of projections, voice-overs, masks and so on. Foon also uses these theatrical elements expression-istically to embody a problem, as in his use of life-size dummies to represent a parent's alcoholic alter ego in *Liars*, or forcefully to convey a character's perceptions of his environment, as in his portrayal of a physically abusive father as a giant silhouette in *Mirror Game*.

As an idealist committed to social change, Foon sees his issue-ori-ented child advocacy theatre not only as a means to help young people cope with the complexities of their own lives, but also as a vehicle for broader social reform: "What we're breeding is a new kind of citizen," he asserts. "We're empowering these kids."[18] By using theatre to make young people aware of their personal right to control their own bodies, as in *Feeling Yes, Feeling No*, or their entitlement to equal opportunities in education and employment regardless of their skin colour, as in *Skin*, Foon hopes to effect societal attitudes to such endemic problems as racism and the exploitation of children:

> If a huge segment of our population—children—who didn't believe that they had any rights suddenly do have rights—because they are aware of them, the whole fabric of our society is going to be changed.[19]

Foon believes that the potential for social reform in Canada and elsewhere through theatre for young people far exceeds that of conven-tional theatre, due to its distinctive "populist" audience; whereas main-stream adult professional theatres play for the most part to select "middle-class, homogeneous audiences who have very ingrained atti-tudes,"[20] young people's companies like Foon's own Green Thumb Theatre play annually to thousands of Canadian public and private school children from every socio-economic, religious and ethnic back-ground. In addition to being more flexible and open-minded than conventional theatre audiences, young people's audiences, Foon main-tains, are more open, honest and communicative, benefits which out-weigh the disadvantages of lengthy tours, poor working conditions, and low professional status often facing actors working in the field:

> …Actors are at the lowest end of the totem-pole in the theatre, for the most part…the producers and directors control their lives: they decide whether they will work or not. The actor, therefore, is in a kind of child-like

state—they're not given responsibility over their lives—they're dependent. As a result many actors feel a kind of inferiority complex working in
kid's theatre, because it too is the lowest of the low in terms of theatre. It's
not respected for the most part.... But the thing that makes it very exciting
is that, because of the nature of a young audience, they're very honest,
they're going to tell you exactly how they feel moment to moment.[21]

Foon believes that Canada enjoys "a very free and just society,"[22]
unlike the racially-divided United States where he spent his youth prior
to becoming a Canadian citizen. However, he stipulates that there is still
"a lot of room for improvement." Recognizing that any major social
reform is slow to evolve, the playwright qualifies his own ambitious
objectives in writing socially relevant, self-empowering plays for
children and teenagers with this proviso:

...You watch kids and you are looking at the future. Of course I want to
influence what I see. You can't change the world with a forty-minute
show—but maybe you can be an influence.[23]

Foon's two most recent dramatic works herald a third new eclectic
phase in his writing for the young. "My forthcoming projects in TYA
are an attempt to find a visual vocabulary that can help lift the "realistic"
content to a more visceral level,"[24] the playwright reflected in 1992.
Seesaw, his 1993 child advocacy play about the ups and downs of four
young children's relationships with their peers and their parents, (a
Mirror Game for elementary school kids), marries the conventional
dramatic unities of time and place with expressionistic puppetry. Most
recently, Foon's 1994 stage adaptation of his 1986 children's book *The
Short Tree and The Bird That Could Not Sing* blends the fanciful and the
instructive in a delightful theatrical concoction. The tragi-comic one-act
play for primary school children chronicles the meeting, separation and
joyful reunion of a lonely sapling and a gregarious—if tone-deaf—
migratory song-bird. Using programmatic music, puppetry, elaborate
lighting and rainbow coloured scenery and costumes, Foon exploits all
the magic of theatre in order to convey a subtle message to children
about the nature of love and loss.

Since 1975, Dennis Foon has written more than seventeen plays for
young people, directed more than a dozen works by other Canadian
writers, and commissioned and premièred over thirty-five new Canadian plays. He is a recipient of both the British Theatre Award for Best
Production for Young Audiences (*Invisible Kids*, 1986) and the Canadian
Chalmers Award for Best Children's Play (*Skin*, 1987 and *The Short Tree
and The Bird That Could Not Sing*, 1995). In 1989 the playwright's "outstanding contribution to the field of the arts for young people"[25] was
recognized with the prestigious international "Association for Young
Audiences Award."

As a pioneer in socially relevant, issue-oriented theatre for the young in Canada, Foon has truly earned his status as a "bedrock [playwright] in English Canadian theatre for young people."[26]

NOTES

Since some newspapers have no pagination, page numbers are only given if reference is made to an article taken from either a journal or a book.

[1] Kevin Barker, "Going through a stage," *Books in Canada*, 15 (April 1986), 11-12.

[2] Through his artistic directorship of Green Thumb Theatre and its involvement in the annual Vancouver International Theatre Festival for the Young, Foon was introduced to many European theatre specialists. In 1982, the playwright collaborated with Berlin's Grips Theater's founders Volker Ludwig and Wolfgang Kolneder on an English adaptation of Ludwig's emancipatory children's play, *Trummi Kaput*, performed that year at the Vancouver International Theatre Festival. In 1986, Foon adapted and directed Ludwig's play *Max und Milli* (with the new title *Bedtimes and Bullies*) at Toronto's Young People's Theatre. Foon acknowledges the influence of Grips Theater, as well as other European theatre companies, in the development of his own distinctive style of realistic, child advocacy drama. "The people who can really evaluate what we are doing [at Green Thumb] are in Europe," he reflected in 1983. (Interview with Nicholas Read in *The Vancouver Sun*, April 19, 1983).

[3] Bob Allen, "The Children's Festival at age five," *The Province*, May 15, 1982.

[4] Dennis Foon, "*Trummi Kaput* by Volker Ludwig, adapted by Dennis Foon," *Canadian Theatre Review*, 37 (Spring 1983), 68.

[5] "Real life" is a colloquial expression frequently used by Foon and other individuals working in the field of theatre for young people to indicate "existing, realistic, non-fictional, actual, or true" as opposed to "fantastic, fictional, imagined, or conjectural." The expression can also imply a documentary quality.

[6] Christina Wiser, "A 'New Kid' in a new country," *Philadelphia Courier Post*, March 1986.

[7] Myron Galloway, "FOON! Giving kids a new life on stage," *The Sunday Express*, July 11, 1982.

[8] Ian Chance, "Green Thumb nurtures growth," *Lowdown*, August 1985.

[9] This reference pertains to the original unpublished version of *Invisible Kids*, written for a British audience in 1986 while Foon was visiting Unicorn Theatre in London, England.

[10] A typical tour usually consisted of two shows per day (often in different venues), five days a week, for four consecutive months.

[11] Sets and props had to be moderate in size, relatively few in number, portable by two or three people, and easy to assemble.

[12] Dennis Foon, Interview #2 with Sarah Gibson, August 3, 1988.

[13] Galloway, "FOON!"

[14] "Foon's play gives racism a break," *Community Digest*, March 20, 1986.

[15] Dennis Foon, Interview #1 with Sarah Gibson, June 2, 1988.

[16] Dina Sudlow, "Playwright focuses on realities of young lives," *Victoria Times-Colonist*, May 2, 1989.

[17] Liam Lacey, "Exploring the 'friendships and fears' of modern childhood," *The Globe and Mail*, April 6, 1990.

[18] Chris Wong, "Changing attitudes with theatre," *The Georgia Straight*, May 30 - June 6, 1986.

[19] Chance, "Green Thumb nurtures growth."

[20] Foon, Interview #2 with Gibson.

[21] Ibid.

[22] "Green Thumb presents *Skin*," *B.C. Multicultural Education Society Programme*, April 1986.

[23] Joe Adcock, "Fanfare—Beneath 'Skin' lies hope for the future," *Seattle Post Intelligencer*, May 9, 1986.

[24] Dennis Foon, in a letter to Sarah Gibson, November 16, 1992.

[25] Dennis Foon, Interview #3 with Sarah Gibson, September 5, 1991.

[26] Leslee Silverman [Artistic Director of Manitoba Theatre for Young People], interview with Sarah Gibson, December 19, 1991.

Albert-Reiner Glaap

Family Plays, Romances and Comedies: Aspects of David French's Work as a Dramatist

David French comes from Newfoundland which, in 1949, was the tenth province to join the Canadian Confederation. He is considered to be one of the "senior" playwrights who played a major role in promoting the development of the professional English Canadian theatre during the seventies and eighties. Unlike the late Michael Cook, who emigrated from Great Britain in 1965, lived in Newfoundland for some considerable time and was a lecturer at the Memorial University, and even more unlike Al Pittman, a born Newfoundlander who still lives and writes there, David French has been living and working in Toronto since his family moved there when he was seven years old. Yet this province has remained the spiritual pivotal point around which some of his work as a dramatist revolves. His "Mercer Plays," of which there are four,[1] reveal the culture shock which immigrants suffer when caught up in new surroundings and an unknown way of life. In the case of the Mercer family it is the city of Toronto.

Together with the "Donnelly Trilogy" by James Reaney[2] and *The Power Plays* by George Walker,[3] French's tetralogy—a significant cycle of thematically linked plays—is a milestone in the history of the still young professional Canadian theatre. The first of these plays, *Leaving Home* (1972) made English Canadian drama "presentable" in the eyes of the theatre-going public and was the prelude to a series of neo-realistic plays in the seventies. It also established the co-operation between the playwright French and the theatre impresario Bill Glassco at the Tarragon Theatre in Toronto.[4] In 1971 Glassco had founded this theatre with his wife Jane with the object of putting on new Canadian plays in close co-operation with the authors and actors.

For an understanding of David French's dramatic works, some preliminary background information may be useful; that the "Mercer Plays" and the comedy *Jitters*,[55] for example, include marked biographical traits; that—as in Miller's *All My Sons* and *Death of a Salesman*—the conflict between father and son is of central importance; that some of his plays should not only be interpreted on a personal level but also be seen as statements of political and social criticism (cf. *Salt-Water Moon* and *1949*).

French's work can be divided into four categories. *Leaving Home* (1972), *Of the Fields, Lately* (1973), *Salt-Water Moon* (1984), *1949* (1989) often referred to as the "Mercer Plays" all belong to the first group. *One Crack Out* (1976) and *The Riddle of the World* (1982) form the second group. In these two plays French deals with the methods employed by marriage swindlers, matchmakers, male and female prostitutes in the Toronto subway, or homosexual and platonic relationships as a "solution" for men whose wives have left them. The common theme in both plays is that of sexual failure acting as a motivating force. Neither play was particularly successful. *The Riddle of the World* never did equal the popularity gained by *Jitters* (1980) which enjoyed over one hundred professional productions inside and outside Canada. *Jitters* forms the third group of French's work for the theatre. Many consider this comedy to be the best ever written so far by a Canadian playwright; a comedy about what happens behind stage, about "backstage life." The fourth group consists of two Russian plays which David French partly translated and partly adapted for production in Canada; Chekhov's *The Seagull* (1896) for a successful production at the Tarragon theatre (1977) and Alexander Ostrovsky's *The Forest* (1871) for the production at Centrestage in Toronto (1987). Recently he has written a new stage play *Silver Dagger* (published by Talonbooks, Vancouver 1993), a thriller.

The Mercer Plays

The Mercers, a working class family from Newfoundland, like French's own family, have been living in Toronto since the mid-forties. Their experiences and fate form the framework of the action in all four plays, though not necessarily chronologically with the one play starting at the point where the previous one stops. *Of the Fields, Lately* is the only direct continuation of *Leaving Home*. They were both written in consecutive years; both are set in the Toronto of the fifties. The action of *Of the Fields, Lately* begins two years after the events of *Leaving Home*; the audience is addressed directly at the beginning and at the end of the play and told about what has happened in the past. *Salt-Water Moon* takes us back to 1926 when Jacob and Mary (Mercer) first met. *1949* is yet another flashback; this time the play recalls the critical situation which arose from the decision to make the oldest British colony, Newfoundland, a member of the Canadian Confederation after 481 years of British rule. The action begins three days before April 1st, the day on which New-foundland became the tenth province.

Leaving Home was French's first play; an earlier version of the play had carried the title Keepers of the House, an allusion to a passage from the Bible in Ecclesiastes (12,3). The title of Leaving Home contains a reference to the uprooting of the Mercer family who have left New-foundland behind them and have to cope in new surroundings which, for the older generation at least, are totally uncongenial. Leaving Home is a conventional play in two acts which maintains the classical unities of time, place and action; a realistic play with a clear structure; a "well-made play." It suited the climate of the time in which it was written and first produced, and was a contribution to the psychological realism which dominated the end of the sixties and the beginning of the seventies in Canada. The central issue at the time was the question of Canadian identity and French's plays—in common with those of other authors such as David Freeman's Creeps[6]—rang true with the audiences of the time through the use of authentic action on stage and a language composed of realistic regional varieties. French wrote about the famil-iar, about events and questions which were well-known to him and to the theatre-goer. His characters include "migrant heroes," emigrants and migrants in post-war Canada, victims of social and political devel-opments, "victims" by chance. The "little man," already a familiar figure from the plays of Arthur Miller, Tennessee Williams and John Osborne, is also a central figure here. But he is a "little man" with Canadian characteristics and not just a straight copy of Willy Loman in Death of a Salesman, but the sort of person who considers himself to be a "victim" and sees himself in this role. "I'll give you a revelation! I'm just a piece of shit around here!"[7] says Jacob Mercer. The "little man" who is not just a straightforward copy of any one individual but an amalgam of the characteristics and attitudes of various people, is the "hero" of contemporary plays, though no longer in the grand scheme of things but in the small family framework which, in its turn, might even be dispensed with since the individual members understand neither themselves nor each other. Leaving Home can undoubtedly be considered as a Canadian version of the "modern domestic tragedy," a label under which not only some of the plays by Miller, O'Neill and Williams but also O'Casey's Juno and the Paycock, Peter Shaffer's Five Finger Exercise and the French Canadian equivalent to Leaving Home, Michel Tremblay's Forever Yours Marie Lou[8] can be subsumed.

These plays centre around the themes of family relationships, the conflict between father and son and the break-up of inherited or blindly

---

accepted precepts and structures. In *Leaving Home* the action also takes place within the framework of the outside world within which the Mercers are bound. They have migrated from their remote fishing village to the city of Toronto. The uprooted parents are obliged to look on as their sons, under more propitious circumstances, achieve considerably more in life and considerably quicker than their parents. From the point of view of their higher education—documented by their High School diplomas—they, in their turn, feel increasingly estranged from the world of their parents; the one son, Ben, is even ashamed of his father when he appears in his blue working overalls, bearing the cooking utensils (symbols of the working class) in his gnarled, worn-out hands. A higher standard of education has obviously not equipped the sons with the emotional "tools" with which to understand and tolerate their parents who, through no fault of their own, have only attained a lower level of education. Jacob Mercer is proud of the success of his education. Yet this by no means enables him to come to terms with the knowledge that he is a sacrifice to life, that his "little education"—despite all his hard work, industry and commitment to his family—has resulted in his sons trying to withdraw from the sphere of his influence. He wants to keep Ben with him for a few more years; he cannot exist without his sons. He therefore plays the role of *pater familias* and becomes so completely caught up in it that he finally beats Ben with a belt. Mary Mercer, Jacob's wife, wants to tear down the wall, the barrier, which Jacob and Ben have built up between each other. She understands both of them but also wants them to understand each other; she is a totally reliable character. Mary makes no attempt to hide her liking for her son. But when, at the end of the play, she and her husband are alone after Ben, angry at his father's treatment of him, has left home for good, she can also sympathize with and understand Jacob. The play dismisses the audience with Mary's touching story of the incident which, many years ago, had led her to fall in love with him.

In *Leaving Home* the action is prompted by the decision of the as yet only seventeen-year-old Billy to marry his girlfriend Kathy who is expecting a baby. The older brother, Ben, uses this as an excuse to leave home together with the young couple so as to be beyond his father's reach. Jacob increasingly dissociates himself from handed-down moral concepts and in so doing also abandons his spiritual home as well as the physical one which he had left behind him many years previously. His anger over the fact that Billy, the son of Irish Protestant parents, is to marry a Catholic is comparatively mild compared with the disappointment over the departure of his son. There is no longer any neutral ground on which these two could meet. Other scenes are, however, more important than the episode about the "necessity" of Billy's marrying—which very soon appears in a completely different light when Kathy has a miscarriage—for they determine not only the action of *Leaving Home* but are also integrated, either directly or indirectly, into French's second "Mercer Play."

The title *"Of the Fields, Lately,"* is likewise taken from the Bible:

> As for man, his days are
> as grass: as a flower of the
> field, so he flourisheth.
> For the wind passeth
> over it and it is gone; and
> the place thereof shall
> know it no more.

> (Psalm 103, 15-16)[9]

Death and dying lie, as it were, in the air. Ben has returned home after an absence of two years. But he has only come back to be at his aunt's funeral. In the meantime, Jacob has had a heart attack, which hardens Ben's resolve to stay at home and look for work in Toronto. This would enable Jacob to give up his strenuous carpenter's job. In retrospect, Ben seems to forgive his father and make an attempt to slip into his role. However, he soon realises that it would be a mistake to stay, for his father would never consent to taking a back seat; he has to keep going, to keep working, if he is not to lose his identity. This is why Ben leaves for good.

Of the Fields, Lately is the more rounded of the first two "Mercer Plays." It is free from the comedy inserts to amuse the audience which are included in *Leaving Home*. The play has a structure which immediately identifies it as a "memory play."[10] Ben addresses the audience directly at the beginning and the end of the play. At the beginning he refers to a crucial experience with his father which was the beginning of the end of their relationship. For the first time ever Jacob had got himself ready to watch Ben's team play a decisive game for the baseball championship. However, his twelve-year-old son was ashamed of his father's appearance. He would have preferred his father to be a doctor, or a lawyer, or at least a fireman but definitely not a carpenter. At the end of the play Ben tells the audience that seven weeks after the final break he nevertheless returned for his father's funeral. He says he has learnt to accept Jacob as a person, even if his values had been totally different to his own. The wall is still there and the question whether he had enjoyed the baseball game never passed his lips, although he would have dearly liked to hear his father's answer.

The coherent whole of *Of the Fields, Lately* is not only due to the audience-oriented structuring. "Flashbacks" of past events themselves trigger off new developments. Trivial occurrences such as the baseball game prove, in the course of the play, to be decisive events and so create dramatic tension. Scenes which contrast with, or develop, scenes in *Leaving Home* can, however, also be understood within their own context. When reviewers criticized *Leaving Home* for reducing the naturalistic portrayal to stereotypes at certain points in the play, the same criticism can hardly be applied to *Of the Fields, lately*. Here the tendency is away from realism into the poetic.

The events of *Leaving Home* unwind in less than two hours during a single night. The production lasted for exactly the same length of time it took for the family to break apart. In *Of the Fields, Lately* the interplay of family dependants is determined by the impending death of the father. David French has frequently stressed[11] that he wrote the second "Mercer Play" principally to pursue further the unresolved conflicts in *Leaving Home*. Both plays deal with questions of vital interest to the Canadians of the seventies. How can life be endured under new circumstances in an unfamiliar environment? How can one survive? How can one find one's own identity? French deals with these questions through the wearing differences and irritations experienced by the Mercers from Newfoundland. The fact that the search for a comprehensive Canadian identity and the belief in a unifying symbol such as survival has in the meantime long since been replaced by an emphasis on "multi-ethnicity," the variety and multiplicity of ethnic groups with their own claims, allows us to see French's plays about the Mercers—from a present-day perspective—as a contribution towards an understanding of this variety and multiplicity.

Twelve years after *Of the Fields, Lately*, David French wrote a one-act two-hander which was rather more of a prologue or prequel[12] to the other two "Mercer Plays" than a sequel. It takes us back to the twenties when Jacob was eighteen and Mary seventeen years of age. There were many unanswered questions linked to Mary and her role in *Leaving Home* and *Of the Fields, Lately*. She keeps her sons away from their father so that the family's status quo is at least maintained during the family disputes. She tries to nip the conflicts in the bud, puts them off without improving the situation in the least. Is she a mediator between the battle fronts? Or is she not initially fighting for her own survival as a woman? Or does she really consider herself to be first and foremost Jacob's wife and the mother of her sons?

Salt-Water Moon (1984) takes us back to the beginning of the year 1926 when Jacob was courting Mary. The play shows us why the Mercers left Newfoundland in the twenties, a time of transition in which the people were firmly bound in by their past yet were also on the point of fleeing from this past into a new future. The after-effects of the First

World War were still making themselves felt; the memory of the total destruction of the Newfoundland Regiment in the Battle of the Somme, the continuing mourning over those who had fallen in the war together with the pride over those who had received decorations for bravery and merit, but most of all the atrocious social conditions which prevailed in those days.

Jacob and Mary talk to each other about all these things in *Salt-Water Moon*. His father had returned a war hero but was despised at home on account of his low social standing. Her father never returned. Since Mary's mother was not in a position to bring her up herself, she was put into an institution and the fourteen-year-old Dot banished to a home. Although the old values of courage and valour were still valid and Jacob wanted to cling to them, the fishermen nevertheless became the property of the merchant classes and economic deprivation prevailed throughout Newfoundland. The seventeen-year-old Mary worked as a household servant for the parliamentary member for Coley Point. She had got engaged to the teacher Jerome McKenzie after Jacob had left her at the height of their romance without the least explanation a year before. At the beginning of the play he unexpectedly returns to win Mary back.

The action of *Salt-Water Moon* is simple. Opinions, comments and arguments are exchanged in the course of a simple dialogue. The whole resembles a kind of "verbal tennis" with serves and returns and rapid verbal rallies until Jacob achieves the final break against the strong-willed Mary. They are both sitting on the veranda steps of the house. His arrival had taken her by surprise as she was looking at the stars through a telescope. Jacob was renowned for his storytelling and it also brings him success in this situation. He knows how to put things into words and uses this gift to make fun of his rival Jerome by describing him as a bald-headed, pipe-smoking, old warhorse. Finally he professes to be on amicable terms with a certain Rose Sharon, whom he has taken out dancing and to the cinema. Best of all, or so he says, he likes to watch a twenties Western with Tom Mix, "the king of the Cowboys," the highest paid cowboy film star. And then Jacob describes how he will take Mary to the cinema. They take their seats in the back row and watch *The Lucky Horseshoe*. He describes what is happening in the film and the story starts to come to life, developing into Jacob's and Mary's own story.[13] He has to admit that there has never been a Rose Sharon. It is best to forget the past. He tells Mary that the future counts,[14] and the present of silk stockings which he has brought with him from Toronto testify to his honourable intentions. The fire which had gone out between them has been rekindled.

What effect can a play with such a simple story and a minimum of action have on a theatre audience? After Urjo Kareda, the director of the Tarragon Theatre, had adapted the play for radio, some critics were of the opinion that the play's essential intimacy could be better expressed and was more suitable for this medium.[15] As a play, French's work above all comes alive through the choice of words which oscillate between the poetic and the earthy Newfoundland dialect reflecting the emotions as well as the subtle thought processes of an ordinary man, producing comic effect equally well as expressing serious intentions with conviction. Linguistic and narrative techniques and details play an important part in the conversation between Jacob and Mary. The dialogue and the set give the audience an insight into the context of the action on stage. The author's meticulous attention to detail makes French's plays easily accessible. The aforementioned Urja Kareda, who has known the playwright for many years, says of him:

> In a French play, you know exactly the colour of the wallpaper, what people are eating for dinner. You can relate to these details—and feel through them to the universality of his themes.[16]

In 1988 David French added a further play to the so-called "Mercer Trilogy" using a date as its title: *1949*. Newfoundland and its people shaped from "rock, fog and cod" find themselves on the eve of April 1st, the day they joined the Canadian Confederation—April Fool's Day, as some Newfoundlanders ironically commented. Opinions were divided at the time; some emphasized the economic necessity of joining the Confederation while others drew attention to the threat of losing their own Newfoundland cultural identity.

In their modest Toronto house, Jacob and Mary Mercer are getting ready for the celebrations to mark the union of their native region with Canada. In the course of these preparations they receive an unexpected visit from a newspaper reporter from St. John's who is gathering opinions and reactions from Newfoundland families who no longer live there for a newspaper article. The newspaper reporter turns out to be Mary's former fiancé, Jerome McKenzie, and Jacob soon realizes that the old bonds between his wife and Jerome were partly responsible for this visit. The individual characters are portrayed partly through their impassioned, partly through their humorous comments which their views on the union with Canada draw forth. However, the relationships, romances and prejudices of former days are revived in the subplots. Mary's sister, Dot, has by now separated from her husband, Will, because they cannot have children and he refuses to submit to a test. The family doctor, Dr. Hunter, has a soft spot for Dot but for reasons of medical ethics feels himself obliged to bring the two together again. The sons, Ben and Billy, hold forth about a sadistic teacher called Miss

Dunn. These and similar stories and episodes show aspects of the Mercer's life in Toronto at the end of the forties. The details are sketched unpretentiously and with great sensitivity, and interwoven with the far-reaching political implications of the topical events thereby preventing *1949* from turning into a political polemic. As always, French is primarily concerned with people, their reactions to and against each other, self-determination and reconciliation. David French once told me in an interview[17] that he does not consider *1949* to be his "Free Trade Play." Yet parallels did, and still do, suggest themselves between the events in Newfoundland in 1949 and the present Free Trade Agreement between the USA and Canada; an agreement which for many Canadians—like those in Newfoundland at the end of the forties—seems not only to promise economic advantages but might possibly also entail an as yet unforeseeable loss of cultural identity. The audience's spontaneous applause during the première of *1949* in Toronto's Bluma Apple Theatre after Jerome's rhetorical questions and statement of the problems left no room for any doubt:

> Take Canada. How would the average Canadian feel if he climbed out of bed tomorrow and found he wasn't Canadian anymore? That Canada suddenly belonged to the United States? Christ, look what happened this morning, Grace. There's a prime example of what the future holds.[18]

1949 works on three levels; an emotional, a historical and a contemporary political one. It deals with all those things which bind a family together and which also divide it, with guilt and regret and with the power of love to overcome all divisions.[19] *1949* refers to a historical event which gave rise to both high expectations and deep disappointments. *1949* recalls how Newfoundland started down a new road which some regarded as a dead end while others saw in it an open freeway with no speed restrictions. The year 1949 belongs to the past but *1949* throws light on the past and on the present which—each in its own way—were and are signposts to the future. As a part of Canada, Newfoundland has become a political reality; the Free Trade Agreement points towards a new departure into a pan-American home market as a future reality. Yet, it must be restated that for David French the year 1949, despite all the reminiscences and visions of the future which might be aroused in the minds of a Canadian theatre audience, was just an excuse for the portrayal of his characters, for the description of human relationships which make it a "tremendous dynamic play."[20] *1949* is a collage of photographs which capture how the members of a family come to terms with each other—or not, as the case may be.

Jitters

The première of *Jitters* took place in the Tarragon Theatre in 1979. This comedy marks an important stage in the development of modern Canadian theatre. For it not only examines the theme of how the Canadian playwrights of the seventies strove to free themselves from Broadway and The West End, it also illustrates the fact that the Canadian theatre scene could by then laugh at itself. *Jitters* is a play about the institution we call theatre but at the same time it is also a satire on certain specifically Canadian attitudes. David French commented on his own attitude towards *Jitters* in an interview I conducted with him in 1984.

> The play has to do with stage fright (jitters), with fear, failure and success.... But the characters are rooted in a *Canadian* reality. *Jitters* is very much a Canadian play. I'm satirizing specifically Canadian attitudes—the desire to make it in New York, because you almost have to make it in New York in this country, or you are not accepted. You have to have the stamp of the United States.[21]

With regard to the author, *Jitters* marks a new departure in his career as a playwright. After *Leaving Home* and *Of the Fields, Lately* he wrote his first comedy, a so-called "comedy-of-the-stage," which can be compared with the extremely successful farce *Noises Off* (1982) by the English playwright Michael Frayn,[22] or to *A Life in the Theatre* written by the American author David Mamet[23] in the mid-seventies. In a "comedy-of-the-stage" the action centres around what is happening on stage and behind the scenes. *Jitters* has a great deal in common with *Noises Off* written three years later. Both plays deal with show business; both consist of three acts of very similar structure; in both plays there is a "play-within-a-play." Yet there are marked differences. In *Noises Off* everything finally comes to a halt, the play ends in a farce which, so to speak, explodes in its own face. In the second act of *Jitters* things seem to get out of control, yet in the end the show goes on despite the remaining jitters which the actors try to cover up.[24]

When the curtain rises at the beginning of *Jitters* a play is already in progress; a "play-within-a-play." After a few minutes the audience slowly realises that they are watching the rehearsal for a production of a sentimental comedy with the title of *The Care and Treatment of Roses*. Suddenly the director leaps up like a Jack-in-the-box and calls out, "Stop! Cut. That's terrific. We'll stop there. We'll run it from the top now in costume."[26]

The play-within-the-play is an excuse for showing an extremely funny rehearsal scene with the actors also engaging in a bit of backstage hanky-panky. Ambiguously comical situations arise when the actors slip into their designated roles on stage.

During the first act there is hardly any development in the action. The rehearsal conveys the impression of hysterical hustle and bustle. The actors complain about all sorts of things including each other. The second act takes place at 8:30 p.m. in the actors' dressing rooms forty-five minutes before the curtain is due to go up on the first night. In the third act the director and the actors are perusing the somewhat mediocre reviews. When an actor who had fluffed his lines several times during the course of the performance is even praised in one of the articles, the audience becomes aware that this is a parody on theatrical reviews.

The very "Canadian-ness" of *Jitters* is clearly shown in the characters, through the things they say and the things they do. Jessica Logan, a Canadian actress, had taken part in a Broadway production which the New York critics had completely torn to pieces. Jessica is now back in Canada preparing to return to New York. In addition to this fading Broadway star for whom New York is the measure of all things there is the very flamboyant Patrick Flanagan; a Canadian of Irish decent. He is not in the least interested in whether or not he can make it in New York. He has never left Canada. He is satisfied with his success in his own country and wants a reasonable degree of privacy. Modesty and self-restraint are more important to him than a Broadway sinecure. He untiringly gives voice to his abhorrence of American theatre yet cannot conceal a certain sense of insecurity arising from the fact that he has never been offered the opportunity of working in New York. He incessantly moans about Jessica. Another actor, Phil Mastorakis, pins all his hopes on Bernie Feldman, an American producer, who has been invited to the première of the play which they are this minute rehearsing in Toronto. However, now of all times when Phil has had particularly good reviews, he fails to turn up. Phil himself, his fellow actors and the director are not only disappointed but also completely at a loss, since they must now rely on their own judgement in deciding on whether the play could possibly be a success in New York. This mirrors the schizophrenic attitude characteristic among many Canadian theatre people in the seventies.[26] They condemned Broadway commercialism while at the same time envying its success. In *Jitters* David French puts satirical and provocative statements into the actors' mouths. We hear Patrick Flanagan saying the following:

> I am totally against the American star system. No, really. That's why I prefer Canada. Where else can you be a top-notch actor all your life and still die broke and anonymous.[27]

And Phil Mastorakis expresses his disappointment about Bernie Feldman's absence in this way:

George Feldman was my only hope: he was an American. Down there they embrace success. Up here it's like stepping out of line.[28]

David French with his straightforward and yet meaningful plays has had a formative influence on contemporary English Canadian drama. Jerry Wasserman considers David French's development to be a "miniature version" of the development of Canadian drama. Wasserman's anthology includes the following lines:

If a single playwright can be said to epitomize the success of modern Canadian drama, it would be David French. From his apprenticeship with the CBC and his early identification with alternate theatre in Toronto to the current status of his plays as a mainstay of the regional theatres and a cultural export, his career has coincided with the growth and maturation of Canadian theatrical art.[30]

NOTES

[1] David French, *Leaving Home*, Don Mills, Ontario: General Publishing Co., 1972; *Of the Fields, Lately*, Toronto: New Press, 1975; *Salt-Water Moon*, Toronto: Playwrights Canada, 1985; *1949*, Vancouver: Talonbooks, 1989. Excerpts from these plays are taken from these editions.

[2] James Reaney, *The Donnellys*, Victoria/Toronto: Press Porcépic, 1983.

[3] George F. Walker, *The Power Plays*, Toronto: The Coach House Press, 1984.

[4] Cf. Denis W. Johnston, *Diverting the Mainstream: Bill Glassco and the Early Years of Tarragon Theatre*, Copyright Denis W. Johnston, 1988 (53 pages). This paper which was first published in the journal *Canadian Drama/L'art dramatique canadien* contains no further bibliographical details.

[5] David French, *Jitters*, Vancouver: Talonbooks, 1980.

[6] David Freeman, *Creeps*, in Jerry Wasserman (ed.), *Modern Canadian Plays*, Vancouver: Talonbooks, 1985, 85-100.

[7] David French, *Leaving Home*, 29.

[8] Michel Tremblay, *Forever Yours Marie-Lou*, Vancouver: Talonbooks, 1975.

[9] Two versions prior to this quotation (103, 13) one reads:

"Like as a father pitieth his children, so the Lord pitieth them that fear him." In French's play, the elder son slipped into his father's role not before he was able to pardon him. Cf. Robert Wallace/Cynthia Zimmerman (eds.), *The Work. Conversations with English Canadian Playwrights*, Toronto: The Coach House Press, 1982, 307.

[10] A memory play recalls past thought processes, models and symbols connected in some way by time and/or place. Cynthia Zimmerman considers *Of the Fields, Lately* to be a memory play. Cf. Wallace/Zimmerman, 307.

[11] In an interview I conducted with the author in Toronto on May 11, 1984.

[12] In British reviews the term *prequel* is used as opposed to *sequel*.

[13] Cf. French, *Salt-Water Moon*, 57-61.

[14] Cf. French, *Salt-Water Moon*, 76.

[15] Cf. Henry Mietkiewitz, "The play's the thing on CBC," in *Toronto Star*, April 6, 1985, H8.

[16] Quote in: "Romancing the Rock. David French builds on his Mercer Saga," in *Maclean's*, October 31, 1988, 58.

[17] The interview was given in Cablehead, Prince Edward Island, on August 22, 1988.

[18] French, *1949*, 160.

---

[19] Cf. Robert Reid, "*1949* a powerful family portrait," in *Kitchener-Waterloo Record*, October 21, 1988, C1 and C3.

[20] Cf. Philippa Shepard, "*1949*: tremendous dynamic play," in *The Varsity*, October 27, 1988 (no pagination).

[21] The interview was given in Toronto on May 11, 1984.

[22] Michael Frayn, *Noises Off*, London: Methuen, 1982.

[23] David Mamet, *A Life in the Theatre*, New York: Samuel French, 1975.

[24] Further details can be found in *Noises Off*, *A Life in the Theatre* and *Jitters*. Cf. Albert-Reiner Glaap, "*Noises Off* and *Jitters*: Two Comedies of Backstage Life," in *Canadian Drama/L'Art dramatique canadien*, 13, 2, 1987, 210-215. Also in: Albert-Reiner Glaap, "Was ist kanadisch am (Englisch-)Kanadischen Drama?," in *Zeitschrift der Gesellschaft für Kanada-Studien*, 8, 2, 1988, 7-15.

[25] French, *Jitters*, 11.

[26] Cf. Neil Carson, "Towards a Popular Theatre in English Canada," in *Canadian Literature*, 85, 1980, 311.

[27] French, *Jitters*, 31.

[28] French, *Jitters*, 139.

[29] Jerry Wasserman (ed.), *Modern Canadian Plays*, Vancouver: Talonbooks, 1985, 311.

Geraldine Anthony

John Herbert's
Fortune and Men's Eyes
and Other Plays

John Herbert is one of the most controversial playwrights in Canadian theatre. Both his style of life and his plays have often been the subject of adverse Canadian criticism from his early career to the present day. Yet his play, *Fortune and Men's Eyes*,[1] won high praise from the New York critics, and has been produced in countries throughout the world.[2] Through this play, John Herbert has become known internationally.

Born in Toronto, Ontario, in 1926, the son of Claude Herbert Brundage and Gladys Reba (Kirk) Brundage, John was educated in the public schools of Ontario. As a brilliant and artistic teenager, he early accepted the fact that he was a homosexual. The narrow prejudices of the 1940s forced this sensitive youth to hide the fact from family and friends. In 1946 he was unjustly accused of making advances to a group of teenage boys who were, in fact, attempting to rob him. Their testimony was accepted in court and John Herbert was imprisoned in Guelph Reformatory for six months. It was his bitter experiences at Guelph that were later refined into his most noted play, *Fortune and Men's Eyes*. It was from the innocent, the fearful and the hardened young criminals who were his cellmates, that he created the characters for this play.

Herbert is the author of many plays, essays, short stories as well as one novel. However, his main interest has always been in theatre where he has worked successfully as director, actor, set and costume designer, prop man, lighting, stage and house manager and theatre critic. For some years he was also a university lecturer in drama. Herbert thus brings to the writing of plays an enormous knowledge of stagecraft. Never wholly accepted in Canada because of his life style, the controversial nature of his plays, and his many fearless attacks on Canadian social problems, and, in particular, Canada's penal system, John Herbert has received recognition largely from the United States and European countries where his plays have been widely produced on stage, radio and television. To see his finest play, *Fortune and Men's Eyes*, within the context of his entire dramatic work, is the object of this essay.

Fortune and Men's Eyes, a play dealing with the corruption of youth and individuality, set within a reformatory, a prison for young men, was a logical outgrowth from the author's earlier writings. As far back as the age of fifteen, he wrote a short story entitled "The Chinese Proverb" (published in *Wee Wisdom Magazine*, a monthly periodical for children printed in Kansas City, Mo., U.S.A., 1942), centred on racial prejudice in North America. The tale looks at the problems of a boy born of Chinese immigrants and his difficulties in finding acceptance by his schoolmates. In the end, the boy's personal salvation lies in his love for drawing and painting. The proverb spoken of in the title and the story translates from the Chinese into "Within four seas, we are all brothers and sisters."

It was the second story by the young author to be published in *Wee Wisdom*. The first, titled *A Boy and His Queen*, was printed in 1941, and deals with the plight of a young minstrel in the time of Queen Elizabeth I. In the story, a boy from a poor family earns money by singing in the streets of London. He has a beautiful voice and is heard one day by the Queen of England, who invites him into the palace, where he is dubbed by her as Sir Nightingale, made a page in her court and given money to help his family. (Copies of all John Herbert's works, both published and unpublished, reside in the John Herbert archives, in the University of Waterloo Library, Waterloo, Ontario, Canada. The following references to his writings can be found in those archives. The documents are all extant).

In dozens of unpublished short stories and hundreds of poems from the years of adolescence and early manhood, the subject matter reveals the writer's concern with poverty, prejudice, racism, violence, war, social injustice and the other ills of humanity as it struggles towards civilization. A poem published in the *York Memo* (a secondary-school annual publication) in 1942 and titled, "The Dawning," speaks of the ugliness and cruelty of war, but admits the need of fighting against tyranny. The conflict between a love for peace and harmony and the urge to rebel against cruelty and injustice would struggle to find common ground in all the writer's plays.

A play (unpublished and unperformed) written in the 1950s and titled "Felice" (John Herbert Archives) tries to come to grips with the emotional isolation of a physically handicapped woman, who has difficulty in finding consolation in her chosen art, her marriage or a long-lasting friendship. Only the great love and sacrifice of a friend brings the woman back to a passion for life as she discovers her own worth. It is a story of the spirit triumphant over the limitations of the body.

This theme, in different forms, would become the long line on which John Herbert would hang many works of art. At the heart of his drama there beats, always, the life of the outcast, the misfit, the individualist, the victim and the forgotten person in society.

"Private Club," a one-act play, written in 1960, was performed at the Bohemian Embassy, a coffee-house in Toronto, in 1962, and again in the Newmarket Play Festival in Newmarket, Ontario, in 1963. The play presents the picture of racial prejudice in a Canadian private club. We see the situation through the plight of an immigrant from Austria, a Jewish girl named Poldi Dahl, who finds herself exposed to the restrictive attitudes and rules of the club's members when she departs from her role as a waitress in the club's dining room. A young member of the club falls in love with Poldi, and both she and he are forced to pay a bitter price for defying the racial and religious bigots who control the life of Canadian society, in the author's 1960 view.

The companion piece, produced at both the coffee-house and in the out-of-town festival, was another one-act play, written by Herbert in 1961. It is titled "A Household God," and deals with the subject of greed. The owner of a restaurant exploits and finally destroys three members of his own family through his insatiable greed and inability to spend or give. His wife, whom he has made into a kitchen drudge, while ignoring her wishes to spend some time with old friends, turns into a bitter, hate-filled woman who fights only to save her daughter from a similar fate. The son, well-trained by the father, becomes greedier than his sire and consequently the restaurant owner's formidable rival. When performed by New Venture Players, a Toronto theatre company, in 1962, it frightened many people who could see the materialism of Canadian life reflected there.

In 1963 John Herbert would try to interest George Luscombe, Canadian director of Toronto Workshop Productions, in the first version of *Fortune and Men's Eyes*, titled "Christmas Concert." Luscombe, seemingly disinterested in the piece, asked Herbert what other work he might do for Toronto Workshop Productions. Both liked the unfinished and last play of Georg Büchner, the nineteenth-century German playwright's *Woyzeck*.

Herbert worked for many months in 1963 on an adaptation and development of Georg Büchner's unfinished play. The timeless power of Büchner's philosophy is revealed in the sketchy scenes that survived a fire after Büchner's premature death in Poland. There one finds a clear questioning of war and revolution as the solution to any human problem. In those short scenes, it was clear to Herbert that Büchner protested the violence done to individuals in an ugly chain of man's inhumanity to man. The army officer exploits the little soldier Woyzeck's need for money by having Woyzeck do humiliating tasks for the officer. The army doctor does experiments, using Woyzeck as a human guinea-pig. Woyzeck eventually goes blind.

But the chain of violence does not end at Woyzeck; the young soldier has a woman friend and a child. Marie, without money enough to care for her child and herself, runs off to have an affair with a handsome drum major, who uses her and casts her aside. The drum major also beats Woyzeck in a fight in a tavern, adding physical injury to emotional torment. When the starving, bleeding, betrayed Woyzeck can bear no more of life, he gives his few cherished personal belongings, a wooden cross, a bible and ring that belonged to his mother, to his friend and fellow-soldier, Andre, then goes to murder Marie and to drown himself in the lake. At the end of the tragedy, the child is left alone, playing a war-game on stage.

Herbert wanted to develop the play into a full-length stage piece that would be true to the spirit of Büchner. He decided to research the German playwright's life and the history of Büchner productions in German. Though Büchner wrote relatively little, much has been written about him. Herbert read *Leonce and Lena* and *Danton's Death*, as well as other writings by or about Büchner.

Fortunately, among papers that survived, there was a letter written to the woman in Germany whom Büchner loved. Herbert used many lines from this letter in the last scene between the soldier and his woman before the murder of Marie. Surviving, too, was a satirical essay on the subject of modern science, written during Büchner's days as a university student. His professors were displeased with this essay. Herbert used certain aspects of this satirical piece to colour the character of the diabolical and ridiculous doctor who uses the soldier in scientific and sadistic experiments. (It was as if Büchner, almost a century before, foresaw the experiments that Nazi doctors would perform on prisoners in concentration camps.) Herbert came to see Büchner as a prophet.

It was this discovery, so vital to the understanding of Büchner's vision, that enabled Herbert to understand certain characteristics given to Woyzeck in the original writing; in my view the visions or hallucinations the little soldier has of skies filled with fire and of mushrooms (the nuclear cloud?) are trying to tell us something of importance. Consequently, Herbert heightened the quality of prophecy in *Woyzeck*, and so the suffering figure becomes Christ-like in his own simple way. At last, Herbert had a two-hour play that could be performed in two acts. The Canadian playwright developed and finished songs that had been promised with a line or two here and there in Büchner's script. The style of the play, in the end, was and is expressionistic and poetic, in the manner of Brecht's play, *The Caucasian Chalk Circle*.

Although George Luscombe rejected the Herbert version, which the adapter had titled *World of Woyzeck*, it was produced in 1969, when Herbert staged and directed his own production at his Garret Theatre, in a second-floor space on Yonge Street (at Maitland) in Toronto. *World of Woyzeck* was one of the Garret Theatre Company's very successful productions, running for seventeen weeks to enthusiastic audiences.

Having become fascinated with mid-nineteenth century drama, art, science and politics, Herbert adapted another play. He saw Alexandre Dumas fils' play, *La Dame Aux Camelias*, as a turning point in European theatre, a play that heralded the coming of Ibsen and Shaw. Despite its florid language and romantic surface, the play about a prostitute dying of consumption, was, in its time, a startling departure from that kind of popular play of the era where nothing need be taken seriously, except, perhaps, the artifice of forced wit.

Herbert's work on *The Lady of the Camellias* may have been a foreshadowing of choices he would make in the future creation of central characters in his own plays. After *Fortune and Men's Eyes* would follow a series of plays, each taking its shape from the life of a woman doing battle against forces that would destroy her.

"Born of Medusa's Blood" (1972): Clio Cain, the central character is an aging singer, once successful as an artist, who has fallen on difficult and dangerous days. She is one of two black characters in the play, and it is Clio, the older woman, who teaches Polly, a young black girl, to fight the forces of racism in their world. When the play made its debut at Theatre-In-Camera, Toronto, Clio was played by the jazz singer and actress, Jodie Drake, member of the Jazz Hall of Fame in New Orleans. The play points out the historical fact that black women in North America have always been betrayed by both men and white people.

"Omphale and the Hero" (1973): Antoinette, the central character in this play, is a prostitute in a small Canadian town on the border between an English-speaking province and a French-speaking one. As a young woman, she had been a librarian in the town's public library, but was dismissed from that post when the townspeople became scandalized by Antoinette's love affair with a Canadian Indian. The forces of prudery and bigotry push Antoinette to survival's sharpest edge, then to death. "Omphale and the Hero" had a workshop performance with the Forest Hill Chamber Players in 1974. It has been translated into French and German. It was published in English in *Canadian Theatre Review*, Summer 1974.

"The Dinosaurs" (1974) is an hour-long one-act play with only two characters, Monique Dominique, a Canadian-born actress who has an international reputation in theatre, and Rudolph Nabob, a newspaper critic who has become a dictator of theatrical tastes in Canadian theatre. Both characters are veterans in their fields and the play puts them together at a midnight supper, after the critic has written a scathing review of the actress' latest performance in Canada. The play was first produced in Toronto with the Forest Hill Chamber Players. This and three other plays were published by Talonbooks, Canada, in 1976. The action of the play follows a battle to the death between the artist's view of her world and the critic's desire to dictate the destiny of her career. (Herbert would use both characters again in a full-length play titled "The Token Star"—Poor Alex Theatre, 1979.)

The three other one-act plays published in the Talonbook collection were pieces written earlier in the playwright's life:
— "Pearl Divers" (1965): a four-character play about a young homosexual man looking for a job as a dishwasher and his encounters with three very different women employed in the large city restaurant.
— "Beer Room" (1966): a five-character play about an actor and a painter, their hopes and disappointments, observed during a single evening of drinking and talking in a tavern.
— "Close Friends" (1969): a two-character play about the painful parting of two young men who lived together.

A few years after the first edition of these four one-act plays had been published under the umbrella title, *Some Angry Summer Songs,*[3] Talonbooks opened an office in California, so that copies became available to the American public. Since then, many universities in the United States have presented student performances of the plays, with special attention to the one called "Close Friends." This interest in Herbert's plays other than *Fortune and Men's Eyes* has not been echoed, for the most part, in Canadian institutions.

Fortunately, young and new directors in Canada have become interested in Herbert's latest works. Most notable of these new directors is one who has worked as both actor and director internationally, Thom Sokoloski, a young Canadian who has directed plays and operas in the Netherlands, France, the United States and, more recently, Yugoslavia.

After workshopping two of Herbert's new plays, "Magda" (1983) and "The Power of Paper Dolls" (1984), Sokoloski chose to present a professional production of "Magda" at the Adelaide Court Theatre in Toronto (February and March of 1985) in a Canadian edition. Audience reception of the play was enthusiastic and appreciative, offering the cast of eight actors several curtain calls on each evening. The enthusiasm of the Toronto audience was not reflected in the newspaper's reviews, with the exception of the *Canadian Jewish News*. The critics seemed uneasy with the subject matter of the play, and Ray Conlogue of *The Globe and Mail* virtually attacked the right of the author to deal with this subject.

"Magda" is the story of a Jewish survivor of Auschwitz Concentration Camp, a woman who lost her whole family to the holocaust. She returns to Germany after forty years in America, and takes revenge on the family of the S.S. officer she holds responsible for her own torture and the death of a sister, Naomi. At a picnic, she poisons the food that kills eight people. Those who perish are the children and the grandchildren of the couple who were Nazis, Hans and Christine Wagner. Magda purposely leaves the grandparents to live out their lives, finally knowing what it is to lose an entire family through violence and hatred. The play is in the German expressionistic style that Herbert used to adapt Büchner's *Woyzeck*. The setting in "Magda" is a modern-day courtroom in Berlin, where Magda is on trial for the eight murders. As the play progresses, it is Naziism which goes on trial, memories strengthened by the presence of flashback scenes of Magda's past, a life haunted by fascism and genocide.

Three of the important friends in John Herbert's life are women, born in Europe, who are all survivors of the holocaust. His play "Magda" is, in its essence, based on their lives and memories. The act of revenge was the playwright's own particular choice of dramatic invention. The idea gives an air of Greek tragedy to the play, which is brought forward in a shocking curve to the more recent human destruction in Vietnam, El Salvador and the Philippines. The growing fascism in American thinking is the frightening note on which the play ends. Herbert sounds a warning. He said that he would most like the play to be shown in South Africa, where his *Fortune and Men's Eyes* was the first play to be staged with a racially mixed cast at the The Space theatre club in Cape Town. At the time, Herbert stipulated that the play's rights included the written contract that the performance could not be shown to a segregated audience. The producers in Cape Town agreed and the show played to a racially mixed audience. The South African Government forbade any royalties to leave the country to go to John Herbert, so the author instructed the producers of his work to use that money to assist a fund for development of black theatre artists in South Africa.

Fortune and Men's Eyes, the prison play, has, in fact, become something of a theatrical barometer of the political climate in countries of the world. The play has been translated into more than forty languages and played in over a hundred countries, but never in a totalitarian state. Russia and the other former Eastern Block countries have never seen the play, and it was not performed in Greece, Spain or Argentina until those lands rid themselves of their military governments. In each case, with the departure of fascism, the societies of those countries saw a production of Herbert's play within weeks of the changes that brought some artistic freedom. It was as if there was always someone waiting for a chance to put the play on stage.

If Herbert is to be placed within the context of Canadian playwrights, one might say that if Robertson Davies is the most British of Canadian writers, David French the most domestic and Michel Tremblay the most French, then Herbert must be the most international.

Herbert's decision in 1963 to rewrite *La Dame Aux Camelias* as his company worked on the Dumas play, was a very wise exercise. His immersion in the style and structure of the well-made play strongly influenced the shape of *Fortune and Men's Eyes* which is, in the words of one European critic, "as carefully structured as anything written by Racine."[4] "A Lady of the Camellias" played at the Victoria Auditorium, on downtown Queen Street in Toronto, in January and February 1964. Audiences were charmed and approving. Herbert, like Sarah Bernhardt, knew that the only "sacred monster" to be reached and delighted was the audience. He still trusts in that belief and refuses to pander to any of his critics. In the next year, 1965, when Herbert opened the Garret Theatre he began to present plays that would bring critic Nathan Cohen to observe his work favourably.

In the play, *Fortune and Men's Eyes*, John Herbert was one of the first English-speaking playwrights to deal openly with the theme of homosexuality. Presented on February 23, 1967, at the Actor's Playhouse in New York, it was received enthusiastically by the audience and critics. In John Herbert's chapter on his life and work published in the book *Stage Voices*, he says:

> I felt...that the bullies of the world were in love with death more than with life. To me, life was always 'growing things' and I was horrified at the sight of the things lost to life: dead animals, broken limbs, destructive adults, cruel teachers, hunger, poverty, crippling....[5]

This quotation gives the reader the essence of John Herbert's work. His plays deal with broken people whose wounds he seeks to heal. *Fortune and Men's Eyes* offers a vivid, realistic presentation of four wounded young men whom John Herbert yearns to make whole: Smitty, the honest, good person whose prison term inevitably changes him into a hardened criminal; Rocky, the insecure, fearful bully who is sadly incapable of change; Queenie, the homosexual, who uses the reformatory's unfeeling and unjust regulations to advance his own needs; Mona, the sensitive boy, forced to accept homosexual advances in order to survive. In these four young men, John Herbert sees suffering humanity and he longs to offer wounded human beings compassion. Herbert uses drama to assuage the wounds of others. Angered by the unfeeling indifference to the human problems surrounding people on every side, he uses his rhetoric to awaken them, to reveal to them their negligence, to force them to face the human condition. This is possibly why Torontonians dislike John Herbert; it is why he has always been such a controversial figure.

The title, _Fortune and Men's Eyes_, is taken from the quotation by Shakespeare, "When in disgrace with fortune and men's eyes I, all alone, beweep my outcast state."[6] Love shared will bring surcease to the wounds of damaged people. To those whom society refuses to acknowledge, who have no chance for so-called success in this life, love will obliterate the pain and bring peace.

Each of the characters in _Fortune and Men's Eyes_ has his redeeming qualities; seventeen-year-old Smitty, a "clean-cut youth of clear intelligence...strong and masculine with enough sensitivity...to soften the sharp outline. He is of a type that everyone seems to like almost on sight;"[7] nineteen-year-old Rocky, "He has a nature, driven by fear, that uses hatred aggressively to protest itself...;" twenty-year-old Queenie, "...a strange combination of softness and hulking strength. For a large person he moves with definite grace and fine precision...;" (7) eighteen-year-old Mona, "His effeminacy is not aggressive...just exists.... If he had been a woman, some would have described him as having a certain ethereal beauty." (8) Thus does John Herbert describe his characters before the opening of the play. Only Smitty has no negative qualities but it is Smitty whose change is the most drastic. It is Smitty, the non-criminal, whom the prison system changes into the most hardened of them all. Rocky "lives like a cornered rat, vicious, dangerous and unpredictable." (7) Queenie is: "coarse, cruel, tough and voluptuously pretty." (7) Mona is "A youth...of a physical appearance that arouses resentment at once in many people, men and women. He seems to hang suspended between the sexes, neither boy nor woman." (8)

Act One, Scene One, of this two-act play is set in mid-October in a Canadian reformatory school of a penitentiary, with young inmates in their late teens and early twenties. The setting is a four-bed dormitory. "Rocky is stretched on his bed like a prince at rest; Queenie sits on his own bed up-stage; Mona leans against the wall of bars...." (9) The dialogue is sharp, unsavoury, realistic for prisoners, and sets the tone for the admittance of the innocent newcomer, Smitty. He is made party to their degrading dialogue on their gay exploits. Rocky forces Smitty into the shower and into becoming his buddy. In Act One, Scene Two, Smitty is learning to protect himself as he observes and listens to the others. Queenie urges him to fight Rocky and thus liberate himself. Smitty complies. The scene ends on this act of violence. Act Two opens on Christmas Eve. There is only one scene and it involves a rehearsal for the Christmas play. Queenie enacts the role of a confident transvestite and is completely happy doing so. Mona rehearses the speech on mercy from *The Merchant of Venice* and there is pathos in the attempt, much as he is derided by the others. Smitty is now a hardened criminal, giving the others orders, but he defends Mona. When the guard comes to take them to the play, Smitty and Mona remain behind. Then it is that Smitty propositions Mona in the same way that Rocky had originally propositioned him. Mona (and the audience) are shocked. Smitty has descended to the level of his cellmates. Mona, in his refusal, quotes the passage from Shakespeare, "When in disgrace with fortune and men's eyes...." (90) At this most unfortunate time in each man's life, he has then only to think of the one he loves, to rise above misfortune. "Haply I think on thee, and then my soul/(Like to the lark at break of day arising,/From sullen earth) sings hymns at heaven's gate...." (90, 91) Both Mona and Smitty come to an understanding through these poignant words. A physical relationship will destroy rather then enrich their friendship. The play ends almost immediately with Rocky and Queenie's return, their jealous reprisals, the guard's intervention, and Mona's torture by the guard. Smitty is reduced to bitterness, indignation and hatred, as he threatens in the last words of *Fortune and Men's Eyes*, "I'll pay you all back." (96)

A textual study of the play shows some revealing characteristics of John Herbert's victims as well as his own compassion for wounded and damaged people. His hapless young men, imprisoned either unjustly or because their family life brought them to criminal acts, exhibit all the reactions of victims: fear, hatred, jealousy, revenge, blackmail, cruelty, despair. Only Mona possesses positive qualities. Fear is behind the actions of all the characters—fear of punishment by the guards, reprisals from fellow prisoners, gang torture and rape; fear of the prison world itself so utterly unlike the free society outside. Smitty says on entering prison: "I feel like I'm in another country." (19) Even the guards are full of fear. Queenie describes one: "When he's out of that uniform, he's scared to death o' any eleven-year-old kid he meets on the street." (14) The prisoners hate the straight society to which they had no chance to belong. Queenie says: "I hate them gutless bastards who go to work eight hours a day, to parties and shows the rest of the time." (26)

They are jealous of each other, particularly anyone who develops a friendship with another prisoner. These liaisons cause sadistic violence among prisoners. The desire to have a buddy, whether he be friend, victim or political ally, is so powerful that much of the criminal interplay between characters proceeds from this basic human need. Both Rocky and Queenie want to be Smitty's "Old Man." They vie for his friendship and use fear to entrap him. Rocky tells him "You're sittin duck for a gang splash if y'ain't got a old man." (33) And Queenie tells Smitty, "Nobody'll bother you while you got a old man." (47) To Smitty's astonishment, being somebody's buddy means accepting his sexual advances. Only a liaison with the so-called "politicians" seems safe and Smitty eventually becomes one of them, a hardened criminal, revealing that he is finally Baldy's boy with an office job and the power to victimize his fellow prisoners.

The play very realistically reveals the cruelty of both guards and prisoners alike. A Canadian Indian prisoner is beaten up by the guards because he is a "redskin." Mona, the young, gentle person, is the butt of their torture. He is given rags to wear like a clown and is constantly punished by the guards. Rocky says of the gay person: "Never let a fruit scare ya.... The cops don't like them either, so underneath they're yellow as a broken egg." (31) The guard refers to Mona as "It" and takes out his revenge upon this innocent victim. Mona is the catalyst in this play, unwittingly bringing out both good and bad qualities in his cellmates and guards. Smitty, the new prisoner, is the central character, the representative of all new, unjustly accused, young prisoners, who begin life in prison as straight, principled people, and end as hardened criminals. The note of despair throughout the play cannot be silenced. Queenie says: "I learned before I was twelve that nobody gives a crap about you in this cruddy world." (26) The future holds nothing for these damaged, young men. Rocky tells Smitty to find some devious way of making money later on, because the Morality Squad will tell everyone of his past in prison and so prevent his ever getting honest work.

Only Mona exhibits sensitivity, independence and compassion. About Smitty he says, "They won't do it to him. He doesn't look gay, and he's probably not here on a sex charge." (23) Regarding Rocky, Mona says to Smitty who plans to destroy Rocky: "Rocky can destroy himself soon enough." (83) Rocky's parents were both imprisoned for drug peddling and bootlegging. His sixteen-year-old brother has become a pimp. There is no future for these damaged people. Mona has never really surrendered his mind to the sadistic people around him.

He maintains his independence. Queenie says of Mona, "I coulda got her a real good old man, but she told him she like her 'independence' if you can picture it." (23) Mona is sensitive to Smitty's character and crushed by Smitty's turning into a hardened criminal. At the climax of the play when Smitty propositions Mona, he rejects Smitty, pointing out that what Smitty needs is a girl. Mona then reveals his secret for being able to live in this hell of a prison: "I separate things in order to live with others and myself. What my body does and feels is one thing, and what I think and feel apart from that is something else." (89)

John Herbert's capacity for participating with compassion in another's suffering reveals itself as he gives Mona the speech made by Portia in *The Merchant of Venice*—the plea for human charity and mercy. The highlight of the play is the scene between Smitty and Mona, when Mona refuses Smitty's advances because true love cannot issue from such a brutal relationship. Mona makes Smitty see that love is a spiritual quality dependent on respect for one another. When Smitty draws out Mona's secret regarding his imprisonment, it is John Herbert's story—the reason for his imprisonment—the young man being robbed by a gang, who, when the police move in, accuse the victim of homosexual advances. The play ends with the guards cruelly punishing Mona, and with Smitty's avowal "…to pay them back. I'll pay you all back." (96)

Fortune and Men's Eyes not only received high praise from New York and European critics but also from renowned playwrights and actors when it was performed in Europe. Included among these New Yorkers and Europeans were: Tennessee Williams, Lee Strasburg, John Gielgud, Noel Coward, Simone Signoret, and Melina Mercuri. In 1975 Canadian critics belatedly acknowledged John Herbert's work by giving him the prestigious Chalmers Award for the best play produced that year in Canada.

As director and writer, Herbert has been drawn to the outrages of tyrants as some people are hypnotized by the weaving and ominous movements of the deadly, poisonous cobra. Anyone who has ever been the victim of bullies remains watchful and distrustful of people who like to have power over others. This concern reveals itself in many of the plays mentioned earlier; the desire to fight back and to remove the evil of tyranny is most pronounced. Perhaps this is the result of his homosexuality. John Herbert is something of a rare phenomenon in Canadian life. There are many homosexual writers, directors and actors in the present world of Canada's artistic expression, but Herbert did what others at that time dared not do. He proclaimed his sexual orientation as openly as he did his politics and philosophical inclinations.

It is not possible to fit John Herbert into a style of theatre: he has always mixed the elements of tragedy and comedy. He has dealt with fantasy in a television play called "Time to A Waltz," absurdist theatre and satire in his many topical revues, "The Wonderful Whores" (Poor Alex Theatre, 1976), "The Great Schmaltz" (Poor Alex Theatre, 1977), "Hollywood, Here?" (Poor Alex Theatre, 1980), and a satirical three-act play on Canadian theatre titled "The Token Star" (Poor Alex Theatre, 1979); realism and expressionism in "World of Woyzeck," "Magda" and "Close Friends;" romanticism and naturalism in "A Lady of the Camellias," "Felice," "The Power of Paper Dolls" and several other plays, including some of the one-acters, such as "Beer Room," "The Dinosaurs," "Private Club" and "A Household God." He has also ventured into the realm of Grand Guignol with a 1959 play titled "A Ruby Fell."

It is unlikely that scholars of the future, when examining Herbert's full output of work, will be able to fit him into any school of writing or style of theatre. He is an adventurer and explorer, and has long had the habit of finding a fitting way to do things. He would say that he operates on the motto Sarah Bernhardt adopted early in her career and to whose directive she held through the ups and downs of a passionately experienced life; "Quand même," a phrase that translates into "even though" or "in spite of all." Such an attitude enabled her in her old age, disabled with only one leg, to say that she would continue to play on stage, if it meant strapping herself to the scenery. In earlier years it meant "in spite of criticism and ridicule." For many years, Herbert has kept near him the copy of a letter written to Sarah Bernhardt when she was a young actress by an older fellow actress, Madeline Brohan:

> If you want to keep the YOU you're creating, be prepared to rise on a platform constructed of calumnies, gossip, adulation, flattery, lies and truths. But once upon it, stay and cement it with your work and excellence. Then the malicious ones who unwittingly furnished the materials for the edifice, will try to knock it down. But if you remain true to your art, they will be made powerless. That is my wish for you, dear Sarah.[8]

No doubt this is John Herbert's hope for his own fate.

NOTES

[1] John Herbert, *Fortune and Men's Eyes*, New York: Grove Press, 1967.

[2] See John Herbert Archives, University of Waterloo Library. Waterloo, Ontario.

[3] John Herbert, *Some Angry Summer Songs*, Vancouver: Talonbooks, 1976.

[4] John Herbert, in a letter to this writer, March 16, 1985.

[5] John Herbert, in Geraldine Anthony (ed.), *Stage Voices*, New York and Toronto: Doubleday & Co., 1978, 170.

[6] Shakespeare, *Sonnet 29*, as quoted by John Herbert, *Fortune and Men's Eyes*, 90, 91.

[7] John Herbert, *Fortune*, 1967, 7. All further quotations will be taken from this text.

[8] Madeline Brohan, in a letter to Sarah Bernhardt, as quoted by John Herbert in a letter to this writer, March 16, 1985.

Richard Plant

The Deconstruction of Pleasure: John Krizanc's *Tamara*, Richard Rose and the Necessary Angel Theatre Company

As an introduction to the work of Necessary Angel,[1] this article provides brief commentary on several stage productions and culminates in a reading of *Tamara* with reference to some of its performances. My point about *Tamara* is that the naturalistic elements of its stage production urge audience members to construct the most pleasurable experience possible from the illusionistic performance circumstances. Simultaneously through its deconstructive mode, the metatheatrical semiosis prompts the audience to interrogate the nature of that construction of pleasure. Those Necessary Angel productions which I mention as context for *Tamara* can be seen to urge, to some degree, a similar consideration of the "truth" of pleasure—both the pleasure derived from mimetic illusionary stage performance and from ethically questionable behaviour in daily life.

Consistently among the most exciting work for the stage in Canada over the past decade or so (1978-1989) has been that of Richard Rose and the Toronto-based Necessary Angel Theatre Company founded in 1978. Their seasons have been highlighted by innovative stagings in a variety of styles and venues, environmental to proscenium, and have included rivetting productions of challenging plays, such as *Jacques and his Master* (1986) by the Czech author Milan Kundera or *The Castle* (1987) and *The Possibilities* (1989), these latter two by British playwright Howard Barker.

Many of their shows have been generated from within the company itself, as for example, was *Mein* (1983, remounted 1985), a collectively created, expressionistic handling of the inner world, the "fears, desires and impulses,"[2] experienced by "I," a young business executive on the way to the top. Marked by wittily choreographed movement, the play fragmented "I" into five performers (three men, two women, all in dark grey business suits) who presented the ironic iconography of his/her triumph over another applicant for a job, "I"'s subsequent promotion in which the displaced boss committed suicide, and then "I"'s fall from grace. Available to the audience throughout the imagistic, allusive *Mein* was an ironic, theatricalized experience of the "struggle" (*Kampf*) obliquely suggested in the puns of the title. The pleasure found by the materialistic, corporate mentality in "success," that is, dominating and possessing (mein/mine), was seen to be undercut by the pain of those oppressed and the shallowness of the "lifestyle" gains.

In 1989 Necessary Angel staged an adaptation by noted author Michael Ondaatje, dramaturge D.D. Kugler and Richard Rose of Ondaatje's novel *Coming Through Slaughter*, centred around a search for the tormented jazz musician Buddy Bolden who has disappeared. The Silver Dollar, one of Toronto's low-end bars, was an appropriately atmospheric site prompting the audience to enter an illusion of New Orleans jazz life. And clearly some audience members were transported, as Robert Crew's review might signal:

> The audience is plunged straight away into steamy New Orleans in about 1906. On the small stage, a glistening, nearly nude woman is performing the Oyster Dance. The malleable mollusc starts on the forehead and slips slowly past some interesting slopes and valleys before ending its journey around about the knee. Phew![3]

But the illusion was often strained, sometimes by limitations in the production, for instance the terrible sightlines experienced by some of the audience. At other times, the presentational mode was foregrounded by strategic theatrical devices, as for instance when the actor playing the tormented Bolden moved into his other role of the rational Narrator and recited passages clearly identifiable as part of the novel, while the performers enacted them in various presentational modes. One of the effects of this conscious theatricalism was that the audience's attention was directed out of the naturalistic illusion toward the metaphorical resonances of the performance—questions about pleasure, pain, loss, madness, creativity, identity.

Just before *Coming Through Slaughter*, the production of Rose's own play *Newhouse*, (April 19-30, 1989; also created with D.D Kugler) in a Toronto hockey arena allowed audience members to walk about a cityscape formed in the shape of a body[4] by a number of "stages" on the arena's perimeter and at its centre. The fast-moving action they followed was an ingenious interweaving of an imagined Canadian sociopolitical reality, *Oedipus Tyrannus* and Tirso de Molina's *The Trickster of*

Seville, with material from Molière's *Don Juan*, Seneca's *Oedipus* and Diderot's *Rameau's Nephew*. Described as a "speculation about possible, but avoidable, future events,"[5] the play centres on two people, a Canadian Prime Minister (Oedipus) and Newhouse (Don Juan), the son of the Minister of Foreign Affairs. The Prime Minister's liberal-minded attempt to deal with a national epidemic of a sexually-transmitted disease leads him into conflict with conservatives and fundamentalists, and to the discovery that he has the fatal illness himself from an undisclosed extramarital affair years before. In a climate where promiscuous sexual activity could be deemed a criminal offence (some of the Prime Minister's opponents want legislation to that effect), Newhouse's profound allure and insatiable sexual appetite lead to clandestine affairs whose volatile implications—he has contracted the disease also— threaten the government and raise weighty issues for everyone: "Is he an irredeemable menace knowingly infecting others with a deadly disease? Or is he the last vestige of devil-may-care spontaneity in an increasingly paranoid and suffocated society?"[6]

The performance was shaped by dramatic tension between, on one side, the "timelessness" of the mythic echoes of *Don Juan*, *Oedipus* and the other works, as well as the allegorical, quasi-medieval world of multiple staging. On the other side was juxtaposed the immediate reality of the audience, the theatrical actuality of the individual playing spaces, and the references to everyday Canadian society, politics and personalities (for example, the actor playing the Prime Minister looked like Brian Mulroney). Within this diachronic/synchronic tension other conceptual frames were at work. As Richard Rose has said: "The audience members are voyeurs in the intimate scenes [the 'private', hidden political dealings, sexual and domestic affairs] and in the *Oedipus* story they become part of the public."[7] In performance, this public world existed amidst the audience, for example in news scrums where media figures with microphones and television recording equipment interviewed the politicians. As designer Graeme Thomson commented before the show: "...the piece will really be moving through the crowd a lot. At various times, when the Prime Minister and Minister of Foreign Affairs are being hounded by the press from all quarters, the audience will be forced to scatter."[8]

These images of a "you are there" reality gained part of their public identity, their authority, from being "broadcast" throughout the performance space on screens, which ranged from ordinary televisions to large videotrons. (The "private" moments were not caught on camera.) The result was the creation of not only different sizes but different layers of reality: the theatrical illusion of the private world established a dialectic with the authenticated or documented public reality, and expanded into self-reflexive scenes where the audience could see itself on the screens watching events being recorded.[9] These reverberant images were poised to operate in a fashion dramaturge D. D. Kugler has explained:

> Thematically...we're looking for much more complex material that doesn't give simple answers, that in fact makes the complexity of real issues apparent.
>
> I think that spills over into the form. You really want to pull out of a proscenium context because it gives you a framed, two-dimensional reality in a way. If you open the form out and get the audience inside the story structurally, they can see that that story spills over into their lives—that it affects them and they have an effect on it.[10]

The artists may have been overly optimistic in their vision of the interactivity of *Newhouse*, particularly the audience's power to impact on the "story," since the production offered no openings in its mimetic narrative for audience intervention. The performance made clear that the production was aimed at exploring serious issues:

> ...how fear and ignorance are used as tools to manipulate social policy and political structure....alternative views of the public and private person....the ruthless pursuit of knowledge [and its implicit] arrogance that assumes all knowledge is attainable.[11]

However, the predominant impression, as Natalie Rewa argues,[12] appears to have been that of audience excitement generated by the novelty of the decentralized, multi-matrixed staging. This is certainly not an inconsequential artistic achievement in its challenge to proscenium theatre, but clearly not all the artists envisioned.

As successful as works such as *Mein* and *Newhouse* have been, the most fruitful collaboration for Necessary Angel has been that between Richard Rose and his high school friend, the playwright John Krizanc, also a founder of the Company. In addition to *Tamara*, to which I shall return shortly, they have worked together on Krizanc's *Prague*, which was a runner-up for both the Chalmer's Best New Canadian Play Award and a Dora Mavor Moore Award in 1984. *Prague* also earned the 1987 Governor General's Award for drama. In it, the director of a Prague theatre, motivated by guilt over betraying his father to authorities years earlier, endangers his company and family in an attempt to stage his own subversive play. *Prague* is intellectually and emotionally rich, a "critique of fascism"[13] with wit and complexity in the manner of Tom Stoppard's works, such as *Professional Foul*. Unlike *Tamara* and other of the Necessary Angel plays, *Prague* takes metatheatrical advantage of a proscenium stage but deconstructs the illusions of that theatrical idiom at the same time, it examines the nature and function of art in an oppressive state. The subject is one on which Krizanc has commented outside of his plays:

> It's wrong for writers to be heroic. Ours is not an age of heroes. Every hero, or moralist, creates more and more victims, and totalitarianism can eat up as many people as want to throw themselves at the wall.[14]

Krizanc has expressed concern about the responsibility of artists, as well as the costs involved in "heroic" action:

> I was intrigued by Vaclav Havel and Pavel Kahout and the other Czech writers who were standing up against Communist totalitarianism. I really admire those writers.... I was saddened because the dissident movement had been so successfully crushed. But I also have to question the consequences of those actions, of the stands that were taken. For example, Pavel Landovsky, who signed the Charter of 77, is now in Vienna and he's been told not to return. But as a result of that action, his first wife lost her job, the son from that marriage was kept out of university, and the daughter was not allowed to graduate. Her apartment isn't heated, so she has a hacking cough and goes around like Camille. You think, so he's a better man for this because signing the Charter was the right thing to do. But what is the human cost? How many people have to fall in order for there to be goodness?[15]

One of the links which has joined Rose and Krizanc has been their mutual interest in creating theatre which is interactive in ways that traditional theatre is not and in which the experience of the form is inherently that of the play's socio-political and ethical concerns. Their highest profile work has been *Tamara*, the unheralded, unassuming hit—loosely referred to as "environmental" or "promenade" theatre—of Toronto's "Onstage Festival" in 1981. Since then, *Tamara* has had "successful" productions in Los Angeles, Mexico City and New York, and is being considered for performances in other countries.[16] In Los Angeles where it won numerous awards, the production developed a cult following of "Lifers," those who came back five times or more. Overall, *Tamara* International has grossed somewhere in the vicinity of $10,000,000 (including the sale of T-shirts and other memorabilia), an unheard of sum for a Canadian play from the small theatres.[17] The script has been printed by a major publishing house and, tangentially, there has even been a *Tamara* novel released in the United States, although John Krizanc has not allowed his name to be connected with it. An irony of all this is that the more "successful" *Tamara* has become at the box office, and the larger the production has grown, the less successful it seems to have been in achieving what its author and director have expressed as their serious intentions.

The action of the play occurs on January 10 and 11, 1927 in Il Vittoriale degli Italiani, the country home of Gabriele D'Annunzio, on the occasion of a visit by Tamara de Lempicka, the captivating artist from Poland who was portrait painter to many prominent individuals at the time. D'Annunzio has been carrying on a passionate correspondence with Tamara, and has invited her to paint his portrait. But, as the other eight members of his household know, he is attempting to add Tamara to his long list of lovers which already includes Eleanora Duse and Isadora Duncan.[18] In the play as in history, D'Annunzio is the world-famous, nationalist Italian poet and hero whom Il Duce keeps out of political circulation and in a life of cocaine and sexual indulgence under a "protective" house arrest at Il Vittoriale. But Krizanc's D'Annunzio is the antithesis of the figure Isadora Duncan describes from personal experience:

> Perhaps one of the most wonderful personalities of our time is Gabriel D'Annunzio, and yet he is small and, except when his face lights up, can hardly be called beautiful. But when he talks to one he loves, he is transformed to the likeness of Phoebus Apollo himself.... When D'Annunzio loves a woman, he lifts her spirit from this earth to the divine region where Beatrice moves and shines. In turn he transforms each woman to a part of the divine essence, he carries her aloft until she believes herself really with Beatrice, of whom Dante has sung immortal strophes.
>
> Only one woman [Duse] in the life of the poet withstood this test...and so before her D'Annunzio could only fall on his knees in adoration, which was the unique and beatific experience of his life.[19]

Also at Il Vittoriale are Gian Francesco de Spiga, an "inebriated composer, dillettante"; Dante Fenzo, a valet and ex-gondolier; Mario Pagnutti, a "mysterious new chauffeur"; Luisa Baccara, a former concert pianist; Carlotta Barra, a young dancer; Aélis Mazoyer, head housekeeper and D'Annunzio's confidante; Emilia Pavese, a "light-fingered" maid, and Aldo Finzi, a Fascist Captain stationed by Mussolini to guard D'Annunzio.[20]

Like D'Annunzio, whose liberty and artistic creativity have been compromised, the members of the household are each seeking freedom from forces oppressing them, but ironically each person has fixed on an ideological goal which denies freedom and overwhelms his or her integrity and creative potential. Krizanc's view is clear in this regard: "What I hate is people who let truth become subservient to political ideology. I think it has to be a personal truth."[21] De Spiga, who is not above passing off another composer's work as his own, has become a secret member of Mussolini's Fascist Party believing that in this way he can protect art and his music. He is in love with Luisa, who gave up her art to become D'Annunzio's mistress, but she is now rejected and broken. Carlotta, a religious, racist fanatic (the Italian equivalent of a member of the Aryan Youth movement), seeks D'Annunzio's letter of recommendation to dance for Diaghalev; Aélis has sexual designs on Carlotta. Emilia comes from embittered poverty and will do whatever is necessary to rise in the world: steal, sleep with Finzi or with Mario. Dante is blindly in love with Emilia and has secretly had a child with her. Finzi, in love with Luisa, is surviving as best a Jew can at the time by joining the Fascisti. Mario, whose father is the Fascist Duke of Milano, is secretly a communist attempting to convince D'Annunzio to turn in that direction, but who will kill D'Annunzio as a last resort if he refuses. Tamara believes, or appears to believe, in art for art's sake.

When audience members arrive at Il Vittoriale (in Toronto a Victorian mansion; in Los Angeles the Hollywood American Legion; in New York the Seventh Regiment Armory), they are issued passports and greeted by Dante. Capitano Finzi stamps the passports and explains that they must be carried at all times, that anyone not able to produce his or her papers when asked will be deported. The audience, in Toronto a total of about 40, in Los Angeles about 125, and in New York approximately 160, then congregates in the "Atrium" where de Spiga is playing the piano (in New York champagne was served). Various members of the cast carry on a dialogue which introduces the characters and explains the house rules: in essence, each audience member is a guest at Il Vittoriale and is expected to act as a guest. Each person can follow whatever member of D'Annunzio's household he or she chooses throughout the evening, but no one is to go through a closed door nor follow any performer who shuts a door behind him/her. At the Intermezzo, everyone will be invited to enjoy refreshments and share information.

By the end of the evening, the audience has been close witness to dark political and sexual intrigue. Some spectators have seen Tamara reject D'Annunzio and humiliate him by calling him syphilitic. Everyone has seen D'Annunzio at the end of the play raving about his past glory in Fiume and snorting cocaine poured on the floor and a dead body. That body is Mario's, whose communist identity has been revealed and who has been shot accidentally by Finzi in a struggle with Emilia. (Not everyone has seen that, nor anything else except D'Annunzio's raving.) De Spiga has triumphantly crushed Finzi by announcing untruthfully that Luisa was always de Spiga's, but he is subsequently crushed himself on learning from Tamara that Luisa has committed suicide. Tamara, after revealing Luisa's body to de Spiga, leaves the house calling everyone (including the audience) "Fascistes" (Tamara speaks French throughout much of the play). Emilia refuses to leave Il Vittoriale, so Dante flees by himself to find their daughter. Carlotta had departed earlier with a letter from D'Annunzio, without knowing that it explained he had written only because he owed her father money.

Despite careful plotting, everyone's plans have been brought to ruin by accident, human error or unforeseen awareness on someone else's part. The ending can be seen as chaos and devastation for the characters in the play.

For the audience, there is a parallel experience to the characters' chaos. The performance itself might be described as the enacting of ten plots, each centered on a person in the house, which intersect with one or another at various times in the evening. Because of the nature of the performance (noises off, actors visible in hallways and so forth), audience members will constantly be aware that action is going on simultaneously in other parts of the house—and, able to follow only one character, will be aware that they cannot see it all. Moreover, each plot is incomplete in itself because it depends in part on the actions of characters in other lines of the narrative. The overall experience fosters in the audience a sense of being unable to comprehend exactly what is happening, a sense of fragmentation and confusion. Intermission provides a kind of relief: sharing experience allows the pieces of the puzzle gathered by one person to join with those picked up by others resulting in a greater sense of what has occurred. But ultimately audience members are foiled in their Aristotelian detective work. Narratively, there are just too many loose ends, too many events unexperienced, unexplained to get a sense of the whole.[22]

Published reaction to *Tamara* in performance has been generally favourable, at times ecstatic, if not very perceptive, as John Krizanc's "the incomprehension of the reviewers drove me crazy"[23] would indicate. In Toronto reviewers called it a "surprise hit," commented that it was "brilliantly staged" and described the experience in terms of watching like "a fly on the wall." They spoke of the vicarious thrill of taking part in romance and intrigue, and of the joy in trying to put the pieces together. Many acknowledged the aforementioned sense of chaos and fragmentation; some treated that as a flaw. In Los Angeles, published commentary was much as in Toronto, but in addition, expressed interest in what stars were involved, both on stage and in the house. Attention was drawn to the catering by Ma Maison, and to the paintings by Tamara De Lempicka (Jack Nicholson, among others is a collector) adorning the walls (until they were withdrawn for safety reasons). There were references to the $500,000 budget (in contrast to $28,000 in Toronto which swelled to $40,000 before the six months were finished), to the fact that Karen Black could fill the house at $75 a seat, and eventually to the cult of "Lifers." Mexico had a special interest: Tamara had lived there, somewhat ingloriously, in her later years, replicating her earlier paintings. Published commentary spoke of the Mexican who invested in the production, of the $117,000 spent to buy the house in which it was played, and of the nationally famous soap opera stars who filled the lead roles. Reviewers described the piece as novel and passionate, and very enjoyable. New York, where an elegant buffet of Il Vittoriale-style food, champagne and even a "Tamara Cocktail" was part of the evening, was not greatly different, albeit larger in all respects, and on occasion somewhat jaded:

> Come to think of it, "Tamara" rather resembles one of those misguided sight-seeing tours at the end of which nothing is more welcome than the waiting bus. (The armory amenities include plenty of well-distributed settees.).... Beyond the novelty and the refreshments, perhaps it appeals to the Peeping Tom instincts of an age when supermarket tabloids and slick gossip magazines have made a major industry out of publicizing other people's scandals.[24]

The overall impact might be indicated by the subsequent opening in New York of other "promenade" theatre events.

As time goes by and scholars have a chance to study the performance in light of the published and unpublished scripts, as well as printed criticism and other resources, this response is changing. Richard Paul Knowles, in his usual perceptive fashion, points out how the play and its language deal with the failure of the artist to take a stand.[25] In his "Foreword" to the published edition, Alberto Manguel offers an insightful analysis touching on several of the points mentioned here. But in short, the performance response seems to have centred on the novelty of the staging, the "good natured decadence"[26] of the food and drink, and the fun of piecing it all together. It has generally dismissed the play's serious intentions and profound disquiet.[27] As John Krizanc says, "if you go for the sex you miss the climax."[28]

In retrospect, this is understandable. The experience of the play can be seen to depend on two counteracting impulses. On one side are the results of John Krizanc's and Richard Rose's attempt to construct a "democratic theatre" that allows the individual in the audience freedom to make choices, to create his/her own work of art: "I thought the best way to write a critique of Fascism was to give people more democratic freedom than they've ever had in the theatre.... For the audience, the intermezzo is important because it's about freedom of information, which you don't have in a Fascist state."[29] Yet the performance mode simultaneously deconstructs the move toward apparent freedom, denying the audience completion of any artistic vision. The spectator creates his/her art within what is at root a manipulated set of circumstances, a state of artistic "fascism" where the choices are dependent upon the conventions set up by the production. At the same time *Tamara* is breaking with traditional theatre, the performance mode calls for an illusionary art, the "willing suspension of disbelief" by the audience, in

---

a realistic (I might argue naturalistic) theatre where the house, props, costumes and the characters are aimed at re-creating the place, people and events of January 10 and 11, 1927. This illusionist form invokes our perception of the illusion in "Aristotelian" terms of a beginning, middle and end, a narrative linear plot, and a resolution of issues—an invocation of closure. Ironically, the choices available to the audience all end in the same state of chaos and incompleteness. On the other side is the non-illusionary world, the world of theatrical event, deliberate artifice or falseness. The audience is constantly made aware that these are actors in front of them; the spectators bump into other spectators; they consciously walk about a house they do not know; they consciously (self-consciously?) stand in a room watching representations of life at Il Vittoriale. The theatrical mode is foregrounded urging them to be critical or detached about what they are experiencing, and ultimately to think about it.

And what might they think about? Signs communicate entrapment, sterility, over-indulgence and selling-out. Just as D'Annunzio has sold out to his own rhetoric, Fascism and lust, and just as the other people in his house have sold out to their respective ideologies, so the audience has sold out to the novelty of the artifice, its form, the promotion, voyeurism and the pleasure of "good-natured decadence." The tendency to seek the "illusionary"—that is in both the usual "misleading impression" sense and the theatrical realism sense of the word— world of pleasure has kept them from fully taking part in the serious discoveries to be made. As John Krizanc points out: "*Tamara* is the only play I have been to where people actually talk about the play [at intermission]. But on the other hand, *Tamara* is destroyed by the sum of its parts, because the subtleties of the play, its implications, are overwhelmed by the experience."[30]

Tamara serves as an example of the work of Necessary Angel, chiefly that shaped by Richard Rose and John Krizanc or D.D. Kugler, which has been concerned with creating performances where the audience—and often characters in the performance—seemingly have their cake and eat it too. The various Necessary Angel productions have challenged the limitations of realistic theatre—there are lots of people who get pleasure from this critical action— while often treating the audience to the pleasures of theatrical illusion. At the same time, this metatheatrical mode has been the performative envelope for questioning the pleasure-oriented moral, ethical and political values of a middle-class, English Canadian audience.

NOTES

[1] Favourable conditions rarely exist for even short-term maintenance of a theatre company in Canada. Nonetheless, several artists, including founders Richard Rose (Artistic Director) and John Krizanc (Resident Author), have worked extensively with Necessary Angel: performers Tanja Jacobs, Elizabeth Hanna, Mark Christmann, Bruce Vavrina and Denis Forest; designers Dorian Clark (also a founding member) and Graeme Thomson; stagemanagers Sarah Stanley and Cheryl Landy (also an Assistant Director).

[2] Henry Mietkiewicz, "Mind-boggling *Mein* still fascinates," in *Toronto Star*, February 22, 1985.

[3] Robert Crew, "Engrossing play features fine lead performer," in *Toronto Star*, June 8, 1989, C1. A woman reviewer, Isabel Vincent, may have been less affected; she wrote simply, "…a racy performance of the infamous Oyster Dance…by Denese Matthews, who manages to make a raw oyster slither down her body" in *Globe and Mail*, June 9, 1989.

[4] Designer Graeme Thomson explained the design as follows: "Because the show deals with the body in a number of contexts—the physical body, the body politic and so on—an overhead view of the arena would show a stick figure of a human form with a number of raised platforms. The head is the seat of government, the church and the press sit on a shoulder, the bedroom is placed in the groin. The physical set as well as the props will be scaffolding, to suggest the skeletal nature of the body" (Jon Kaplan, in *Now*, April 13-19, 1989, 49). It is unfortunate that the conditions of performance, one of which was an inadequate source of funding, did not allow an over-head camera shot of the playing space. I would be very surprised to learn that many of the audience were aware of this significant three-dimensional metaphor.

[5] "Director's Notes," Programme for *Newhouse*, 2.

[6] Vit Wagner, "Drama packs arena with sex, plague and politics," in *Toronto Star*, April 14, 1989, D5.

[7] Quoted by Vit Wagner, ibid.

[8] Ibid.

[9] I am grateful to my colleague Dr. Natalie Rewa for enlightening discussions on *Newhouse*, and for a chance to read an unpublished version of her article, "All News Newhouse," which has subsequently appeared in *Canadian Theatre Review*, 61 (Winter 1989) 40-42, along with a text of *Newhouse*.

[10] Quoted by Vit Wagner, Drama packs arena, D5.

[11] Jon Kaplan, "Dramaturge Kugler redesigns the body," in *Now*, April 13-19, 1989, 49.

[12] Rewa, ibid.

[13] Quoted in Richard Paul Knowles, "'The Truth Must Out': The Political Plays of John Krizanc," in *Canadian Drama/L'Art dramatique canadien*, 13, 1, 1987, 28.

[14] From an interview with Richard Paul Knowles cited by Knowles, ibid., 30.

[15] Ann Jansen, "Interview John Krizanc," in *Books in Canada*, March 1988, 34.

[16] *Tamara* opened in Toronto on May 8, 1981; it was remounted at Dundurn Castle in Hamilton, Ontario in November 1981. The productions in Los Angeles (script revised), which opened in July 1984, and in New York (script revised again), which opened in November 1987, were still running in October 1989. The production in Mexico opened in November 1986.

[17] One of the ironies of *Tamara*'s history is that out of the gross income, John Krizanc has earned only approximately $24,000 (as of the date of the writing of this article). He has been advised that to claim the $60,000 he is entitled to would likely cost about $40,000 in legal fees.

[18] John Krizanc, *Tamara*, Toronto: Stoddart, 1989, 29.

[19] Isadora Duncan, *My Life*, New York: Liveright, 1955, 5-6.

[20] These characterizations are taken from the cast list published with the text of the play.

[21] Ann Jansen, Interview, 34.

[22] The publication of *Tamara* allows readers the opportunity to deal with the narrative in a linear fashion tying loose ends together. To some extent this linear experience is available to audience members who return, (as did the "Lifers" in Los Angeles) many times. But linearity is denied in a single attendance at performance.

[23] Ann Jansen, Interview, 36.

[24] John Beaufort, "If you don't warm to the play, maybe you'll like the buffet," in *The Christian Science Monitor*, December 21, 1987, 22.

[25] Knowles, 27-33.

[26] Mel Gussow, "The Stage: 'Tamara,'" in *New York Times*, December 3, 1987, Section 3, 24.

[27] Typical examples: Martin Hunter reviewing the play in publication referred to the production as a "gimmick" in *Toronto Star*, July 1, 1989; Mel Gussow in the *New York Times*, December 3, 1987: "There are references to politics and also to art of the period, but 'Tamara' is not to be taken too seriously. It is basically a clever diverting whodunit."

[28] John Krizanc, "Innocents Abroad," in *Saturday Night*, November 1984, 38.

[29] Ann Jansen, Interview, 34.

[30] Ibid.

Denis Salter

Ancestral Voices: The (European) Plays of John Murrell

Although he lives in Western Canada, which provides the setting for many of his major plays, John Murrell's imagination draws much of its sustenance from the intellectual and cultural preoccupations of nineteenth-century European romanticism. He has written adaptations of Ibsen, Chekhov, Sardou, Feydeau and Rostand; he has a passion for the operas of Puccini, Verdi, Wallace and Wagner; and his plays often require the kind of heightened acting styles and *tableau vivant* effects commonly employed in the staging of nineteenth-century opera and melodrama.

This indebtedness to nineteenth-century European culture contributes significantly to one of his recurring themes: the relationship between the artistic and moral values of the old world, on the one hand, and the new world, on the other. He tends to develop this theme through elaborate variations on the stereotyped characterization of the "fallen woman," whom Murrell depicts as a social misfit or alienated outsider, hemmed in by outmoded conventions of thought and behaviour and victimized by power-hungry men. Fundamentally a romantic spirit, she asserts her unique self-worth by flouting proprieties and by daring to search for her own utopian vision—no matter the personal cost. Predictably, Murrell imagines the old world as a place of limited opportunity, moribund traditions, and sexual and imaginative denial; the new world, in formulaic contrast, is treated as a place of infinite possibilities, innovation and sexual and imaginative freedom, where "isolation and longing"[1] force people to come to terms with who they are and who they might become....

Murrell's 1977 (and subsequently revised) play *Memoir* is a compact summary of all these themes and also reveals several of his typical

---

dramatic techniques. The main character is the nineteenth-century French actress Sarah Bernhardt who in 1922, at the age of 77, is sitting on the terrace of her estate on an island off the coast of Brittany. While dictating her memoirs to her secretary, Georges Pitou, she grows impatient with mere dictation and insists that she and Pitou enact together some of the important scenes and famous characters from her adventurous theatrical past. Gaining dramatic immediacy and concentration of effect from its single setting, as well as from its compressed twelve-hour time-span from dusk until dawn, the play, like memory itself, ranges widely in time and place. It allows us to see Bernhardt's whole life at a glance as a form of performance in which she has literally acted herself—or her various contradictory 'selves'—into existence. Her life has been spent as a form of romantic defiance against Puritanical strictness, bourgeois complacency, type-casting, and the dated acting conventions of the Comédie Française. During an imaginary vignette with Pitou playing Oscar Wilde, she says, "We are the last of our kind, Oscar Wilde! The last Romantics. The last bright banners of ego and happy selfishness.... We lived exactly as we chose, every moment of our lives" (118). Now, however, everything is changing: old, infirm and often bewildered, she is forced against her indomitable will to bear witness to what critic Keith Garebian has memorably described as "a single organic complex of existential decline."[2]

The play's image patterns are effective in their deliberate simplicity: the island (Belle-Île-en-Mer), possibly meant to remind us of Shakespeare's setting for *The Tempest*, represents Bernhardt's own isolated yet still powerful character; the sea, heard now and again throughout, conjures up the inexorable passing of time, and the hot glare of the sun is likened by Bernhardt herself to her own dynamic energy and to her own (inevitable) decline: "The sun. Engaged in the long process of burning itself to a cinder. So I'm told." And then she adds in what is essentially a moment of self-recognition: "Well—she won't be easy to replace!" (10). In a lighting pattern worthy of Adolphe Appia or Edward Gordon Craig, the setting sun at the start symbolizes her own coming death, the darkness of the night emblematizes her deepest fears of dying, and the rising sun of dawn, at the close, is a tribute to both her enduring strength of character and her ennobling art. (To highlight these symbolical connections, actress Siobhán McKenna was "swathed in a gigantic red silk robe"[3] during the second half of the 1978 London, England production.)

Despite the ever-present evocations of death, we are always being reminded by Murrell that this is the *Divine* Sarah. Through the lyrical intensity of her art, she can leave commonplace reality behind, to carry her audience into sensuous dreams and fantasies, into a world transfigured by her radiant spell. The play's dominant ethos of romantic existentialism remains unchallenged throughout, especially in the closing moments when she stares boldly at the morning sun and asks if it is afraid of death, then *"laughs, as though in acknowledgement of a positive response"* before posing her final equivocal question: "Yes?" (124).

From Murrell's romantic perspective, Bernhardt's life has been a form of secularized martyrdom in which she has sacrificed *everything* for the sake of her art. Her amputation, which is described in gruesome clinical detail by Pitou in the role of the surgeon, is merely another obstacle for her spirit to overcome. The play tends to suggest that art has a paradoxical function. Art's passionate intensity leads to moments of extraordinary self-realization (a kind of 'divine' consummation of the soul) and yet these moments can *only* come about when the self dies or pretends to assimilate itself into a transcendent moment out of time. Bernhardt has spent much of her career acting Marguerite Gauthier, Tosca and Phaedra, among others, in deeply felt scenes of protracted death which she repeats during the play. She believes that by dying well one can experience the pleasure of living well; that death can be cheated through the pretence of performance. In dictating and enacting her memoirs, she can retheatricalize her life, repudiating the normal limits of time, space and character to achieve the illusion of eternity.

For her, the old world of Europe is not to be feared or hated: its classic plays constitute her repertoire; her mercurial temperament is quintessentially 'French'. Nevertheless, the stages of Europe are too small for her dreams: she makes numerous tours of the whole world, including the United States, where she discovers hidden parts of her complex personality. American audiences are so mesmerised by her dance-of-death as Marguerite Gauthier, her "Lady of the Camellias," that she finds herself reaching ever higher states of irradiating ecstasy. In Oregon, moreover, she shoots a huge brown bear that grins at her as he dies, teaching her to do likewise. She keeps the fur, wrapping herself in it now and again as a reminder of what she has learned—as a powerful theatrical image it conveys the dark and ancient mystery of death. Bernhardt is effectively a transitional figure for Murrell; her romantic quest for herself is enhanced by her willingness to cross back and forth between the old and new worlds.

Murrell's Bernhardt is of course not literally a 'fallen woman,' but she is a variant of the type: remarkably independent for her time, her early decision to abandon the convent for a life in the theatre gives off a strong whiff of fire and brimstone, of *danger*. The only substantial obstacles to her 'martyr's creed of the self' are her unscrupulous manager William E. Jarrett and her degenerate husband Ambroise-Aristide

Damala. This theme of the man as a constant threat to a woman's integrity is more fully developed in Murrell's subsequent plays, including *Waiting for the Parade* (1977), which dramatizes the lives of five Calgary women as they await the ending of World War II. The five women—Marta, Catherine, Janet, Margaret and Eve—are much more conventional in their beliefs and actions than Sarah Bernhardt, but just as effectively, *Waiting for the Parade* raises some troubling (and ultimately unanswered) questions about the problems that strong-minded women have faced in trying to break free from male oppression.

Men never actually appear in the play but their presence is felt at almost every turn. They are all preoccupied with what Murrell tends to suggest are mainly old world ideas about war and heroism. The women, despite their repressed doubts, are also carried away at times by these jingoistic ideals. Eve's husband Harry is so upset by being declared too old for active service that he compensates by childishly making the noise of a machine gun every morning at breakfast and by joining the local constabulary; Catherine fears that her husband Billy, who goes missing with his battalion at Dieppe, has been killed or taken prisoner of war; and Janet's husband Jack remains behind in Canada in 'essential service' as a radio news announcer but wishes, as does his embittered wife, that he had been sent overseas. One of Margaret's sons serves on the convoy ships criss-crossing the Atlantic to avoid German U-boats; but the other is imprisoned for joining an anti-war campaign, and she is so exhausted by worry and shame that she dies near the end just as Armistice is declared. Leslie Howard's film *Intermezzo* provides a model of *gentlemanly* heroism that the women admire but which the men deprecate: Eve's husband Harry calls Howard "'[t]oo fussy and feminine'" (11) and is jealous of his wife's infatuation with a mere film star. When Leslie Howard himself dies in his plane during enemy action, however, Eve's naive faith in the war as a kind of romantic game is somewhat undermined, although she never reaches the point of asking hard questions about what the war is really meant to achieve.

As its title suggests, the play is a Beckett-like study of the phenomenon of 'waiting' as experienced by characters who are essentially passive. A European war, thousands of miles away, directs every event in their lives, while they fill Red Cross boxes with medical supplies, make up packages of treats for the soldiers, or go through the absurdity of rehearsing emergency procedures in the event of a direct enemy attack. As they wait, they dream of a different life (Eve), pray to God for help (Margaret), work unreasonably hard, becoming stern and unyielding (Janet), flirt a little (Catherine) or rail against the stupidity of the Canadian government (Marta). There is little they can do to alter the outcome of the war, or at least change the supportive roles to which they have been assigned. Nonetheless, they say or do a number of subversive things that suggest that they would like to do a good deal more than merely await the arrival of a military parade signalling the war's end. Catherine, for instance, is proud when her husband Billy is one of the first men to enlist, yet she observes that "somewhere inside a man's big skull, along with the honour and the glory—and the charm—there ought to be some space for good sense and—a little mutual respect" (9); and in a particularly poignant moment, Eve cries out: "They're bombing Great Britain! They're bombing France! They're bombing Norway! They're bombing Belgium! We're back in the Dark Ages! Wasting lives, spilling blood all over Europe!" (25).

The play's title is *not* a celebration of war but is meant to be darkly ironic. Through a *tableau vivant* at the beginning and a variation of it at the end, Murrell makes it clear that the women, despite their elation over the Armistice, are nonetheless wondering if their protracted waiting has in fact meant anything useful at all. In the first tableau, to the sound of a Glenn Miller swing tune, Janet tries to dance with each of the women in turn; but none of them dances with her for long, because she is too stern and because they are reminded that their husbands are not there to dance with them. In the second *tableau vivant*, to the sound of a contemporary 1945 swing tune, Janet again tries to dance with the women, and again they are reluctant—this time they cannot concentrate because they keep listening for the sounds of the long-expected military parade. However, when the parade finally comes their reaction to it is not as jubilant as we might expect. As the military march, with symbolic significance, drowns out the swing tune, Marta is motionless, Janet *"can't believe what's happening"* (96), Eve cries, and Catherine waves, presumably to her approaching husband Billy. The scene then suddenly goes to blackout while the march gets *"louder and louder"* (96). The elegiac tone here, together with the women's mixed responses and the aggressive noises of the military march, are very much at odds with the celebratory atmosphere of a victory parade.

As in *Memoir*, these dance-tableaus are in effect dances-of-death in which the playwright visualizes his recurring theme of the life-force in paradoxical search of itself. Contrary to its initial critical response,[4] *Waiting For the Parade* is *not* merely a documentary excursion into World War II period nostalgia. Instead, it takes a moderately sceptical view towards the brutality of war, and the male ethos of heroism; and it articulates a number of *incipient* feminist ideas about the establishment of peace, the overthrow of both public and personal forms of tyranny, and the need to resist stereotyped modes of behaviour.

European perspectives dominate in both *Memoir* and *Waiting for the Parade*; in his 1982 play *Farther West*, however, Murrell tries, as the title indicates, to separate himself from these influences by examining some of the distinctive historic, mythic and moral characteristics of the Canadian West. Loosely based on a real-life incident, the play dramatizes the experiences of a prostitute called May Buchanan as she travels ever 'farther west', from Rat Portage (now Kenora), Ontario in 1886 to Calgary in the Northwest Territories and then onward to Vancouver on the Pacific Coast where she dies in 1892. Much of the writing in the play is accomplished; but much of it is also embarrassingly awkward. The central question, at every point, is this: in what kind(s) of dramatic language are the characters meant to be speaking?

As a nineteenth-century version of the romantic existentialist, May Buchanan's first (interrogative) word in the text is "Next?" (15). She is in fact referring to her 'next' lover, but as a refrain throughout the text, it summarizes her obsession with leaving both the past and the present behind in order to embrace an uncertain future. Her name, May, is meant to suggest eternal rebirth in the spring, the person she 'may' become as she travels ever westward, fully experiencing the 'farthest' reaches of her own identity. Who am I? What kind of person can I be? What, after all, is the self I assume as my own? These are the kinds of questions that she asks, both implicitly and explicitly. May Buchanan is modelled after Sarah Bernhardt. Yet there is at least one significant difference between them. A self-styled romantic, Murrell's Bernhardt never feels compelled to question the premises by which she has so fiercely lived. Thus in the re-enacted scene with Oscar Wilde, she disparages contemporary, (merely) democratic values and asks: "Do you think they will understand what it was like, for us, to live without knowledge? To be so *alive* that *Death* was the only thing impossible to imagine?" (118). But for May Buchanan, the bedrock moral certainties of the nineteenth-century have given way to twentieth-century doubts: as she journeys ever farther westward, she experiences several existential crises of identity.

But despite this significant difference, the characterization of May Buchanan throughout the play is often hobbled by Murrell's excessive reliance on the Bernhardt prototype. At times a ludicrously overwritten character with a limited emotional and intellectual range, May often amounts to nothing more than the stereotype of the seductive whorehouse madame. As she is dying, her prostitute-friend Violet refers to her as "Angel," "baby" (84) and indirectly as "Mother of Christ" (86); the deranged Seward, a symbol of traditional moral authority and shame, has only moments before likened her to Babylon and the Devil (79); and her lover Thomas Shepherd (the good shepherd?) idealizes her as a woman redeemed, an image supported by the frequently repeated song, "The Bluest Eyes," with its key words, "A skin so fine, /Divine" (90).

Murrell has described Martha Henry, who played May Buchanan in the 1982 première at Theatre Calgary, as ideal for the part, because she "is an extraordinary combination of the mysterious and the earthy. I would like to think that when I'm writing my very best, my characters have that combination, too. I think that anybody who has seen Martha in film or on the stage would agree that she's very sexy yet, finally, enormously unavailable to the rest of the human race. It's a terribly exciting combination that has fascinated writers throughout history."[5] In keeping with this emphasis on earthiness and mystery, two of May Buchanan's prostitutes—Violet Decarmin and Lily Reeves—have flower names, and a third, Nettie McDowell, is compared early on to an idealized golden-haired woman in a medieval picture book (24). The play never allows its women characters to become anything more significant than deified and/or defiled: these are intractable categories and interfere with Murrell's occasional attempts to liberate his text from nineteenth-century dramatic conventions.

A related difficulty is Murrell's weakness for overstatement and his self-confessed love affair with words.[6] Urjo Kareda's introduction to the published edition of *Farther West* praises Murrell's rich use of language and notes the influence of Murrell's versions of *Uncle Vanya* and *The Seagull* on his work (8). Murrell himself has acknowledged his debt to Chekhov, particularly in learning how to differentiate behaviour and dialogue in exterior and interior scenes.[7] Although *Farther West* is obsessively logocentric, Murrell has felt compelled to elaborate the text with sound effects, musical reprises, and snatches of song, along with heightened *tableaus*—such as the rushing train at the end of the first act or the image of the dead May floating out to sea in a row boat, going ever 'farther west' at the close. He also creates a visual poetry of interrelated image-patterns—for example, Seward's burnt hand representing the fires of retribution and purification that haunt his fundamentalist imagination, along with Shepherd's bleeding hand, emblematic of both the blood-money with which he tries to buy May Buchanan for himself and the spiritual "hellfire!" (72) of his unrequited love for her. Despite these evocative images, the actual words of *Farther West* are often disappointing. They can be hackneyed, as in May's line, "No rules, no laws, no judges" (47) to explain why she needs to travel farther West; or inflated, as in Seward's description of the dead whore Lily Reeves, "Bloated and burst like a poisoned dog!" (7); or simply pedestrian, like the dialogue in a John Wayne cowboy film, as in Shepherd's attempts to persuade May to marry him: "May! Nothing's changed! Not a thing! You traveled on, like you thought you had to! But I traveled on too! I found you! We can go on traveling, if that's what you want! But together! I love you! Nothing has changed!" (73). As in this last quotation, the text bristles throughout with exclamation marks, suggesting that it lacks the courage of its own convictions and so is forced to compensate through ludicrous over-statement.

Despite—or perhaps because of—its verbal preoccupations, *Farther West* also asks questions about whether May Buchanan can find a way 'to speak' her identity in a language commensurate with her existential search for herself. Early in the play, the prostitute Lily Reeves (who functions throughout as a symbol of sin, decay and, finally, death) sings some lines from Wallace's romantic opera *Maritana* about how language can be deceptive, giving little more than false hope: "Words cannot scatter/The thoughts we fear, / For though they flatter, / They mock the ear!" (23). Later, May Buchanan recognizes that words, contrary to her expectations, *cannot* set her free from the social conventions which she defies:

> Words! Nettie McDowell had a few words, like bubbles on her lip, sweet! Words can't free her now! ...Lily Reeves! Had words and songs too—enough to howl, to cry for help! But she's dead, helpless, rotten, and quicklime at her cry!! Violet Decarmin, swiping at men and demons with a tongue like a razor! But I could tell her, men and demons always come back! (80-81).

May's insight that words are coined and manipulated by men to acquire power over women is given horrifying expression in the scene in which Shepherd rapes her at pistol point because she has refused to submit to his (sexual) will; at one critical moment, he says: "I'll make this flesh hear me then! I'll make the inside listen—since the outside wants to be deaf!!" (81). Meanwhile, the disembodied voice of Violet 'the flower' comes from the next room, singing the refrain, "'A skin so fine, / Divine—'" (82), a refrain that creates a deeply ironic complement to this act of brutalization. How can May Buchanan liberate herself, then, not merely from the past and the aptly named Rat Portage with its hidebound morality, but also from both Shepherd and Seward, the two men who want to destroy her, with violent actions and violent words, as each of them is driven by a rigid system of male-dominated values?

The answer is an old-fashioned one: here, as in *Memoir*, Murrell makes his characters yearn for dematerialized transcendent experiences in which the normal self dies and is redeemed through a kind of quasi-mystical transfiguration. May Buchanan is inspired by a spiritual sensibility: though she spends most of the play on the western prairie, she is drawn, in quasi-spiritual affinity, to water. Water, for her, cleanses the world of sickness, purifies the soul, and accounts for her ineffable desire for the Pacific Ocean, for the 'next' phase of her quest romance. It also reminds her of evanescence and death, as things, events and people dissolve, as it were, into the past. Defining herself in relationship to the ever-receding frontier she has only one certainty, however tentative, and that is herself: "It all gets washed away," she explains to the confused Shepherd. "Except myself" (48).

The text has a complex image-pattern in order to schematize its pervasive life-in-death theme. At key moments, the text expresses a powerful sense of disgust: towards death, sin and illicit desire, articulated through images of mud, dust, marsh, worms, maggots and blood-suckers; and yet, at the same time, it expresses an equally powerful mystical yearning towards beatitude and redemption, a kind of Bernhardt-inspired secularized 'divinity', conveyed through images of silk, flowers, skin and, of course, water itself. The première, directed by Robin Phillips at Theatre Calgary in 1982, dressed the women in white during the laundry scene in the backyard of May's house and also during the scene at Nose Creek, just before the end of the first act, where Shepherd and Seward wind up fighting over May. This deliberate idealization of the 'feminine' made itself felt in many parts of the *mise-en-scène*, giving a paradoxically rarefied quality to the theme of repressed eroticism. Other productions, like Duncan McIntosh's at the Tarragon Theatre in 1986, have instead chosen to emphasize the images of mud, blood and sweat, to underscore the counter-balancing theme of sexual defilement and death.

Despite his efforts to locate his play within both the reality and the myth of the Canadian West, at the end Murrell falls back on a clichéd final liberation for May through the deliberate reworking of the conventions of nineteenth-century romantic opera and melodrama. After the crazed Seward pushes May's dead body out to sea in a rowboat, he says, as he watches her disappear into the distance, "Free now. Safe. Pure.... Go on. Go on. Go on. Go on. That's it. Go on. Go on." (88), as his insistent repetitions seem to buoy up the rowboat itself. Phillips suggested in an interview that Murrell's May Buchanan does in fact find her liberation "'perhaps not unhappily, in death.'"[8] The final moments are like the ending of *Memoir* or any number of nineteenth-century operas: "[*Darkness. Seabirds, ships' horns and bells, as though dawn were approaching.*]" (88). This traditional *tableau vivant*, in which the self yields itself up to the mysteries of the great beyond, does not allow May to embrace the new world for which she has been searching, but effectively returns her to the values of the old world from which she has sought to escape. Is Murrell perhaps trying to suggest that the old and new worlds are inseparable? Or is this a case in which his nineteenth-century Eurocentric dramatic methods and his 'modern' Canadian character-drawing remain disturbingly incommensurate?

Murrell is on surer ground with *New World* (1984), which is literally set on the shores of the Pacific Ocean, at China Beach, beginning, in other words, at the point at which *Farther West* comes to an end. The play is a literate comedy of (bad) manners, in which three different nationalities test out their reactions to the new world: the British (Bet, Bob and Larry Rennie), the Americans (Larry's wife Carla and their daughter Linda), and the Canadians (Jean, from Québec, who has been Bob's 'companion' for a number of years and Peter, an aspiring poet). As in *Waiting for the Parade* and *Farther West*, the characters try to disengage themselves, to a degree, from European (or European-derived) assumptions and behaviour. Bob has become a photographer, rather than a painter, taking pictures of the rich and famous in Hollywood; Larry has become an obnoxious Californian, and gets his kicks from technological gimmickry, suntans, and gee-whiz expressions; and Bet, the most impressively drawn character in the play, is a failed painter who is at home in the damp greyness of English life but nonetheless yearns for the high-energy openness (but not the vacuity) of this brave new world. Carla and Linda are set up as stereotypes of American trendiness, naive optimism and shallowness. Jean and Peter are lacklustre Canadians: it is hard to tell if this is just inadequate playwriting or a satire on a so-called national trait.

The dominant imagery in the play is similar to *Memoir* and *Farther West*: the ocean itself represents a fresh start, and also invites much wished-for oblivion. Bet, for example, weary of her old self, wants to be swallowed up by an enormous "black wave!" (114)—like Bernhardt, by destroying herself, Bet hopes to realize herself more completely than ever before. In frequently referring to other works of art, the text locates itself in a wider cultural context so that each character's spiritual dilemma takes on symbolic importance. Carla and Jean, for example, flirt with each other by listening to Puccini's *Girl of the Golden West*, which Carla's husband Larry, ever the contemporary technophile, jealously tries to drown out with the noise of one of his video-cassettes. Bob is fond of reciting Whitman on the joyful possibilities of life in the new world; and, at the close, Bet starts reciting from *The Tempest*, to express the "sea-change" which she and some of the play's other characters have been undergoing in the transformational atmosphere of China Beach.

Here, as at the end of both *Memoir* and *Farther West*, the desire to celebrate what one has been—and what one might become—is symbolized by the arrival of dawn. In a high comedy version of *entente cordiale*,

Linda the American, Peter the Canadian and Bob the Brit invite Bet to join them in a sleeping bag on the beach by a dying fire. As Peter and Linda hum some Puccini and continue gesturing hopefully towards her, Bet hesitates, for as she had remarked earlier on, she is a person who can "sometimes stand at a threshold for hours" (101). Yet there is a sense that she is now at peace with her new found self, and that she does not need to acknowledge this insight with the histrionic gestures and triumphant death-throes of Sarah Bernhardt or May Buchanan. Nonetheless, like both of her prototypes, she is a mediating character who seeks to embrace old and new forms of experience, as the 'ancestral voices' of Shakespeare and Puccini, and the 'new voices' of Whitman and the Pacific Ocean sound deep within the 'farthest' reaches of *her* being. Through that exacting combination of "isolation and longing" that Murrell sees as central to the experience of the new world, Bet is now ready to cross over that intractable "threshold" to become absolutely anyone she wishes to be....

NOTES

For financial assistance with the research on which this article is based, I am grateful to the Social Sciences and Humanities Research Council of Canada.

[1] Brian Brennan, "The theatre world according to John Murrell," in *Calgary Herald*, January 18, 1986.

[2] Keith Garebian, "The Magic Craft: John Murrell's poetic theatre," in *The Canadian Forum*, 66 (May 1986), 36.

[3] Bernard Levin, "The secret life of divine Sarah," in *Sunday Times*, January 15, 1978.

[4] Brian Brennan, "Play about wartime Calgary mainly of historical interest," in *Calgary Herald*, February 5, 1977 and Jay Scott (Scott Beaven, pseud.), "Locally written play has abundance of blessings," in *The Albertan*, February 7, 1977.

[5] Quoted in Robert Wallace, "Interview: John Murrell," in *Books in Canada*, 15 (April 1986), 40-41.

[6] See Louise Bresky, "Profile: John Murrell," in *CityScope* [Calgary] (January-Febrary 1986), 47.

[7] Cf. Wallace, "Interview: John Murrell," 40.

[8] Quoted in Brian Brennan, "Phillips praises Murrell as 'best,'" in *Calgary Herald* (April 10, 1982).

BIBLIOGRAPHY

Brennan, Brian. "Phillips praises Murrell as 'best,'" *Calgary Herald* April 10, 1982.

———. "Play about wartime Calgary mainly of historical interest," *Calgary Herald* February 5, 1977.

———. "The theatre world according to John Murrell," *Calgary Herald* January 18, 1986.

Bresky, Louise. "Profile: John Murrell," *CityScope* [Calgary] (January-February 1986), 46-47.

Garebian, Keith. "The Magic Craft: John Murrell's poetic theatre," *The Canadian Forum* 66 (May 1986), 34-38.

Levin, Bernard. "The secret life of divine Sarah," *Sunday Times* January 15, 1978.

Murrell, John. *Farther West/New World*. Toronto: Coach House Press, 1985.

———. *Memoir*. New York: Avon Books, 1978.

———. *Waiting for the Parade*. Vancouver: Talonbooks, 1980.

Scott, Jay [Scott Beaven, pseud.]. "Locally written play has abundance of blessings," *The Albertan* February 7, 1977.

Wallace, Robert. "Interview: John Murrell," *Books in Canada* 15, 3 (April 1986), 38, 40-41.

Patricia Keeney

James Reaney:
Playmaker

In his study of James Reaney, Ross G. Woodman identifies this artist's major motivation as "an attempt to make imaginative sense out of the various props provided by the accidents of his birth, family, and environment."[1] These include a long, loving residency in southwestern Ontario, Ulster ancestry, and an evangelical family. It is Reaney's mode, especially in his earliest work, to universalize the personal, to leap from the anecdotal to the mythic; therefore he turns many aspects of an individual history to poetic and dramatic purposes.

In much of Reaney's early writing, the recreation of his "Souwesto," as described by his son J. Stewart Reaney in his profile for Gage, is accomplished through patterns of imagery. This is as true for the poetry in *The Red Heart* (1949), as for early plays like *The Killdeer*. Critics have described the emotional content of these as aesthetic, feelings more in response to imaginative form than to the plight of people. Yet this world, as Margaret Atwood points out in an article for *Canadian Literature*, is not an innocent one. It is often violent and macabre, full of spiritual exiles. Atwood writes that it was probably Northrop Frye (most often associated with the so-called mythopoeic school of poetry), under whom Reaney studied as a graduate student, who made him realize that escape from a terrifying world could be made through the imagination, through the agents of memory and verbal magic.[2]

Until the writing of his Donnelly trilogy, however, Reaney seems to step directly from the hell of earth right up to transcendent vision. It is in this major tragedy that he manages to unite not only poetic impressionism with the earthy details of rural life, but also his antiquarian and teaching abilities with his verbal wizardry. Reaney sees the Biddulph tragedy as an attempt to apply the techniques he's collected through years of drama workshop experiments to a story in the past with all its longhand archival detail. The trilogy weaves together many disparate strands of Reaney's various talents and interests. He is equally poet and playwright, as well as historian, improvisor and master of ceremonies whose entertainment is profound enough to alter the way we see things.

For James Reaney, play *is* life, poetry and theatre. Imaginative play, through which the child learns and the adult rediscovers, infuses Reaney's very individual art. He can never get enough of "games...imitation itself. The instinct to just 'have fun'—to make a pattern simply because like a whooping crane we can't help doing a spring dance with our bodies."[3] Twice, though, first in the long poem, *A Suit of Nettles* (1958), and then in his Donnelly trilogy of the mid-seventies, the game itself got serious, became richly imaginative in its power to produce works of tragic proportion. The joyful dance, the rapturous free-flowing celebration of life through language more characteristic of the writer's early children's plays like *Names and Nicknames*, finally insisted on its birthright as tragic drama. Thus with his sweeping tragedy, *The Donnellys*, James Reaney found himself playing for keeps. Between the two, however, there winds a long and adventurous yellow brick road.

Colours in the Dark, Reaney's first major script to be generally praised, parades life—"an endless procession of stories, an endless coloured comic strip, things to listen to and look at, a bottomless playbox."[4] It takes place in the head of a boy confined to a bed in a darkened room with measles. His sea of consciousness brings him from a personal past to future, like a journeying everyman. Reaney associates freely against the grid of our commonplace controls: days of the week, colours, the alphabet, street names. As always, he uses the techniques of total theatre—song, dance, choral work, fragments of poems, slides that bring his central character from child to hero to the edge of social awareness. It's drama in an original sense—ritual born of multiple vision, an enchanting, mesmerizing imitation of the life process, expressed like a refrain, through the "existence song"—existence gives a pebble, a dewdrop, a piece of string, a straw. They become respectively a menacing hill to be climbed, a lake to be crossed, a hidden road, an obscure sign; by play's end, they return to their initial simplicity. In this way, Reaney invents his own creation myth. From his own background he draws the local, specific items that stubbornly will not render up their identities, but stand out, embossments on a fading circular frieze: glacier, forest, Indians, Britannica, gooseberries, the history of a set of dishes, Orangemen's Day. Yet, *Colours* feels static, only a blueprint for dramatic action rather than a fully realized drama.

In his early plays, then, Reaney's methods are dazzlingly, even distractingly theatrical; what they lack is the force of story and character, as the author seems satisfied to conjure with impressions. His very subject *is* play, the magic of the medium exuberantly evoked. His people travel from innocence to innocence, only dreaming the intervening experience, rehearsing for actual life. The passions of a Medea or a Lear are not to be found. Reaney has yet to travel from the games people play to the joyful freedom born of real suffering.

With *Listen to the Wind* (written by 1966) Reaney has still not taken that step towards tragedy; the tragic fall remains child's make-believe (it is, of course, a children's play). Reaney has consistently found his inspirations for the stage while working with young actors. And in this play-within-a-play, a group of youngsters spend their summer enacting their adaptation of a quintessentially melodramatic Victorian novel, *The Saga of Caresfoot Court*. In a production for Althouse College, London, in 1966, he used fourteen child actors as his set and props. They were "trees in the forest, the wind, a pack of mad hound-dogs"[5] and so on. This practice of using actors as props has become a stumbling block of Reaney's drama for many critics who regard his enthusiastic pantomimes as over-explanatory.[6]

Certainly Reaney has baffled, even alienated, elements of the professional theatre. Practising what he preaches, the man doesn't just talk community theatre, he *makes* it, often using amateurs to investigate through his workshops facets of their own psychic and social pasts. In the early, somewhat transparent pieces, the playwright's visual literalizations call attention to themselves. When embedded deeply in the texture of his Donnelly trilogy, however, such techniques, once dismissed as heavily contrived spontaneity, are as right as masks and elevated shoes were to classical Greek Theatre.

The rich vein of tragedy in Reaney's imagination can be traced back to its beginnings. Jay MacPherson, a fellow writer in the so-called mythopoeic school, connects the slight story of Owen in *Listen to the Wind*, fighting illness and trying to get his parents together again, with the Branwell of Reaney's long poem, *A Suit of Nettles*. Branwell takes on the mantle of the poet-soul. In her *Canadian Forum* article of 1966, MacPherson goes further to identify the "explosive confrontations" that characterize the Caresfoot Court episodes of *Listen to the Wind*. The same contrast between wistfulness and brutality animates *A Suit of Nettles* and culminates in Reaney's Donnelly trilogy where the author's tragic muse is most impressively evident.

Tragedy is not inconsistent with the optimism of games and play since it finds ultimate release in a liberating joy. After the massacre of the Donnellys, for instance, Reaney could not possibly have missed the chance to bring them back as ghosts, full of mischief to work on modern souvenir hunters, who (according to the actual legend) revisit the graveside annually, drinking beer and waiting for visitations. Members of the dead clan oblige. And at the end of the visitation Johannah and James Donnelly unite in a lyric that fixes their place as the progenitors of fruitful, elemental life: "I was a child once, a spring/I became a river when my body united with his/hers/From that river came seven sons and one daughter." Tom, the youngest son and a true seer, continues: "look we are everywhere/In the clouds, in the treebranch, in the puddle."[7]

Like the trilogy, *A Suit of Nettles* encompasses real life. It does not evaporate into light and air before you have got a handle on it, or rely on tricks of illusion the way many of Reaney's theatre pieces seem, ingeniously, to do. Though populated by the barnyard geese of south-western Ontario, the poem gives us genuine personalities, riddled with idiosyncracy. Essentially the theme of *Nettles* is one Reaney never abandons—the forces of creativity, of human potential battling to convert a cold and hostile world.

From the outset, one can *hear* Reaney's poem—the primitive chanting of ancient drama in which participants drum up fertility (now poetic imagination) from the very earth itself and beat it "into a sterile land" with a stick that replenishes itself, a cut vine. Reaney's violent Muse of Satire must beat the four senses of all dullards into blossoming.[8] Similarly, the Barley Corn Ballad that provides the lyrical substructure of *Sticks and Stones* (Part I of the Donnelly trilogy) returns us to Dionysian dismemberment, which for Nietzsche signified the very birth of tragedy. The reeling Irish tune, merrily innocent in its praise of whiskey, is ultimately about the cycles and seasons of the natural year and of human existence which, in a rural community, are almost synonymous. And it prefigures the martyrdom of the sovereign Donnellys, as well as their subsequent triumph: "They sold me to the brewer/and he brewed me on the pan/But when I got into the jug/I was the strongest man."[9] The Donnelly individuals leap forward from Branwell's quiet, serious questing ("is there purpose in the pulse one gathers/Wristful by wristful?")[10] to definite, if inchoate self-knowledge. They know who they are and why they're alive, but must finally sacrifice everything to retain the uniqueness which is their birthright. Without this essential struggle, tragedy is not possible. Arthur Miller extends this idea in an essay called "Tragedy and the Common Man," where he identifies the heroes as those who "act against the scheme of things that degrades them." The figure of real stature is "intent upon claiming his whole due as a personality," for the achievement of which he may have to wield an indestructible, even inhuman will.[11] Keith Turnbull, for years a very sympathetic director of Reaney's work, voices similar sentiments about the Donnellys: their ability to create a world from within themselves that would counter external pettiness was an irresistible magnet for him.

Though the trilogy's philistines of Biddulph township may be blundering, self-centred, brutal men, they are no more sinister than the icy Mopsus of *Nettles* who tempts Branwell from the sting of his five senses: "Come to my ferny groves by calm canals / Where all is bland correct and rational."[12] The latter's imaginative fires seem sadly extinguished ("I used to see a rat and then observe a robin, / But now the bird seems but a rat with wings"),[13] especially when he is compared to the Donnellys who retain their proud selfhood to the end. It is captured many times in the trilogy; strikingly in the image of Mrs. Donnelly, her arms raised for the dance she cannot, despite the worst adversity, stop dancing.

In *A Suit of Nettles*, restrictive mentality is represented at one point, by "two strange geese of the scientific variety"[14] busily dispensing birth control information. They are farcically trounced. In contrast, James and Johannah Donnelly produce from their loins brave and troublesome sons, impishly pictured throughout as shirts flapping assertively, hauntingly on a constant clothesline. In *The Donnellys*, Reaney's originality is partly due to the risks he takes in investing the ordinary and the domestic with tragic significance. By comparison, the poem's inventiveness seems clever and literary. In both books, savage destruction is inevitable and almost equally terrifying. For geese, it's the almost cartoon-like grotesquerie of the farmer's chopping block at Christmastime, on which heads are severed from plump bodies for the greasy feast. The Donnelly family experience an extermination, as dark as anything in the old revenge chronicles. There may be those capable of a stoic acceptance in death, but Reaney writes no such consolation into his Donnelly story. That family must be bloodily uprooted from their deep clutch on life; their suffering is real and intense, despite foreknowledge, or rather because of it.

The Donnellys are dimly aware of their fate from the beginning. The trilogy repeatedly foreshadows events, a technique that in no way diminishes the terrible tension along which it stretches and strains. This is no conventional murder mystery; nevertheless, there are thrills, portents, an atmosphere full of threat where each word and each step might bring down the heavens or convulse the earth. The problem arises because one is different in the close, claustrophobic world of Biddulph, a largely Irish township in nineteenth century Ontario. Maintaining a free private life, let alone Olympian isolation, is virtually impossible. On stage, interconnections are menacingly imaged by means of ladders that square off farms and lives and provide obstacles to be crossed. The country was divided into concessions, the boundaries of which crackled with family feuds. Roman Line, Church Line, Chapel Line; as Mrs. Donnelly, in the weighted prose of Reaney's play, puts it, "the road you lived on could destroy you, just like that."[15] And destroy her family it does.

The Donnelly trilogy documents a time when politics and religion marked a man for life. James Donnelly has come from Ireland to escape violent factionalism, secret societies, Blackfeet, Whitefeet and vigilante committees. Like a whirlwind these follow the family to an already infested New World, where their instinctive independence drives the community mad. Reaney, ever an advocate of creative community, here exalts the solidarity of the individual family. Reprisals for irregular behaviour are swift and primitive—non-conformists are rolled around in a barrel of thorn tree branches until they learn obedience.

So, the playwright has taken a single gruesome episode in Canadian history—the butchery of five Donnellys at Lucan on February 4, 1880—recreated it dramatically and imaginatively in a manner that none the less rejected histrionic, popular/sensationalist versions such as T.P. Kelley's 1954 Black Donnelly. Sticks and Stones premièred in 1973 at the Tarragon Theatre in Toronto to reviews that regarded it as totally unique. The amazement did not cease with Part II, The St. Nicholas Hotel, which opened at the Tarragon in 1974, nor with Handcuffs, the third part, in 1975. Then in 1975 members of the NDWT (Ne'er-Do-Well Thespians) theatre company joined hands and decided, as James Reaney puts it, "to tour the trilogy from sea to sea."[16]

The catalytic event of Sticks and Stones is Jim Donnelly's drunken, angry (accidental?) killing of Pat Farl at a logging bee. The slaughter is no surprise, having been preceded by Farl's taunts and goads. As Jim Donnelly puts it to Johannah after an earlier confrontation with his enemy: "ever since that day you told me they'd been calling our son that [i.e. Blackfoot] in the churchyard it's as if a thousand little tinkly pebbles keep batting up against the windows in my mind just when it's a house that's about to sleep. I didn't kill him, this time."[17] Inevitability is the long connecting thread. Donnelly gets a jail sentence of seven years; his wife, a dusty road-fighting woman, makes her valiant pilgrimage between Biddulph and Goderich to plead for her man. Certainly, the woman here represents gritty truth brought up against the oily mendacity and commercialism of official civilization. Certainly she and her brood inspire in us all what Keith Turnbull called a need to rise above the greyness. What we remember of her trek are ladders, short and long, over which she must climb, the hardship endured, and her stubborn tenacity. As he concentrates on the sensations of her trip, Reaney manages to universalize Johannah's mission in a spare poetry, which, as always, transforms the coarse homespun event into myth.

Reaney's muse weaves in and out of time, and specific activities become leitmotifs, revisited again and again. For instance, Mrs. Donnelly's journey anticipates the essence of *The St. Nicholas Hotel* which gives us life as a race, a rollicking, dangerous relay between beginning and end. With its stagecoach war and its shivaree, the second play lightens grim foreboding somewhat by accenting lusty hijinks and youthful spirits. The playwright's heroes, possessing a natural superiority, are able to express his tragic muse exuberantly. Indeed, the Donnelly's carry with them more than a little of that classic sin, *hubris*, precisely because they overflow with energy and power. The stifling world of nineteenth century southwestern Ontario cannot contain them and they know it. So their moments of laughter and lyricism, though bound by mortal clay, seem inspired—Will Donnelly, for instance with his appealing, bitter-sweet quality, fiddling down a hostile crowd to the tune of "Boney Over the Alps." There is a scene from *Sticks and Stones* that recalls all the ghosts of Shakespearean tragedy: Johannah is with her spirit, "a ghost lady with a lamp," who chides her [i.e. Johannah = Judith]: "There were ladders with certain rungs, Judith, you could have avoided, you know"[18] and warns her that her nemesis, Cassleigh, will catch up with her because, by night, he can never forget the humiliation she thrust upon him. It's a touching moment recalling that, while Reaney's trilogy is complete, it can never be finished, since, like all masterpieces in the genre, it implies many more acts.

After *The Donnellys,* James Reaney wanted to rein in a while, so he returned to several regional projects. The result was *Baldoon*, a witch-ridden mystery written with Marty Gervais taken from a curious chapter in the history of the Wallaceburg area of Baldoon, settled in 1804 by Scottish families. The following year (1977), Toronto saw *The Dismissal*, presented again by Turnbull's NDWT theatre company, but this time at Hart House, an appropriate setting for a play that tells the story of the University's student strike in 1895 with William Lyon Mackenzie King as a 20-year-old villain. Then there was *Wacousta* (also produced by NDWT). Based on what has been called the first Canadian novel, this historical drama is as theatrical as the rest, set in George III's British North America at the time of the Pontiac conspiracy. It merges images of native lacrosse with shuttlecock and identifies Detroit as a serpent's egg hatching millions of cars into its modern steel megalopolis. Like most of Reaney's work, *Wacousta* evolved out of workshop, that vital process by which community and professionals make theatre, and this time native people also participated.

One of the last landmarks along James Reaney's abruptly shifting path has taken him back to community and local issues. Rather like the dreaming children of his early plays, he has come full circle, but through and not around the mire of experience. After the innocent pleasure of child's play-acting, after ringing tragedy that plays for keeps, where do you go when your imagination insists on creating the whole of life's journey? Well, you go to a factory strike that radically divided people in your own home town over fifty years ago. Indeed, you return to the people at large, to involvement and social awareness. You also, of course, have fun. Hence, *King Whistle!*—produced at Stratford in November, 1979. It brings us back down to the urban, not elemental, earth, for a passionate romp through local history.

Some critics cringe when Reaney gets his hometown spectacles on. Having felt the roaring flame of the Donnellys, they will not settle for a fire in a grate. Consequently, *King Whistle!* has been called by some a documentary pageant of dated style. The content seems anachronistic and reads like a straightforward morality play, with Money tempting people as thoroughly as the devil himself and taunting his victims with a jingle about his insatiable appetite. It's vaguely reminiscent of the "Money" song in *Cabaret*, without the glint of real satire.

However when you check with Stratfordians, the students at Stratford Central Secondary School from whose amateur, eager ranks the show was largely cast, or the devoted members of NDWT who worked on the project with Reaney, you hear another story, and it's an affecting one. While both supporters and detractors wax lyrical over the play's lyrical moments—women in a factory, in white aprons, checking eggs by candlelight—they differ when it comes to relevance. The latter see it as poetic indulgence, the former as inspirational, even mystical. Many among the local citizenry loved and understood what they saw.

With all their surprise, energy and community workshop truth, however, the post-Donnelly plays cannot match the trilogy's force. Somehow, they fly too soon out of the historical mud into fantasy. They seem to miss the natural middle ground of his major work. Reaney is the ebullient jester, a kind of pied piper, rather than a visionary poet. He may again sound the depths of tragedy when he forgets the propaganda of play and allows it to express itself instinctively. In this, he acknowledges a debt to the Greeks who, he feels, were so imbued with the spirit of *homo ludens* that they never considered playfulness a thing separate from life. It's a matter of letting go, losing what is known in order to discover what must be known. Judging by his powerful Donnellys, the formula for a Reaney tragedy seems to be: find the subject that engages your real passions, and then trust your dangerous exploration to the rules of the game that you have played so well, for so long.

NOTES

[1] Ross G. Woodman, *James Reaney*, Toronto: McClelland & Stewart, 1971, 8.

[2] Margaret Atwood, "Eleven Years of Alphabet," in *Canadian Literature*, Summer 1971, 60-64.

[3] James Reaney, "Kids and Crossovers," in *Canadian Theatre Review*, 10, Spring 1976, 28-31.

[4] James Reaney, *Colours in the Dark*, Vancouver: Talonbooks, 1969, 4.

[5] Alvin A. Lee, *James Reaney*, New York: Twayne, 1968, 149.

[6] Several critics have hinted at this including, in a number of reviews, Herbert Whittaker in the Toronto *Globe and Mail*. Whittaker most directly spoke of this in a review of the 1973 production of *Listen to the Wind*.

[7] James Reaney, *Listen to the Wind*, Vancouver: Talonbooks, 1980, 3-4.

[8] James Reaney, *Handcuffs*, Erin, Ontario: Press Porcépic, 1977, 133.

[9] James Reaney, "Sticks and Stones" in *Canadian Theatre Review*, 2, Spring 1974, 43-44.

[10] James Reaney, *A Suit of Nettles*, Erin, Ontario: Press Porcépic, 1975, 1.

[11] Arthur Miller, "Tragedy and the Common Man," in Bernard Dukore (ed.), *Dramatic Theory and Criticism*, New York: Holt, Rinehart and Winston, 1974, 894-897.

[12] Reaney, *Nettles*, 3.

[13] Reaney, *Nettles*, 14.

[14] Reaney, *Nettles*, 22.

[15] Reaney, "Sticks and Stones," 54.

[16] James Reaney, *14 Barrels From Sea to Sea*, Erin, Ontario: Press Porcépic, Introduction.

[17] Reaney, "Sticks and Stones," 71.

[18] Reaney, "Sticks and Stones," 103.

Don Rubin

George Ryga:
The Poetics of Engagement

Less than a decade after he burst on the national dramatic scene with his stunning drama *The Ecstasy of Rita Joe*, a play produced all across Canada in both English and French and subsequently in both the United States and Europe, George Ryga found himself an outcast among Canada's largest theatres, *persona non grata* among the companies with the resources needed to best produce his major works.

Wanted in Hollywood by television studios to crank out weekly series at far greater sums of money than he could ever possibly earn by remaining in Canada, winning awards for his radio dramas in Germany, invited regularly to give readings in the former Soviet Union, and the subject of doctoral dissertations in both Italy and France, Ryga found himself virtually unable to get a major production of one of his plays in his own country.

Why?

Ryga speculated on the answer to this disturbing question in an issue of the *Canadian Theatre Review* in 1974. As he put it:

> Because I refused to divorce theatre from the larger issues of life confronting us, I get punished. My plays are produced less frequently...today. Words written by me have been bastardized and rearranged beyond recognition.... The cause of a viable Canadian theatre has reeled under the counter-attack of a social and political system that viciously defends itself against all criticism and examination. Certainly I've been hurt. And because I've been hurt so have you. Because I do no more than reflect your experiences, thoughts and possibilities through my art.... The role of theatre, as I see it, is to give light, colour and nobility to the quality of our lives.[1]

Ryga's concern for the establishment of a socially-rooted theatre in Canada was not limited to specific political issues. Even Canadian English, like "joual" for the nationalist theatre of Quebec, was a flag of sorts. In *CTR 14* he wrote:

> A qualitative change is taking place in the language of our theatre. The common speech of people, carefully studied and reproduced, is now being elevated into theatrical poetry. Regional speech mannerisms are no longer treated as aberrations—they are examined and integrated into emotional lines not previously explored.... One only has to hear the commonplace thoughts of Newfoundland fisherpeople translate into the soaring poetry of Michael Cook to understand why there will not...must not be, a return to one acceptable accent or language form for this country. [2]

For Ryga, the Canadian dramatist was charting nothing less than the end of a way of life, perhaps the end of Canada as most had come to believe in it and as most tended to perceive it. The plays which most struck him were those which concerned themselves

> with a vanishing landscape. The fishermen working depleted waters...the Nova Scotian family leaving its ancestral fields...the Indian torn between two worlds.... We are...recording in a human way the agonies and triumphs of yet another transition. [3]

If the social message was not clear to his audiences by this time, Ryga spelled it out in still another *CTR* article.

> Despite the fact that for generations the reasonably cultivated Canadian of means purchased his wines from France, his porcelain and silver from Britain, his woolens from Scotland, his entertainment and his hardwood furnishings from the United States—despite the fact that acquisition of a pseudo-English accent adequately fed a national inferiority-superiority complex for longer than one cares to remember—despite the fact that as a nation we appeared to voluntarily submit into a position of cultural subservience by cultivation of tastes which depend entirely on the importation of literature, music, drama and dance—despite all this, all is not as it should be in paradise....
>
> Culture is a living thing, into which the problems of racial inequality, inflation, foreign ownership of resources and unemployment will and must reflect itself.... It pleases and refreshes by isolating problems and proposing resolutions based on daily contact and examination of people. [4]

It is the future, says Ryga, embodied in the next generation, embodied in our own children, which imposes a responsibility on us.

> Once we have opted for children, and the only promise of immortality left to us, the obligations to history, to a piece of this earth, to the generations to come, begins. Only madness exempts us from the responsibilities and rewards of changing the landscape and changing ourselves. [5]

Born in 1932 to a family of Ukrainian immigrants in Deep Creek, Alberta, a farming community composed for the most part of eastern

European immigrants, Ryga's early recollections relate mostly to the primitiveness of his hometown. "In essence," he recalled,

> life hadn't changed from what it was in the seventeenth century in Europe. A lot of impressions of how people live when reduced to bare essentials still persist in my mind.... My father didn't know when the thirties ended and the good times began. He worked this farm for thirty-two years. [6]

Growing up in a home where English was not spoken, Ryga was six years old when he entered the public school system, a one-room school, in fact.

> I remember the first words I heard were "Good Morning." It was like a hammerblow. I had never heard an English word up to that time. [7]

Remaining there for the next seven years, he left school shortly before his thirteenth birthday and began doing general farm labour, eventually drifting into construction work and lumbering. For the most part, the work he found was modest and occasional. Often he had to compete for these jobs with another poor group in the community—the Indians. Years later, Ryga recalled the enormous "interconnection between the thoughts of the white community and the thoughts of the Indian community."[8] Clearly, both were struggling for their economic life, their dignity and their cultural identity in a socio-political environment where concerns for the poor were not paramount.

Over the next few years, Ryga read avidly although his choices were limited to what was available in the local travelling library. What did he read?

> Historical books, do-it-yourself manuals, fiction.... This was my first contact with Shelley and Byron.... Coming into contact with literature and becoming aware of its dignity, beauty and severe discipline was probably the kind of challenge I needed at the time to confront myself. [9]

Ryga's earliest writing dates to the late forties and, like most young people experimenting with writing, he turned first to poetry. He became fascinated early by the Scots poet Robert Burns. For about two years, in fact, he actually rewrote much of Burns, "a very useful learning method that I had evolved on my own."[10] In 1950, he enrolled in a correspondance course and was encouraged by his teacher to pursue creative writing even more seriously. On the teacher's recommendation, he applied for and received a scholarship to attend the Banff School of Fine Arts during the summer sessions of 1951 and 1952.

Banff, however, was not an easy experience for the poor son of an immigrant. Catering heavily to the children of the wealthy and the established, Ryga was far from comfortable at the school. During his second summer there, in fact, he wound up in trouble because of a poem he wrote about the Korean War and attempts were made to withdraw the scholarship. Though this was his first experience with establishment censorship, it would be far from his last.

Moving to nearby Edmonton, Ryga found a job at a local radio station writing news and advertising copy and eventually producing his own radio program called *Reverie*. A program that included music, poetry and prose—much of it original—Ryga stayed with the station in general and *Reverie* in particular for close to three years. Two incidents in 1955 rudely ended his association with the station, however. To celebrate Armistice Day, he aired a program of pacifist poems. About half the audience was enraged and the station owners warned him to be less controversial. The end came a few months later when, as something of a radio personality, he was spending time picketing and making speeches about the Rosenberg trial. Shortly thereafter, the station asked him to resign.

Looking for an opportunity to expand his writing as well as a chance to see the world, he took his life's savings at this point and began an extended and largely unplanned journey through Europe. Beginning in England, and going on to Scotland to explore the countryside of Robert Burns, Ryga recalled that what he really wanted to do was to go deeper into the question of language—heightened language—than he had been able to do before.

> At that time, there were two writers who had a very special significance. One was Burns; the other was the Ukrainian poet, Sevchenko. Both did the same thing with language: they elevated it, they took it from a very colloquial form into a new art form.[11]

While in Europe, the Canadian Peace Movement—well aware of Ryga's commitment to the cause—approached him about being an official delegate to the World Peace Conference in Helsinki. A committed Communist as well by this time, Ryga attended the conference, making innumerable personal contacts there, and was subsequently invited to both Warsaw and Sofia. The following year, however, he broke totally with the Communist Party and lost much of his enthusiasm for the Soviet Union following that country's invasion of Hungary.

The people who seemed to most fascinate Ryga during the Helsinki Conference, though, were not so much the eastern Europeans as the Africans, particularly their experience with independence and literature. They had, he recalled,

> a very no-nonsense attitude to literature, to art, to folk forms like the dance. They were reinterpreting everything and it was like watching a laboratory. It was all part of a larger process.... Years later, this influenced me in many judgements I had to make about my own country, when we caught up with our own anti-colonial struggle. [12]

It was during this same period that he met his future wife Norma, then working at the BBC in London. He persuaded her to return to Canada with him (along with her two children by a previous marriage) where they married, had two more children of their own and adopted still another.

Between 1960 and 1963, Ryga wrote six novels while holding a variety of jobs. One of those jobs—a night clerk in a small hotel—gave him the opportunity to read as well as to write.

For his reading, he turned to Dostoevsky. On the nights he wasn't reading Dostoevsky, he would write for three or four hours. Five of the six novels he wrote during this time, however, remain unpublished. The sixth—*Hungry Hills*—was written in 1962 and published first in England in 1963.

Hungry Hills is the first Ryga work of consequence. About a young man returning home to the Alberta foothills where he grew up, the novel reflects Ryga's growing ability to draw powerful characters, to set scenes clearly and effectively, to reflect the dignity of the poor and disenfranchised in a strong language reminiscent not so much of Burns as of Hemingway. Like much of Ryga's work, *Hungry Hills* is also clearly rooted in "memory."

His career as a dramatist also begins in 1962. That year, he writes two television plays—*Indian* and *The Storm*. The following year, he writes five more, and in 1964, he does his own adaptation of *Hungry Hills* for television.

Indian, the most successful and significant of these television plays, was written, he says, after seeing Edward Albee's *The Zoo Story* on television and feeling he could do as well. The play was sent to CBC-TV which read it, liked it and eventually produced it. Ryga says that he watched it on television—his first produced play—"with fascination, then with discomfort. I finally vomited."[13]

The Albee play is, in its simplest form, a meeting between two strangers who share a bizarre and frightening story and then separate. *Indian* utilizes the same basic structure: an Indian agent, having heard about trouble with a group of Indians who had been hired to do some menial work for a local farmer, shows up to investigate. Beginning as the pursuer, beginning as the power figure, he becomes the pursued after hearing the Indian's frightening tale, becomes the victim and is forced to flee.

Indian is also archetypal Ryga—a tale of someone from the land, someone whose roots go into the earth, someone poor, who finds himself caught in the wheels of a society he does not really understand. The play also contains another key Ryga idea, that of the "semento," an

Indian word meaning someone who has lost touch with the land and through it, with his soul. It is a concept which runs through much of Ryga's later writing including his most famous play, *The Ecstasy of Rita Joe*.

Turning his energies again to the novel in 1964 with his *Ballad of a Stonepicker*, Ryga once more dramatizes the tension between going out into the world while trying to remain true to one's roots. He splits this tension into two separate characters, two brothers pulled in totally different directions.

One of the brothers in *Ballad* remains on the land farming; the other leaves home for an education, to see the world, to experience what's out there. In doing so, he turns his back on his roots. Are these the two halves of Ryga himself? Of any of us? Clearly, one cannot easily make such a split, one cannot be "out there" and "back home" at the same time.

And in the novel, neither brother is happy nor satisfied. The one who works the land, who literally works in the dirt, is certainly more together than the brother who has gone into the world. But neither one feels complete. Existential angst and melancholy pervade the novel as the questions are asked again and again, questions of responsibility, questions of self and one's relation to the world. At what point does one lose one's soul, does one become a "semento?" Interestingly, it is at about this point in his life that Ryga himself leaves the big cities again and moves permanently back to the type of farming community in which he grew up. Though drawn back to the urban centres of Edmonton and, particularly, Vancouver again and again in his career, Ryga's permanent home from this point becomes Summerland, a small farming community in British Columbia's Okanagan Valley.

The year 1967 was an important one in the history of Canada. It was important as well in the development of Canadian theatre and in George Ryga's own career. The celebrations of Canada's Centennial that year were to include, at the urging of the Federal Government which would fund them, cultural events from the outports of Newfoundland in the east, to retirement communities of Victoria in the west. In some communities—including Toronto—Centennial projects were to include the building of whole new theatres while in others—such as Vancouver—special Centennial funds were made available for the commissioning of new artistic works celebrating Canada's glorious history. The fact that Canada didn't have a particularly glorious history didn't seem to matter at all. Centennial fever was in the air. Canada had survived for a hundred years as a nation.

The Artistic Director of the Vancouver Playhouse at that time was Malcolm Black and in 1966 he was already thinking of commissioning new plays for the Centennial season. That year, he came across a short paragraph in a Vancouver newspaper reporting "the murder of an Indian girl, whose body had been found in a rooming house in the slum area of the city. This routine clipping became the seed from which *The Ecstasy of Rita Joe* eventually grew."[14] Black first approached writer Paul St. Pierre with the idea but St. Pierre was unable to accept the commission. A friend, Beverly Simons (not yet known as a playwright herself), had seen *Indian* on television and suggested Ryga's name.

The play went through several drafts. Because it was essentially a memory play and because Ryga was not an established playwright, Black had to convince members of the company to have faith in the new script. Director George Bloomfield—whose career was basically in television—and actress Frances Hyland were key figures in the production. Hyland was to play the title role while Dan George, an actual Burrard Tribe Chief, was to play her father.

Very quickly word got out that something unusual was taking place. To keep both his actors in and the curious out, Bloomfield decided that rehearsals would be closed to absolutely everyone. Opening night, November 23, 1967, was, in Bloomfield's own words, "explosive." The play, a powerful, quasi-Brechtian anatomization of racism and liberal paternalism in virtually every level of Canadian society, was probably not exactly what was envisaged for a Centennial Celebration play. Its very uniqueness, though, made *The Ecstasy of Rita Joe* a landmark in Canadian dramaturgy. The fact that *Rita Joe* was also recognized early on as an extraordinary piece of theatre by Canadian audiences—this at a time when the "new" Canadian play was all but ignored by producers—clearly paved the way for a whole new generation of Canadian dramatists who would no longer be satisfied with either the usual amateur productions of non-controversial plays or with professional careers limited primarily to radio or television. The stage quickly became a viable option for serious writers and the impact of *Rita Joe* on that perception cannot be overestimated.

A muscular, musical, morality play revealing new aspects of Ryga's poetic and dramatic imagination, *Rita Joe* also takes up Ryga's by now familiar ideas once again. From his earliest days as a writer, one finds his interest in developing a heightened language, particularly for those not at the centre of their society. Ryga's political distrust is obvious in his handling of power figures—petty officials and magistrates, generally unfeeling representatives of an entrenched political system. And Ryga's social concern, particularly his disgust with racism, is clear throughout.

But what may not be quite so clear is Ryga's return to his *idée fixe*, the loss of soul and self that occurs when one loses touch with one's roots. Rita, like Jaimie Paul, dared to leave home, dared to leave her land, dared to leave her roots, her family, her people. In this desire to reach out to something larger, to connect to the world, we admire Rita as we admire the wanderlust of all Ryga's heroes. But when we lose touch with the roots, with the earth, with who we really are—when the cement of the city comes between us and it—the loss can be irreparable and our very souls become endangered.

We carry our past with us, Ryga suggests, and when we leave it behind or forget it, we are no match for the urban world or for our collective technological future symbolized in *Rita Joe* by the menacing planes and trains which eventually roar over both Rita and Jaimie. Can we carry the land and the past as we might like into an increasingly complicated urban future? Can we bring the peace of the land to the anxiety and impersonality of the city? Can we really do any more than carry the memory of a time when the world not only seemed but was simpler?

Certainly everyone in *Rita Joe* "remembers." David Joe, her father, remembers the old traditions, the deep love he bore for his wife, his first job *away* from the reserve. All these memories come together in one of the play's most powerful monologues.

> The first time I got work there was a girl about as old as I.... She'd come out in the yard an' watch the men working at the threshing machine. She had eyes that were the biggest I ever seen...like fifty cent pieces...an' there was always a flock of geese around her. Whenever I see her I feel good. She used to stand an' watch me, an' the geese made a helluva lot of noise. One time I got off my rick an' went to get a drink of water...but I walked close to where she was watching me. She backed away, and then ran from me with the geese chasin' after her, their wings out an' their feet no longer touching the ground.... They were white geese.... The last time Rita Joe come home to see us...the last time she ever come home...I watched her leave...and I seen geese running after Rita Joe the same way...white geese...with their wings out an' their feet no longer touching the ground. And I remembered it all, an' my heart got so heavy I wanted to cry.... [15]

Rita too remembers—her childhood, her lost innocence, her blueberry walks with her sister Eileen Joe in the woods, her mother's illness. About the only time in the play when she *can't* remember is when she appears in court (nine different times over a period of more than a year) on charges ranging from vagrancy to prostitution, shoplifting to assault. Rita's real crimes, of course, are her poverty and her unpreparedness for the realities of a culture whose rules were made, as she says, long before she was born.

Clearly for Ryga, it is not Rita Joe herself who is on trial but, as in Brecht's *Threepenny Opera*, Capitalism. For all her memories, for all her struggles to reconcile the polarities of her father (who urges her to return to the roots), and her lover (who dares her to join him in the white man's city) Rita is ultimately destroyed by a Capitalist system that "alienates" even those it allows in. And Rita can't even get in.

One of the questions rarely answered in performance is whose "memory" the play really is, a question complicated by the fact that Rita Joe, in terms of strict chronology, is actually already murdered before the play begins. One is not speaking here necessarily of Ryga's own intentions to make this play "a woman's odyssey through hell"[16] but of the difficulties faced by a director and actors in trying to "place" the script and realize the characters.

It would seem that one clear solution would be to set the play in the mind of Eileen Joe. She is present throughout, from Rita's funeral to the shared memories of the family. As well, she could certainly be privy to Rita's more intimate moments with Jaimie. Even Rita's murder could be her own reconstruction of the brutal events. Too often, however, productions of the play fail to "place" it for the viewer in some per-sonal/historical reality and too often productions leave the viewer without a clear anchor and, deep-down, a vaguely unsatisfied feeling. Such anchoring, therefore, is not only essential but clearly text based.

In thematic terms, Ryga has no real answers for the problems he raises but then why should one expect an artist to have easy solutions to problems that are so very complicated. It is ultimately, as Chekhov has said, the artist's responsibility to simply identify areas of human and social concern and this Ryga has always done brilliantly. If there is any solution proposed by Ryga, it is the need for each of us to under-stand who we are and to realize that "self" as fully as possible. In such understanding lies freedom. It is the old man of the play, as it is in many Ryga works, who understands this best. And it is in *Rita Joe's* central metaphor—metamorphosis—where Ryga comes closest to writing a poem about this dream of self and freedom.

> I once seen a dragonfly breakin' its shell to get its wings.... It floated on water an' crawled up on a log where I was sitting.... It dug its feet into the log an' then it pulled until the shell bust over its neck. Then it pulled some more...an' slowly its wings slipped out of the shell...like that! (He shows with his hands how the dragonfly got freedom.)[...] Such wings I never seen before...folded like an accordion so fine, like thin glass an' white in the morning sun...[...] It spread its wings...so slowly...an' then the wings opened an' began to flutter...Just like that...see! Hesitant at first...then stronger...an' then the wings beatin' like that made the dragonfly's body quiver until the shell on its back falls off...[...] an' the dragonfly...flew

up...up...up...into the white sun...to the green sky...to the sun...faster
an' faster.... Higher.... Higher! (The Father reaches up with his hands,
releasing the imaginary dragonfly into the sun, his final words torn out of
his heart.)[17]

The Ecstasy of Rita Joe was an enormous success in Vancouver and
plans were soon set in motion to have the play seen by as wide an
audience as possible. In 1969, *Rita Joe,* with essentially the same cast but
now directed by David Gardner, played at the new National Arts Centre
in Ottawa. That same year, the distinguished Quebec playwright Gratien Gélinas translated the play into French and in 1970, *Rita Joe* was
seen in Montreal. Subsequently, the play was produced in the United
States and in England and attracted wide attention in eastern Europe.
In 1971, the Royal Winnipeg Ballet premièred a dance version of the
script.

Ryga was immensely popular at this point in his career and his next
play, again commissioned by the Vancouver Playhouse, simply confirmed the earlier success. *Grass and Wild Strawberries,* a play about
alternatives, about power, and youth, premièred in 1969 and played to
over one hundred per cent capacity with seats added for most performances.

Following this second success, the Playhouse again offered Ryga a
commission. It was with this next play, however, that his career as a
playwright began turning sour. Playing once again with the notion of
the socially powerful in confrontation with the disenfranchised, Ryga
encountered problems finding a viable dramatic structure in which to
place his theme.

The events of October 1970 in Quebec, however, gave Ryga a
dramatic handle for his new work. The Front de la Liberation du Quebec
(FLQ), a little-known, left wing radical group intent on pushing Quebec
into independence, began a series of bombings and political kidnap-
pings. The Canadian government, unsure how widespread the movement was in Quebec, responded with the War Measures Act, a law
which essentially suspended the legal rights of every Canadian across
the country and gave the government the right to arrest and hold
virtually anyone it wished. These events were the very stuff of drama
and in 1971, Ryga submitted his new play, *Captives of the Faceless
Drummer,* to the Playhouse.

Focusing on a political kidnapping, the play looks at the position of
the kidnapper, the social outcast, with tremendous sympathy. Even the
wealthy protagonist begins to understand the deeper issues at stake.
Unfortunately, the powers at the Vancouver Playhouse—right up to the
Board of Directors and, depending on the version one listens to, right

into the provincial government—were not much interested in the deeper issues. The subject matter was simply too controversial, too hot politically.

Ryga was informed officially that the *Captives'* script was not ready for production; in fact, *Captives* would not be produced by the Playhouse. Never shy in a fight, Ryga immediately went to the press and said that he felt the play was being censored for political reasons and by political interests. The Playhouse tried to defend itself but the controversy quickly spread across the country through newspaper stories and radio interviews. Eventually, *Captives* was given a bare-bones production at the Vancouver Art Gallery in late 1971, and in 1972 it was produced by Festival Lennoxville in Quebec. But it was to prove to be Ryga's last hurrah for many years on a major stage in Canada. There were many rationalizations made across the country in the months and years to come about the reasons why Ryga's work (including *Rita Joe*) was not produced and there were even a few feeble attempts to challenge Ryga's abilities as a dramatist. The bottom line, however, was that Ryga was gone, his politics finally doing him in as a produceable playwright.

The public, however, was never fully convinced. *Rita Joe* is still studied in virtually every high school and university across Canada and in many universities in Europe. It is the biggest seller of any Canadian-written and Canadian-published play and has never been out of print since it was first published by Vancouver's Talonbooks in February 1970. Nor is it likely to be for many years to come. Among the major theatres in Canada, however, the conspiracy of silence set in, not to be lifted for nearly twenty years. Not a single major Canadian company commissioned a new play from George Ryga—nor produced any of the older successes—between 1971 and 1986. During this time, Ryga wrote close to a dozen plays.

With only small companies seeking out his work and none able to offer him much in the way of financial incentive to rewrite, the results were sadly predictable: no great successes, not even any moderate successes, no major productions. In fact, the only Ryga play to attract any national attention at all was his drama, *A Letter to my Son*, written in 1981 and subsequently nominated for a Governor General's Award for Drama.

Among these post-*Captives* dramas are two produced by theatre students at the Banff School of Fine Arts—*Sunrise on Sarah* (1972), a play about woman as "semento;" and *Portrait of Angelica*, (1973), a drama about a Canadian writer living in a small Mexican town trying to use the experience to define his own identity.

In 1974, the *Canadian Theatre Review* published Ryga's most massive play, *Paracelsus*, an epic drama tracing the life of a medieval European healer in his wars against the rich on behalf of the poor, against the establishment on behalf of those without power. This 24-character play, set on several levels and moving back and forth in time, again asks the old questions about personal identity and social responsibility. In the play, it is ultimately Paracelsus' professional colleagues who destroy him. Interestingly, it took twelve years before a single Canadian company expressed any interest in even attempting to produce the play and then the production was only undertaken because funding was guaranteed not by a theatre but by Vancouver's World Exposition as part of its Cultural Program.

In 1976, Ryga finished three more plays—*Ploughman of the Glacier, Seven Hours to Sundown,* and *Last of the Gladiators* (based on his early novel, *Night Desk*). The first play was produced by a small company in Kamloops, British Columbia; the second by an even smaller company in Edmonton; and the last by a barely-budgeted company in Summerland. Two years later, a small company in Victoria produced his play, *Jeremiah's Place.*

That same year—1978—Ryga, feeling almost totally cut off from the mainstream, chose to do, not surprisingly, an adaptation of the Prometheus legend. The irony was not lost on Canadian cultural commentators. Writing about Ryga's work at that time, critic Mavor Moore—soon to be named head of the Canada Council—wrote:

> It was not unnatural [...] that his attention turned, for subject-matter, to the greatest outcast in mythology, the Titan Prometheus, famous as a benefactor to mankind—nor that he should see in Prometheus bound echoes of Jesus crucified.[18]

The Chorus in Ryga's version has become A Farmer and A Worker. Prometheus himself calls for a change in the system, demands "a new revolution." And, as he is punished for calling Truth by its name, he cries out:

> ...They plan once more
> To crush this earth,
> Burn all the splendid books,
> Silence songs of passion and of freedom—
> Break the backs of upright men and women,
> And look with pride on burning flesh
> ...I am afraid! [...]
> The flames
> Reaching down towards me
> Are more fearful
> Than what God might wish us to endure....[19]

The play ends there with the simple stage directions:

A scream. Silence.

Despite the unkindnesses done to him professionally and the short-sightedness of too many in the Canadian theatre establishment, Ryga was not silent. *A Letter To My Son*, perhaps his best play, proved that his love of theatre as well as his talent continued to burn strongly.

In 1979, following a visit to China, Ryga wrote a novelized documentary about his visit there entitled *Beyond the Crimson Morning*. The dedication—a poem—gives insight into Ryga's state of mind as the eighties approached.

Against speckled heavens
The year's fly
On burning wings
And I
Greying now
And saddened
By this unrelenting earth
Walk hand in hand
Over mountains
With a greying man of China
And joyfully we speak
Of poems
By Chou-En-Lai and Whitman
While overhead
An aircraft
Roars towards the setting sun.[20]

In 1982, Ryga began work on a trilogy of novels, the first part of which, *In the Shadow of the Vulture*, was published in 1984. In his application to the Canada Council requesting a grant to allow him to focus on the work, Ryga said:

I consider it to be the most important work I have yet written.... [It] concerns itself with the plight of five indentured labourers, who through internal and external crises reach a religious and sociological awareness that catapults them into the eye of the social hurricane now sweeping the underbelly of our continent....

The sequel will deal, still through their experiences, with the epic social transformations of the future throughout North America—from the Inuit in the Arctic, to the final liberation from the influences of Cortes in Mexico, the breakdown of the continental USA into principalities, with potential duplications in some areas of Canada and Mexico.[21]

In 1984, Ryga finally admitted the pain of living in a country which seemed to go out of its way to avoid recognizing its own artists generally, and him in particular.

I've been buzzing with a lot of discontent—largely due to living in this country at all. I have a lot to do—have been turning out a book a year for the past few years, with many projects lined up for the future. But it's like pumping water into a void—nobody reads, our national theatre has the frenzy and waste of a low-class whorehouse, nobody THINKS! Once every few months, I get a phone call from Moscow, inviting me to work on a film collaboration with one of their directors, but I lamely postpone the invitation. The Swedes review *Ploughman of the Glacier* from mythological perspectives I have never considered. The Chinese do the same with *Indian*. My novels are now published in the USSR from manuscripts, and not from published texts, as is their practice. The last one came out in serialization to rave reviews. And I am still searching for a publisher in Canada. Awards for radio drama keep tumbling in predictably from Germany. And here I am, stuck, not able to make a decision. I suppose I fear the decision to leave, knowing I will likely be gone a long, long time if I do.[22]

In the summer of 1985, Ryga was asked to prepare a position paper for that year's Congress of UNESCO's International Theatre Institute, a Congress which was to be held for the first time ever in Canada. The theme of the Congress was to be Theatre: New World Visions and Ryga's paper was to set the tone for discussions dealing with the social role of theatre in Canada and how that theatre related to other theatres throughout the hemisphere. In this paper, one finds all of Ryga including his bitterness and sadness. But most of all one finds George Ryga's still unflagging belief in art as an instrument of social change and in the ability of art to affect the world.

To endure—to bring out the best moments in human destiny—despite the twin censors of political expediency or the fashions of the marketplace, is all-important. We in Canada have some running experience of what it means to endure in theatre. Theatre is the revelation of human character in extreme situations. Understanding this, we understand the foundations of each other's origin shaped into understandable metaphors by the building blocks of language and the poetry of ritual. To be born is a ritual. To live with grace and dignity, even in great poverty, is a ritual of hope. And, yes, people die for these privileges even as these words are being considered and written. Such is the pulse of our hemisphere—a revolutionary pulsebeat in which we all move, knowingly or unknowingly.[23]

George Ryga died on November 18, 1987 after a long bout with stomach cancer. Tributes came from all across Canada. Some even came from artistic directors. In the years since, despite the work of a handful of devoted scholars who published several volumes of his early work, few—certainly very few in the profession—seemed even then willing to acknowledge his primacy of place in the development of a viable and important Canadian theatre. Even in death, George Ryga's poetics of engagement were still being strongly felt.

NOTES

[1] George Ryga, "Theatre in Canada: A Viewpoint On Its Development and Future," in *Canadian Theatre Review*, 1 (Winter 1974), 30.

[2] George Ryga, "Contemporary Theatre and Its Language," in *Canadian Theatre Review*, 14 (Spring 1977), 8.

[3] Ibid.

[4] George Ryga, "The Need For A Mythology," in *Canadian Theatre Review*, 16 (Fall 1977), 4-6.

[5] Ibid., 6.

[6] Peter Hay, "George Ryga: Beginnings of a Biography," in *Canadian Theatre Review*, 23 (Summer 1979), 39.

[7] Ibid., 39.

[8] Ibid., 40.

[9] Ibid., 39-40.

[10] Ibid., 41.

[11] Ibid., 42.

[12] Ibid., 44.

[13] Notes from a talk given by George Ryga at York University, 1986.

[14] Christopher Innes, *Politics and the Playwright: George Ryga*, Toronto: Simon & Pierre, 1985, 29.

[15] George Ryga, *The Ecstasy of Rita Joe*, Vancouver: Talonbooks, 1970, 79-80.

[16] Innes, *Politics*, 31.

[17] Ryga, *Rita Joe*, 114.

[18] Mavor Moore, Introduction to Ryga's *Two Plays: Paracelsus and Prometheus Bound*, Winnipeg: Turnstone Press, 1982, 5.

[19] George Ryga, *Two Plays*, 156.

[20] George Ryga, Dedication to *Beyond the Crimson Morning*, Toronto: Doubleday, 1979.

[21] Application to the Canada Council for an Arts Grant "A" dated April 29, 1982, 2.

[22] Letter to Don Rubin dated September 26, 1984.

[23] George Ryga, Discussion paper: "Visions of Theatre in the Americas," draft dated October 1984; final version presented to ITI Congress delegates in Toronto, June 1985.

For Further Reading:

Aside from the plays, most of which were published by Vancouver's Talonbooks, the reader is directed to various essays published by Ryga in the *Canadian Theatre Review* between 1974 and 1982. During this time, Ryga was a member of the *CTR* Editorial Advisory Board and played an active role in its development. Two volumes of previously unpublished Ryga material have more recently been published by Talonbooks as well: *The Athabasca Ryga*, containing fiction from his early years in Alberta, and *Summerland* containing material from his years in Summerland, B.C..

Jennifer Harvie

(Im)Possibility: Fantasy and Judith Thompson's Drama

This could be a dream.

— stage direction in *I Am Yours*

Judith Thompson's plays do not precisely defy description, but they do, enigmatically, confound it. They move unpredictably between the mundane and surreal, the banal and profound, the conscious and unconscious. Their evocation of characters in social and psychic struggle is deeply compassionate and hopeful, but almost equally brutal and horrific. Their resolutions are intense and committed to hope for positive change, indicating certainty, but simultaneously acutely ambiguous, suggesting uncertainty. They entice audiences to intense empathic engagement, but through disruptions and dislocations of structure, character, mood and "logic," they destabilize and shift that engagement. In the Thompsonian *mise en scène* anything is (im)possible.

Critics have employed a variety of strategies, informed particularly by poststructuralism and psychoanalytic theories of subjectivity, to examine the wonderfully strange, unconventional, even grotesque qualities of Thompson's plays.[1] The volume and variety of critical attention paid to Thompson's plays bears testimony to their provocativeness and complexity, and each analytic strategy brings different strengths and emphases to a critical discourse which now elucidates her work in a variety of useful ways. What perhaps none of the previous analyses of Thompson's work has offered, however, is a method adequate to delineating the extreme vicissitudes of desire in the plays, a method which can respond to the way Dee switches with utter alacrity from telling Mack she loves him to telling him she hates him in *I Am*

Yours, or the way Rodney fantasizes his joyous reunion with, and seamlessly his torturous humiliation by, an old school friend in *Lion in the Streets,* and the way Thompson's audiences move with these switches. A method appropriate to re-thinking the play of desire is a theory of fantasy as it has been re-introduced to psychoanalytic theory by Jean Laplanche and Jean-Bertrand Pontalis and applied in feminist film and cultural criticism. Because of its sensitivity to the ambiguity of desire, as well as to the necessity of seeing subjectivity as unfixed and shifting, and to the individual's position straddling the conscious and the unconscious, this theory seems an appropriate tool for analyzing Thompson's plays[2] in particular, but perhaps also many non-"issue-based," more open, but nevertheless politically committed plays in general.

Fantasy

Feminist film criticism has invaluably pioneered analysis of the relation between sexual difference and spectatorship, and a key text in this criticism has been Laura Mulvey's 1975 article, "Visual Pleasure and Narrative Cinema." Linking activity with the male and passivity with the female ("Visual Pleasure..." 11), Mulvey called the gaze active and therefore male and argued the position of active spectator was untenable for women, unless, as she argued in a later article, they identified transsexually as men ("Afterthoughts..."). The rigid determinism of this conclusion was unacceptable for many, usefully provoking a rash of analyses which attempted to theorize the possibility of female spectatorship.

One approach to refuting Mulvey's claim was to demonstrate that the viewing subject's relation to the spectacle was not fixed by his or her gender. In "Fantasia,"[3] Elizabeth Cowie uses a theory of fantasy informed by Laplanche's and Pontalis' "Fantasy and the Origins of Sexuality"[4] to offer another way of considering the fixity, or not, of the sexual positions of cinema-subjects" (150). The fixity of subject positions in Mulvey's "Visual Pleasure..." is guaranteed partly through her emphasis on subjects desiring objects; specifically, active male viewers desiring and, through the gaze controlling, passive female objects embodying "to-be-looked-at-ness" (11). A theory of fantasy changes the stakes by positing desire as something which can never be fulfilled[5] and is therefore not about *obtaining* a *single object.* Removing the term "to obtain," fantasy eliminates that term's controlling, even terminating implications. And unfixing desire's reference to a single object, fantasy accommodates an understanding of desire as shifting, amongst various objects, or not even in relation to objects, but in a *mise en scène* of desire.

> Fantasy involves, is characterized by, not the achievement of desired objects, but the arranging of, a setting out of, desire; a veritable *mise-en-scène* of desire…. [T]he pleasure of fantasy lies in the setting out, not in the having of the objects. (Cowie 159)

And within that setting out, the subject is always present but is not fixed. Constance Penley paraphrases Laplanche and Pontalis: "Although the subject is always present in the fantasy, she or he may be there in a number of positions or in a de-subjectivized form, that is, 'in the very syntax' of the fantasy sequence" ("Feminism…" 439, cf. Laplanche and Pontalis 26, 22-23). A theory of fantasy allows several important possibilities: desire is ongoing and unfixed; the subject is split, multiple and capable of circulating amongst various, even conflicting, positions; and relatedly, the spectator is able to identify in many ways, including across gender, with the *mise en scène*,[6] or with the logic of the text's universe.[7] Anything is possible.

Fantasy also re-evaluates the significance of psychical reality to the subject. Since fantasy refers to a process that is both conscious and unconscious, it is concerned with both social and psychic processes (Cowie 168): "[P]sychical reality of which fantasy is the nucleus has an effect on and for the subject just as much as the material, physical world may have" (Cowie 155). "What is refused here," observes Cowie—in a move which is crucial to analysis of so many of Thompson's characters, like Alan in *The Crackwalker* who is tortured as much by pictures in his head as by his material conditions—"is any privileging of material reality as necessarily more important, more serious" (155), and what is allowed is a recognition of "the complex and ambiguous relationship of real to imagined" (Lyon 247).[8]

Finally, and crucially given my argument that this theory facilitates greater understanding of the vicissitudes of desire in Thompson's plays, fantasy articulates not only unconscious desires but also their interdiction, hence fantasy's powerful, even threatening, ambiguity. In more Lacanian terms, "Fantasy never articulates desire alone but always desire and the law. And even more complexly, it may express desire and the law in a single ensemble" (Lapsley and Westlake 91). In the sense that fantasy is a setting out, a staging, or a plotting of desire, part of that plot, in the dynamic play of desire, is the prohibition of desire. "The fantasy is not only the *mise en scène* of desire, but the *mise en scène* of an impossible desire—the desire for that to which the subject can have no access." (Lyon 269)[9] In fantasy, everything is not only possible, it is also impossible.

The Crackwalker

Thompson's plays are popularly described as being about "social war-fare" (Kareda 9), in which evil powers (what Thompson has called "the abyss" [in Tomc 23, in Rudakoff and Much 95]) confront powers of redemption or grace (Wachtel 40, Rudakoff and Much 103, Knowles "The Achievement..."). Characters have objectives which might be termed worthy or good—to achieve a sense of self worth, and to be able to love, feel, and forgive—but these objectives are often figured as ridiculous, realistically impossible, or simply improbable. Thus, Thompson's plays foil a linear reading strategy centred on the satisfaction of characters' objectives. More appropriate is a reading of the plays as, to a degree, their characters' fantasies—in which characters stage their desires as well as the prohibition of those desires, switch subject positions, factor in psychical as well material realities, and so on, sometimes achieving a provisional sense of fulfilment, but inevitably adapting to the contingencies of their situations. Also appropriate is a reading of the plays as their audiences' fantasies, where audiences identify not necessarily with particular characters, but with the *mise en scène* of the Thompson universe. Thompson's plays present worlds where the possibility of extreme defeat, or prohibition, is acknow-ledged, but where defeat is somehow, miraculously, overcome; indeed, where prohibition almost facilitates some level of fulfilment of desire. And it is with the unlikely but hopeful logic of this universe that Thompson's audiences are prompted to choose, actively, to identify.

In *The Crackwalker*,[10] redemption centres around the idea of achiev-ing and maintaining a sense of personal value. Characters' extreme deprivation inhibits this redemption but does not entirely prevent it. For all four of the play's main characters, ideas of appropriate and valuable belonging seem to be based in the *mise en scène* of the home and family relationships. For Sandy, success means suturing together a life of domestic propriety with her husband Joe: with clean floors, meals eaten together, marital fidelity, and loyalty, to each other and to friends. For Joe it means independent achievement and economic success. For Alan it means being a good father and provider for his family. And for Theresa it means fulfilling her role in a family portrait evoked for her by Alan where she is "that madonna lady" (35), the precisely impossible virgin-mother. In the course of the play, Theresa and Alan become engaged, then married, and have a baby. Superficially, their familial objectives are fulfilled. However, the baby is probably mentally and physically disabled, Alan murders it, and Theresa and Alan split up. Sandy's and Joe's relationship fares little better: at the play's beginning Sandy recounts how she beat Joe with the heel of her shoe after hearing he had committed adultery, he leaves her, and in the end they reconcile in no great tribute to the triumph of romance:

JOE: Come here.

SANDY: Joe it ain't like that no more.

JOE: Who said it ain't.

SANDY: I did. Keep your paws offa me.

JOE: Jeez you're lookin good.

SANDY: I'm doin my eyeliner different.

JOE: Yeah?

SANDY: Makes my eyes look bigger.

JOE: Nice.

SANDY: I know. (60)

But despite the extreme tragedy of Theresa's and Alan's marriage and the tragic farce of Sandy's and Joe's, Sandy and Joe do reach some kind of reconciliation, Sandy achieves a sense of empowerment (Thompson had noted, "[Sandy] believes that you can put on eyeliner a different way and it can change your life" [in Rudakoff and Much 95]), and Theresa acquires a sense of self worth. In the play's final scene, "*THER-ESA runs onstage*" and addresses, offstage, an apparent attacker, "Stupid old bassard don't go foolin with me you don't even know who I look like even. You don't even know who I lookin like" (71). Holding on to her fantasy of being "that madonna lady," Theresa enacts, however provisionally, a personal triumph. *The Crackwalker* acutely delineates the way the grand narrative of the family may be false and even harmful—sexist, exploitative, and so on—but it simultaneously allows its characters to make that narrative real and useful however they can.

In a linear, deterministic reading of desire, where the subject must achieve or acquire his or her object of desire, none of the characters in this play is entirely, or possibly even remotely, successful. But in a reading of desire as it is scripted in fantasy, where pleasure lies in the setting out, not in the having of objects, it is possible to see the useful play of desire in *The Crackwalker*. When Theresa's valued role as mother is terminated with Danny's death, she switches subject positions, setting out and casting herself into fantasies which are still possible. Left alone with Danny's corpse while Sandy summons the police, Theresa "*picks up severed phone, does not dial*," but "tells" Janus she will not be attending her literacy class, then "*hangs up the phone, and picks it up immediately*" to say,

C'I speak to Ron please? Hi Ron, it's Trese. S'okay if we start goin together I love ya. Okay, see you Tuesday. (67)

Theresa desires a new, stable relationship but she enacts her desire and its prohibition—the phone is severed, she does not dial. Theresa's conversation with Ron is "unreal," but it has psychic reality, affirming Theresa's sense of self worth despite her situation. Pleasure, in fantasy, lies in the setting out not in the having of objects. Which is partly how, despite Danny's absence, Theresa "digests the horror...and then she moves on" (Thompson in Tomc 23).

Similarly, Sandy takes pleasure in the "setting out" of the funeral, despite its horrors, and she changes her role in—and the plot or truth of—the *mise en scène* of the funeral, according to her play of desire. The baby is dead, but Sandy claims,

> Youse shoulda seen him lyin there in that casket he looked fine. They had them little pajamas on him Trese got up at the S and R, the ones with all them dogs chasin cats all over, all yellow? They hardly looked sweet. And they had a big wreath of flowers around his neck so's to hide the strangle.... It was kinda nice. (70)

In this portion of Sandy's "review" of the funeral, the child's neck is hidden so that Sandy can reinforce her chosen position as Alan's protector:

> I'll tell ya who else I stood up for at that service...Al, and he done it. Oh yeah, I still consider him a friend. No matter what he done, nobody can say what happened in that room.... (70-71)

While later she claims that she *could* see the child's neck, and that Alan "never done it with a plastic bag he done it with his hands," Sandy's monologue is rife with inconsistencies and contradictions, but one coherent narrative allows her to role play as Alan's defender, and another, specifically as refuter of "[t]hat goddamn holy bitch," Bonnie Cain (71).[11] "What happened" is unknowable, but knowable in the re-enactment of fantasy. Usefully, this prevents the over-determination of material reality, allowing the recognition of contingency, and facilitating the subject's movement in strategies of self-determination. It also provokes the play's audience, particularly through Sandy's direct address, to engage actively and to choose which narrative(s) it will prioritize or believe.

Not all the play's characters reach such satisfactory, if provisional, resolutions. Alan's penultimate address to Joe, "Tell her I could drive a Monte Carlo. Easy" (69), is perhaps logically inadequate to surmounting the transgression of killing his baby. However, if *The Crackwalker* is considered not only as its characters' but also as its audience's fantasy, and if it does not achieve resolution for every character, then it may be seen as enacting both its audience's desire for that resolution and the prohibition of that desire. Inhibiting complete resolution and closure, *The Crackwalker* allows its audience an ongoing play of desire so that the audience can take its will to change (to change, for instance, the oppression of working class characters like Alan) beyond the play's ostensible end.

White Biting Dog

White Biting Dog, like *The Crackwalker*, can be read as a confrontation between the powers of good and evil (Adam 23), where good is seen predominantly as the ability to save (oneself and others) and the ability to feel (empathy and care). These overall desires are again profoundly inhibited, not least because the ability to feel achieved by Cape and his mother Lomia is, perhaps, dubious, despite the sacrificial deaths of Glidden (Cape's father and Lomia's estranged husband) and Pony (Cape's lover), and the scapegoat expulsion of Pascal (Lomia's lover). At the same time, Cape's and Lomia's ability to feel is not altogether impossible. Closing stage directions read, "*LOMIA looks at CAPE. They both feel, hope, that a change is taking place; deep within them something has cracked*,"[12] suggesting a desire to feel may be inhibited but not entirely prohibited.

With the decisive but often weird logic of a dream, the play turns around Cape's desire to save himself by saving his dying father: "...If I save HIM, I save my*self*, get it?" (7) Cape desperately commandeers a stranger, Pony, to help him identify what to do and, in a trance, Pony discovers Cape's mother "coming back is the only thing gonna save [his] dad" (20). So Cape recklessly goes about achieving this, ultimately seducing Pascal so that he will leave Lomia and she, in desperation, will go back to Glidden. When Glidden dies in spite of Cape's efforts, and Cape is unsure whether or not he has saved himself, his desire is not necessarily fulfilled, but *White Biting Dog* has enacted the play of that desire and its prohibition, potentially usefully for Cape, he "*just does not know*," but more hopefully for Lomia, who also could not feel: "*Her hope shows in her eyes*" (108).

Desire and its prohibition are enacted in many more subtle ways throughout the play, linking these terms, indicating their co-dependency, and rendering that co-dependency somehow less threatening. Glidden, for instance, "*is dying of a disease contracted from the handling of sphagnum moss—gardening was one of his chief pleasures*" (n. pag.). The moss—embodying at once decay and fertility—is both destructive and regenerative, as is Glidden's relationship to it, but he still derives pleasure from its handling, as from the setting out of a fantasy. It thus plays a useful role in the *mise en scène* of his illness. Similarly, despite the fact that Glidden is dying, he and Lomia can script him into fantasies which allow the migration of his subject identification between useful positions, accommodating his death but rendering it less awful. Glidden councils Cape, "Look at the kettle and think of me, I'm water now,

I will be steam" (7). And after Cape has tried to persuade Lomia to come back to Glidden by revealing to her that Glidden is dying, Lomia says, "I know it would be—nice—for him to die believing that I loved him the way he wanted…. [B]ut I respect him far too much to lie to him." And then she describes her fantasy of Glidden in death: "He'll—he'll never have to sleep alone, again, think they'll all sleep together inside a—peach!! Glid and all the dead mothers. Just think, admiring him… and…" (54). In Cape's response, "What creepy bullshit," *White Biting Dog* acknowledges the unorthodoxy of Lomia's customized heaven, but the play does not annul that heaven's possibility, depicted as it is with such detail and implications of Lomia's profound care for Glidden. The "evil" of death may be a reality, but so may be the "good" of Glidden's and Lomia's fantasies of death.

Many more elements of *White Biting Dog*'s *mise en scène* are extreme or unusual but nevertheless deliberate, as though willing a belief in their validity. The play, thus, builds an internal logic which admits unlikely possibilities. An author's note, for instance, acknowledges the play's "musicality" may be "extreme," but it is also "deliberate" (n. pag.). One could similarly call Lomia's vision of Glidden's heaven in a peach extreme but deliberate; likewise, Pony's final self-sacrifice for Cape; and correspondingly, character names, which are overtly symbolic, deliberately reinforcing characters' roles. For instance, two "sacrificial" characters are called Pascal (like the paschal lamb) and Pony (another diminutive, "innocent" animal), and Lomia's name is much like "lamia" (typically a seductive monster-woman). Events too are unlikely but nevertheless occur: no sooner has Pony predicted Lomia's return is essential than, like a neon-festooned *deus ex machina*, "[t]he doorbell rings," heralding Lomia's arrival (21). *White Biting Dog*, like *The Crack-walker*, acknowledges the "evil," the extreme, and the prohibition of desire, but once again confounds them, delineating a hopeful logic with which the audience is almost provoked to identify.

I Am Yours

In an interview, Thompson has commented on the similarities between the subject's relation to his or her dreams and to theatre in "the ideal theatrical experience": for the dreamer, "They're your dreams, but it seems as if they're just happening to you" (in Tomc 19). Julie Adam has concluded, "This…implies that in a dream one is narrator, actor / character and observer, both insider and outsider, both active and passive, and it is this configuration that Thompson tries to replicate" (24). There are striking similarities between this conception of theatre and a conception of theatre as fantasy (where the subject is similarly mobile, acted upon and active). *I Am Yours* poignantly introduces the possibility that its *mise en scène* is a dreamscape. The play begins with Toilane, Dee, and Mercy simultaneously having the same dream,[13] a dream of being exiled from the home. Later, Mercy re-enacts through a dream a rendez-vous between her schoolgirl self and Raymond (120-122), and later still, in a scene which "*could be a dream,*" Mercy and Raymond meet in the present (171). Other scenes, like Raymond's recitation of the poem (156-157), and the scene with "*RAYMOND speaking to MERCY, but it doesn't matter if she is on stage or not. He should NOT be speaking directly to her*" (174), are not specified as dreams, but nor are they acutely realistic. Like fantasy, the play straddles the border between the conscious and the unconscious, acknowledging the import of both. Also like fantasy, this composition allows the play's audiences a range of engagements with the play, so that they must choose whether to engage with a theme of love, or of love's prohibition.

The overarching desire in *I Am Yours* is the desire to love and, concomitantly, to be loved. "I want…to be the centre," says Mercy, "I want to be the centre of somebody's life" (150). The prohibition to this desire, hate, is present throughout the play, as signalled perhaps in the title which may refer to who possesses the baby at the play's end, but also to love and its aspects of giving, taking, vulnerability, manipulation—shading into hate. As *White Biting Dog* was the story of Cape coming, or not, to feeling, *I Am Yours* is the story of Dee and others coming to loving and being loved, or not. Once more, the play's conclusion is radically uncertain, unreadable in and of itself, but perhaps readable as hopeful, again, given the odd but eloquent and hopeful logic built up through the rest of the play.

The play's most central characters are Dee and her apartment superintendent Toilane. Dee and Toi have a one night stand, Dee conceives, and after almost having an abortion, she decides to have the child but give it up for adoption. Toi and his mother Pegs fight for custody of the child but have to give up the case when Dee, with her sister Mercy's support, counters by charging Toi with assault. Finally, Toi and Pegs preside at Dee's delivery and kidnap the child. Ironically, despite the fact Dee's baby is not in the hospital nursery, in the play's penultimate scene, Dee "*sees the baby somewhere in the audience*" ("*The audience, to her, is the nursery*"), and addresses it: "I want you baby I want you forever because I…love you. I LOVE you" (176). Also ironically, as soon as Pegs, Toi and baby Tracy Meg have triumphantly escaped to Sudbury, Pegs subsides into a chair, "*passed out or maybe dead*" (176). When Dee has learned genuinely to say "I love you," it is to an absent other. And when Toi has reached a state of peace with his mother and attained the child, emblem of his "true love" for Dee, Pegs becomes possibly absent, as, in a sense, does the child, left with so inexperienced a parent asking, "(*bewildered*) Mum??" (176) This might be a tragic ending, a tribute to the prohibition of love, were it not for the litany of tribute paid to hope in the face of prohibition enacted throughout the rest of the play.

Pegs is in many ways out with love. She is patronized by her doctor (130) and "the high classes" (160), avoided by her putative friends, (130) and often barely tolerated by her son (150-151). Motherhood, for Pegs like Theresa, is an important *mise en scène* of desire, bringing immense reward— "you're the most powerful thing there is, a mother, with young kids"—but also the potential for painful rejection—when children get older "ya never see em, and ya wonder if they hate you" (151). Despite this prohibition to experiencing pleasure in motherhood and in other areas of her life, Pegs finds and embraces love and pleasure where she can; for instance, in talking. Told by Toi, "ya talk too much," Peg replies,

> It is not true. It is in no way true, and if it is, if it is, I don't care. Because I happen to love the sound of my voice. I think it's very nice and.... I am gonna talk and talk till our feet freeze off and our hands get frost bite cause when I am talking I am swimmin in a *big vat* of English cream— cream—and talk and I want to swim and cream and talk and talk till we all fall over and freeze. (131)

Apocalyptic imagery of freezing suggests talking is a source of everlasting love for Pegs, and references to plenteous cream (or milk) intimate talking even offers her an idealized maternal love. The logical inconsistencies of Pegs' tirade—again recognized by an incredulous son, as Toi says, "Jesus. You running a fever? Mum?" (131)—acknowledge that, on one level, what Pegs says is untrue. But, on another level, the rhetorical power of her ode to talking affirms the truth of what she says.

Mercy almost hyperbolically enacts her desires and their prohibition: attempting to seduce Mack at the bus station and berating herself when he rejects her (135); and not only allowing herself to be humiliated by her television-watching husband, but re-enacting that humiliation before her sister. (140) But she, again, finds and enjoys love however she can—in television. "Don't put down television," she warns Dee.

> DON'T YOU FUCKING PUT DOWN TELEVISION, YOU SNOT, TELE-VISION HAS SAVED MY LIFE. IT HAS LITERALLY SAVED MY LIFE.... THE TELEVISION IS A SAVIOUR. IT IS A VOICE A WARM VOICE. THERE ARE FUNNY TALK SHOWS WITH HOSTS WHO THINK EX-ACTLY LIKE I DO.... I...I love television. I love it. It makes me happy so don't put it down. (145-146)

References to "hosts" and the television as "saviour" again evoke a Christian imagery of timelessness and, what Mercy feels painfully excluded from by her sister (133), paternal love. The fact that Mercy's love is articulated towards television, however, acutely grounds this love in the secular and ephemeral. Both Pegs' love of talking and Mercy's of television invoke a belief in true love but base that love in the contingent, thereby recognizing contingency, and with that insight, *choosing* to believe. The practice of choosing to believe evidenced throughout *I Am Yours* facilitates the recognition of contingencies— contingencies such as the baby's absence and Pegs's possible death—at the play's end, but also provokes the play's audience to choose to believe, in both Dee's and Toi's coming to love.

Lion in the Streets

In *Lion in the Streets*, the overriding desire carried by Isobel like a baton through the play's relay structure is the desire to return home. This desire and its metaphorical implications of love, forgiveness, comfort, and so on, are echoed throughout the play by many other characters in their individual scenes. For example, Joanne wants to "die good,"[14] Scarlett wants to escape her boredom and dependency (45-47), and Sherry wants to secure a stable home life (62). But, again, these desires are severely inhibited by "the lion in the streets"—psychical or material conditions which prevent fulfilment of desire, a return home, or, what Richard Paul Knowles has recognized as central to Thompson's plays, "the achievement of grace." Asked by Cynthia Zimmerman about "the cruelties present in each of the episodes in *Lion in the Streets*," Thompson responded, "They are a series of soul murders or physical murders" (191). Both desire and its prohibition are enacted in the play, emphatic- ally recognizing the co-existence of the two and spurring both charac- ters and audiences to choose which they will actively favour in the *mise en scène* of desire.

Joanne is dying of bone cancer and, fearing her immanent expulsion from her home into death, she constructs a vision of herself "dying good"; that is, beautifully and without fear, as she perceives Shake- speare's Ophelia dying in a poster she "had in [her] bedroom growing up" (34). Joanne describes her impression of Ophelia's death to her friend Rhonda:

> And she got this heavy heavy blue dress, real...blue and then she wrapped all these pretty pretty flowers round and round her body, round her head, and her hair, she had this golden wavy hair, long, and then she steps down the bank, and she lies, on her back, in the stream. She lies there, but the stream runs so fast she's on her back and she goes.... [S]he dies, Rhon, she dies...good. She dies good. (34-35)

Joanne concludes, "I want to die like that," and asks for Rhonda's help. Rhonda hesitates but eventually replies,

[H]ow the hell do you think that I could live with that after, eh?? I mean it's all very lovely and that, your picture, in your room but that's a picture, that's a picture, you dimwit! The real of it would be awful, the stalks of the flowers would be chokin you, and the smells of them would make you sick, all those smells comin at you when you're feelin so sick to begin with, and the stream, well if you're talking about the Humber River or any stream in this country you're talkin filth…. (36)

Rhonda catalogues the material prohibitions to Joanne's desire. But again if pleasure lies in the setting out of fantasy, and not in the having of an object, then Joanne may experience pleasure in the telling of her fantasy of death despite Rhonda's arguments that it is realistically unachievable as an object. Simultaneously, Rhonda may take comfort (a form of pleasure) in her fantastic telling of the impossibility of Joanne's fantasy because she could not cope with abetting Joanne in the fulfilment of the fantasy. Both women's stories are mutually exclusive, mutually unobtainable, but they nevertheless provide comfort for Joanne and Rhonda, somehow overwhelming prohibition.

When David walks into church on "a whim" and finds himself giving confession to Father Hayes, the two characters again end up constructing "duelling narratives which perhaps prohibit the obtaining of any kind of resolution but do not erase the play of each character's desire (Knowles "The Achievement…" 34). For Father Hayes, David has returned after drowning as a young boy. Father Hayes could have prevented the drowning had he not been guilty of "the sin of pride," selfishly carving the Canada Day chicken instead of watching David "dancing on the water" (40-41). Father Hayes's narrative of David's return allows the former to ask the latter's forgiveness and absolution; in a classic role reversal, Father Hayes says, "Forgive me Father for I have sinned" (40). Of course David replies,

I'm sorry but I never died. You got the wrong guy I knew you…some other time—I mean, shit, I wish I had died, I only wish, it would have made my life so much more interesting…. I grew up, I grew up.

But David segues into a narrative in which his life (or death) is "more interesting":

I forgive you, I forgive you Father, it was nice on the water, you know? It was neat, so calm, as I slipped underneath I wasn't scared, I'll tell ya. I wasn't scared a bit. The water was so…nice!! (42)

Narratives which are duelling in one sense are compatible in that they both negotiate "happy endings" for their respective characters. They may not resolve the situation, but they do make that situation hopeful.

Scenes like Joanne's and Rhonda's and Father Hayes's and David's are repeated throughout the play, so that when the murdered child Isobel finally says, "I take my life," this is believable, again, despite the

---

"fact" she is dead. And when she tells the audience, "I want you all to take your life. I want you all to have your life" (63), this is desirable, making it—if only through the play of pleasure it allows and not the object it obtains—possible.

Reading Thompson's plays as fantasies means being able to read the prohibitions to desire—the lions, the cracks, the evils, the abysses—that Thompson relentlessly portrays, but to do so within a Thompsonian *mise en scène* where good, the fulfilment of desire, is nevertheless triumphantly possible. Usefully, this allows Thompson's audiences to acknowledge the possibility of evil, but actively to choose the triumph of good. Thompson has characterized *Lion in the Streets* as being about "the power to confront evil and walk away with something" (Kaplan 55), but this is a summary which applies equally to all of her plays. Reading Thompson's plays as fantasies does not mean treating them as less than real, but rather treating reality as something more than the purely material and obvious. It means recognizing diverse realities. If we can accept Thompson's plays as, in many ways, fantasies, then we can learn to see their dynamic subjects, interactions of desire and its prohibition, and combinations of material and psychic realities as not merely fanciful, unrealistic, or contradictory, but as effectively real and useful, presenting a world where many things are realistically impossible, but where positive change is imaginatively possible.

NOTES

[1] George Toles relies upon such terms as "mystery," "love" and "grace" to discuss the plays, echoing Thompson's own commentary on her work (cf. Thompson in Zimmerman 192, and in Rudakoff and Much 103), and apparently mimicking the plays' resistance to categorization, but perhaps endorsing the humanist assumption, not necessarily shared by Thompson's work, that these terms are, finally, knowable and universal. Invoking discourses more specific to dramatic criticism, Julie Adam analyzes the plays' anti-naturalism, and Richard Paul Knowles, their "perversion" of both Aristotelian and modernist dramatic conventions ("The Dramaturgy of the Perverse"). Emphasizing thematic analysis, Diane Bessai studies Thompson's work alongside that of Sharon Pollock, explaining that she has chosen to focus on these authors "for the uncommon and contrasting approaches to family themes of their mature work, which they often, although not always, approach from feminine points of view" (98). With a debt to post-structuralism, I have elsewhere assessed the anti-essentialism of Thompson's plays in general ("Problematizing 'Truth'...") and *Lion in the Streets* in particular ("Constructing Fictions..."), and Knowles has looked more closely at how her plays evoke characters', and invoke audiences', split subjectivity ("The Achievement of Grace"). Finally, Robert Nunn has employed Lacanian psychoanalytic theory to examine the plays' depiction of various psychic levels.

[2] For reasons of length, this article will focus on Thompson's four published full length stage plays: *The Crackwalker*, *White Biting Dog*, *I Am Yours*, and *Lion in the Streets*. Please note that Thompson also writes for television and radio, two other scripts are published in *The Other Side of the Dark* (the short *Pink* and the radio play *Tornado*), the radio play *White Sand* has been published in *Airborne*, and *Perfect Pie* has been published in *Solo*.

[3] This article was first published in 1984.

[4] This article was originally published in French in 1964 and in English in 1968.

[5] Jacques Lacan has written: "The phantasy is the support of desire, it is not the object that is the support of desire" (*The Four Fundamental Concepts of Psychoanalysis* [Trans. A. Sheridan. Hogarth P., 1977] 185, cited in Cowie 158).

[6] See, for instance, the way Cowie reads the staging of desire not necessarily through specific characters, but across the films *Now Voyager* and *The Reckless Moment*.

[7] And see, for instance, the way Penley incorporates into her reading of *Star Trek* slash fandom the importance of the fans' adoption of the governing philosophies of the *Star Trek* universe ("Feminism...").

[8] As Penley has pointed out, an appreciation of psychical reality through fantasy usefully breaks down the binary opposition real/illusory: "Fantasy has nothing to do with an opposition between 'reality' and 'illusion' but rather interjects a third term—psychical reality—that structures both" ("Feminism..." 93).

[9] "From the beginning Freud rejected the banal thesis which attributed the unpleasure provoked by sexuality to a purely external prohibition. Whether they are of internal or external origin, desire and prohibition go hand in hand" (Laplanche and Pontalis 30, cited in Lyon 271).

[10] *The Crackwalker* was first produced in 1980, first published in 1981, and republished in Thompson's collection of plays *The Other Side of the Dark*. All references will be to this edition and will appear in parentheses in the text.

[11] Bonnie Cain perhaps encapsulates the way good and evil, and desire and its prohibition, go hand in hand—"Bonnie" meaning good and beautiful, and "Cain" alluding to the Biblical murderer of his good brother Abel. Bonnie herself sounds gratuitously malicious, but her malice sometimes provokes others to kindness, as here, where Sandy defends Theresa and Alan at Danny's funeral.

[12] Thompson, *White Biting Dog*, 108. All further quotations will appear in parentheses in the text. *White Biting Dog* was first produced in 1984.

[13] Thompson, *I Am Yours*, 119. All further references will appear in parentheses in the text. *I Am Yours* was first produced in 1987.

[14] Thompson, *Lion in the Streets*, 35. All further references will appear in parentheses in the text. *Lion in the Streets* was first produced in 1990.

BIBLIOGRAPHY

Adam, Julie. "The Implicated Audience: Judith Thompson's Anti-Naturalism in *The Crackwalker, White Biting Dog, I Am Yours* and *Lion in the Streets.*" Rita Much (ed.). *Women on the Canadian Stage: The Legacy of Hrotsvit.* Winnipeg: Blizzard Publishing, 1992, 21-29.

Bessai, Diane. "Women Dramatists: Sharon Pollock and Judith Thompson." Bruce King (ed.). *Post-Colonial English Drama: Commonwealth Drama since 1960.* London and New York: St. Martin's Press and Macmillan, 1992, 97-117.

Cowie, Elizabeth. "Fastasia" *m/f* 9 (1984). Rpt. in Parveen Adams and Elizabeth Cowie (eds.). *The Woman in Question.* Cambridge, MA: MIT Press, 1990, 149-196.

Harvie, Jennifer. "Constructing Fictions of an Essential Reality or 'This Pickshur Is Niiiice': Judith Thompson's *Lion in the Streets.*" *Theatre Research in Canada* 13.1 and 2 (Spring and Fall 1992), 81-93.

——————. "Problematizing 'Truth': The Stage Plays of Judith Thompson." MA thesis. U. of Guelph, 1991.

Ives, Patricia. "Charting the Abyss." *Stage Press* (Toronto) 7.1 (Fall 1990), 13-15.

Kaplan, Jon. "Mini-fest Probes Thompson's Unsettling Visions." *Now*—November 8-14 1990, (Toronto), 49 and 55.

Kareda, Urjo. Introduction. Judith Thompson. *The Other Side of the Dark*, 9-13.

Knowles, Richard Paul. "The Achievement of Grace." *Brick* 41 (Summer 1991), 33-36.

——————. "The Dramaturgy of the Perverse." *Theatre Research International* 17.3 (Autumn 1992), 226-235.

Laplanche, Jean and Jean-Bertrand Pontalis. "Fantasy and the Origins of Sexuality." Victor Burgin *et al* (eds.). *Formations of Fantasy.* London: Methuen, 1986, 5-33.

Lapsley, Robert and Michael Westlake. *Film Theory: An Introduction.* Manchester: MUP, 1988.

Lyon, Elisabeth. "The Cinema of Lol V. Stein." *Camera Obscura* 6 (Fall 1980). Rpt. in Penley, 244-271.

Mulvey, Laura. "Afterthoughts on 'Visual Pleasure and Narrative Cinema' Inspired by *Duel in the Sun.*" *Framework* 6.15-17 (1981). Rpt. in Penley, 69-79.

——————. "Visual Pleasure and Narrative Cinema" *Screen* 16.3 (Autumn 1975), 6-18. Rpt. in Penley, 57-68.

Nunn, Robert. "Spatial Metaphor in the Plays of Judith Thompson." *Theatre History in Canada* 10.1 (Spring 1989), 3-29.

Penley, Constance, (ed.). *Feminism and Film Theory.* New York: Routledge, 1988.

——————. "Feminism, Psychoanalysis, and the Study of Popular Culture." Lawrence Grossberg *et al.* (eds.). *Cultural Studies.* New York and London: Routledge, 1992, 479-500.

Thompson, Judith. "A Conversation with Judith Thompson." By Cynthia Zimmerman. *Canadian Drama* 16.2 (1990), 184-194.

——————. *The Crackwalker. The Other Side of the Dark,* 15-71.

——————. *I Am Yours. The Other Side of the Dark,* 115-76.

——————. "Interview." Judith Rudakoff and Rita Much. *Fair Play: Twelve Women Speak.* Toronto: Simon and Pierre, 1990, 88-104.

——————. *Lion in the Streets.* Toronto: Coach House Press, 1992.

——————. *The Other Side of the Dark: Four Plays by Judith Thompson.* Toronto: Coach House Press, 1989.

——————. *Perfect Pie.* Jason Sherman (ed.). *Solo.* Toronto: Coach House, 1994, 161-171.

——————. *Pink. The Other Side of the Dark,* 73-77.

——————. "Revisions of Probability: An Interview with Judith Thompson." By Sandra Tomc. *Canadian Theatre Review* 59 (Summer 1989), 18-23.

——————. *Tornado. The Other Side of the Dark,* 79-114.

——————. *White Biting Dog.* Toronto: Playwrights Canada, Rev. ed. 1985.

——————. *White Sand.* Ann Jansen (ed.). *Airborne: Radio Plays by Women.* Winnipeg: Blizzard Publishing, 1991, 1-28.

Toles, George. "'Cause You're the Only One I Want': The Anatomy of Love in the Plays of Judith Thompson," *Canadian Literature* 118 (Autumn 1988), 116-135.

Chris Johnson

"I put it in terms which cover the spectrum:" Mixed Convention and Dramatic Strategies in George F. Walker's *Criminals in Love*

> I put it in terms which cover the spectrum. The political. The philosophical. The poetic. Occasionally I use the vernacular. I talk of the great fuck-up. Of getting shafted, getting screwed up the ass. Without even a kiss. I describe the human condition. I tell you Junior's story. Your story. And if I may be so bold, our story…. Because aren't we all in this together. Aren't we all friends here. Can't you feel the bond. Isn't this the absolute truth![1]

Thus, William the philosophical bum in George F. Walker's *Criminals in Love* describes to Gail, the protagonist's girlfriend, the rhetorical strategies he employs in telling the story of the protagonist, Junior, trying to "end [his] relationship" with his convict father—Junior, a young man growing up on the mean streets of east end Toronto fears that he is destined to follow the footsteps of his criminal father, thus "fucking up" his love for the level-headed Gail and their plans for a life together. In telling this story of "young lovers doomed," the fate/free will and nature/nurture debates as high farce, Walker himself employs similar strategies, covering the spectrum of high to low comedy to serious drama, "naturalistic" to extravagantly theatrical conventions, employing simultaneously a character's preoccupation with "destiny" and a running sight gag in which Junior appears in ever increasing quantities of bandages as a result of his encounters with the vicissitudes of his sad life.

Response to Walker's work also covers the spectrum in Canada. On one hand, he is regarded as one of the country's leading playwrights, performed, anthologized and discussed more than most, twice winner of the Governor General's Award for Drama. His *Love and Anger* was transferred to a commercial theatre after its Factory Theatre première, and enjoyed the longest run in recent Canadian theatre history. On the other hand, his work still occasions a great deal of bewilderment, and some downright critical hostility. A number of explanations have been put forward. One is that Canadians, while good at comedy, are suspicious of comedy, and Walker is the most serious and dedicated comic playwright Canada has produced. Another is that Canadians are suspicious of political theatre, and Walker is one of the few Canadian playwrights who take seriously issues of class—George Ryga, Arthur Milner, and David Fennario do so overtly; Judith Thompson and Walker build class consciousness and conflict into the very fabric of their plays, while refusing to take doctrinaire positions. Yet another is that English Canadian theatre valourizes neo-realism, and Walker's work has always been distinguished by a more theatrical sensibility, his characters frequently larger than life and given to pyrotechnical outbursts of language and self-conscious philosophy. Finding the right scale has frequently been a problem in producing Walker's work, for often directors and actors leap immediately to the operatic size the scripts seem to invite: the result can be a hollow production, all shout with none of the human conflict and the thus implied social critique essential to the plays, because what Peter Blais has called "the truth of the scene"[2] has been left behind (as was often the case, I think, with the Great Canadian Theatre Company production of *Criminals in Love* in Ottawa in the spring of 1993).

But size by itself is not the whole problem with the later Walker plays. Earlier Walker plays seem, in retrospect, of a piece, their inner logic depending on the majority of characters sharing a larger-than-life quality and an element of caricature (although there is sometimes a "touchstone" character, like Victor in *Zastrozzi* and Jamie in *Filthy Rich* and *The Art of War*, whose combination of psychological complexity and empathetic common sense enables the characters to communicate an effect closer to that of "realism" than is usual in plays from that stage of Walker's career). However, in the last five or six plays, the intrusion of "realism," even "naturalism," in some characters and in some scenes, has been more pronounced. The shift certainly occurs in the first of the East End plays, *Better Living* (while a large audience and a Canadian audience first saw *Criminals in Love*, Walker started work on *Better Living* before beginning *Criminals*, and the earlier version of *Better Living*, much different from the one produced at CentreStage in 1986, was given partial production at Cornell University in 1982). I think this shift is also apparent in the last of the Power plays, *The Art of War*, first produced in 1983. In *Criminals in Love*, we have french fries and prostitution on one hand, "destiny" and "the hanging shadow" on the other; relatively realistic younger characters, Junior, Gail and Sandy, contrasted to the more theatrical portraits of the older characters, William, Henry Dawson Senior and Wineva.

This was one of the earliest and thorniest problems encountered when the Black Hole Theatre of the University of Manitoba began rehearsals for a production of *Criminals in Love* in 1988. Heeding Walker's example and advice from the rehearsals of the 1987 tenth anniversary production of *Zastrozzi* at the Factory Theatre in Toronto (which Walker gave me permission to observe), I, too, sought the "truth of the scene" when directing my actors, and only when we had found it to our satisfaction, did we begin to magnify through what Walker calls "raising the stakes." The problem was that the younger characters didn't magnify, or didn't magnify in the same manner as did the older characters; emotional intensity increased, but Junior, Gail and Sandy stayed stubbornly within the conventions of realism. Scenes involving only the younger characters played realistically, scenes involving only the older characters played theatrically, and scenes involving both groups of characters either didn't play at all in earlier rehearsals, or produced a very peculiar, divided effect, unsettling both to us, and eventually to our audiences. Members of the audience tended to favour one group of characters or the other, depending on their theatrical tastes, to a lesser extent on their generational affiliation, and to dismiss the other grouping as inferior, in the writing and in the performance. Yet another portion of the audience simply found the whole experience unsettling, some with relish, some not. It was to my considerable relief that, during our rehearsal period, *Canadian Drama* published Robert Wallace's interview with Walker, for in it Walker discusses that very characteristic of his more recent work.

> WALLACE [inquires]: It does seem to me...that there are two types of characters and, as a result, two types of scenes in your newer work: for example, the scene between Junior and his father [in] *Criminals in Love* achieves a manic, grotesque theatricality, as does the scene where William visits the father to plead on Junior's behalf; yet in the same play, the scenes between Junior and Gail are much more subtle, approaching a quality of naturalism.... Would you agree that there are these two types of characters in your newer plays?
>
> WALKER [replies]: Yeah, and I think they're riding the edges of each other, and they're meeting more carefully now. I think the voice, my writing voice, is with them both, trusting the shifts in tone, trusting those extremes more, trusting that these two types can be together, like different colours. In effect, I'm saying that's what the world is like, and I'm opening up the panel more to see more of the world.[3]

We were relieved because what we were struggling with as a disparity was apparently an intentional effect of the script, and because, furthermore, Walker didn't expect it to work all the time. "Flaws are essential to its strength,"[4] he says of his new approach, in typically cryptic fashion.

Nonetheless, the question remained, "why?" Just as Walker does not exaggerate for the sake of hyperbole alone, it did not seem likely that he was mixing convention simply to confuse, although that was part of it, a new and effective strategy for achieving the dislocation which Walker considers an essential part of the theatrical experience, certainly essential for theatre which successfully conveys the impression of the world as Walker sees it. It also seemed to us likely that the three older characters were intended to be representative to some degree, "representative" and presentational in the Brechtian sense Johnston attributes to *The Art of War*, a play which Johnston says takes its title from a passage in *The Messingkauf Dialogues* (but also a title which borrows/appropriates that of the classic Chinese military treatise by Sun Tzu, and which additionally echoes Machiavelli). Johnston sees in several characteristics of Walker's work techniques of alienation: "Walker's frequently preposterous situations and incongruous epigrammatic dialogue forestall an extended suspension of disbelief. In addition, the characters' periodic verbal reminders of just who stands for what ideologically encourages the audience to critically examine the validity of what these people believe in…"[5] That this is applicable to William, Wineva, even Henry, seemed likely, but our problem was not solved, for the Brechtian solution is not applicable to the younger, more realistic characters. Moreover, this too is a matter of dramaturgical intention, and will not yield playable action.

Further work on relationships between characters, ways in which characters react to each other, particularly the ways in which they see each other, began to reveal an answer which seemed to us provisionally satisfactory: the degree of theatricality in *Criminals in Love* is, in part, a function of point-of-view, particularly the point-of-view of Junior, whose play it is. The older characters, through his eyes, are larger-than-life: his father, not just a father but a classic Freudian rival for the affection of his lost mother as well as "destiny" personified; Wineva, a monstrous semi-incestuous sexual threat and an even more dangerous agent of familial destiny; William, the wise old man, Jungian this time, the stranger/friend/teacher who is not whom he appears to be and who seems to have the power to control destiny. To Junior, these characters are not so much people as primal forces, with enormous power to shape his life, and over which he apparently has no control. William Lane has described *Zastrozzi* as a "modern morality play;"[6] to a large extent, all Walker's plays are modern morality plays, and in *Criminals*, we have a junior Everyman whose soul is the battleground between the forces of "the hanging shadow" and sociological destiny on one side, and the forces of enlightenment and love on the other. Point-of-view lends *Criminals* its shape, its convention of mixed convention, for Walker gives the audience as its "lens" the perspective of a *naif* like Junior, not Junior himself, for the older characters are larger-than-life whether or not Junior is present.

To a lesser extent, point-of-view also affects the presentation of the young women, Gail and Sandy, for in them, Junior sees the classic mother/whore dichotomy early in the play. He is clearly lying when he says, "I have no problem about breasts,"[7] and Gail is obviously a substitute for his lost mother early in the play. Gail's development throughout the play, as she abandons the role of teacher/mother to Junior and begins to confront and accept her own fears and weaknesses, is not only indicative of her own adjustment to circumstances, but of a change in the way Junior sees her, progressively accepting responsibility for her welfare that goes beyond the hysterical separation anxiety of the first scene, finally seeing clearly that she is not his mother. Similarly, his initial, fearful stereotyping of Sandy as "hooker" is subsequently replaced by a more comprehensive vision of Sandy's "realistic" complexity.

The concept of point-of-view was a useful rehearsal tool, as you can't play Walker's dramaturgical intention to dislocate the audience's reaction to the theatrical event preparatory to replacing their version of "reality" with his own, and, if Johnston is correct, to effect a Brechtian alienation. While you can't play point-of-view either, that factor does qualify and justify actions which can be played, and is often useful as an obstacle to a character's objective. Furthermore, the possibility of manipulating perception gives the older characters additional playable action: all three, with varying degrees of consciousness, play roles, deliberately stage events and enlarge themselves in order to impress and influence the world at large, and Junior in particular.

Henry is not a very good actor, but he nonetheless acts. He attempts to play the penitent, the cosmic victim, and the tough guy for William, with no success. For Junior, a much less demanding, more impressionable audience, he plays the father with a capital "F," enforcing sentimental claims to family loyalties which he himself does not feel, dramatizing family ties and transforming the pathetic Dawson clan into a big-time, crime family. Henry has modelled himself on big brother Ritchie, and, diction and style suggest, on gangster movies: "He's your goddamn godfather."[8] "I owe your Uncle Ritchie this favour. If I welch he'll have me knifed. He's got friends inside."[9] "So Ritchie finally knocked over the Sally Ann. He's been planning that job for two years."[10] Henry has watched too many B-Movies; while of all the characters in the play, he is the least willing to assume responsibility for his own actions, the most eager to blame outside forces for his disaster of a life, he has, in fact, embraced a B-Movie role for which he is ultimately unsuited. Unlike early Walker plays, which were, I have argued, B-Movies or versions of B-Movies,[11] later plays, like *Criminals in Love*, instead insert into more readily recognizable "realistic" settings individual characters who are B-Movie characters, or who have modelled themselves after B-Movie characters (like Henry Sr. and Wineva in *Criminals in Love*, or Tom in *Better Living* or Rolly in *Beautiful City* and *Escape from Happiness*). That his father is playing at being a crook is little comfort to Junior: "He's a crook. That's bad enough. But he's so fucking bad at it."[12] Biology as destiny is just that much more frightening: instead of being doomed to growing up a crook, Junior faces the prospect of a life-time playing a crook badly.

Wineva is a much more polished performer. Like Henry, she theatricalizes the Dawsons ("By the way, do you all understand what I really mean by 'family.'"[13]) and like Henry, she manipulates others through spurious claims to family loyalties she herself does not feel, as well as to loyalties of class, group unity, even of sexual and emotional attraction. The kisses, the sexual allusions, the sexual advances to all the other characters except Henry, are not real to the essentially asexual Wineva at all, in the view of Cynthia Hiebert-Simkin who played the role in our production, but performance, a theatre of intimidation. While a more formidable performer than Henry is, Wineva meets her downfall through her madness, which the Black Hole company took as real, and tried to portray realistically, with some if not complete success; Wineva must not be merely funny, she must be dangerous, for her schizophrenia is not part of her performance. Madness misleads her into believing her own performances as she progresses from gun moll to revolutionary, complete with costume for herself and for her supporting players, and by the end of the play, she performs as much to impress herself as she does to affect those around her.

William also comes to grief, at least in part, through coming to believe too much in his own performance. William is the most conscious performer in the play, and the character who finds the most joy in performance. He goes through more costume changes and transformations during the play than does any other character, most of his own volition, most for plays-within-the-play of his own composition: at the beginning of *Criminals*, he says he is just pretending to be a bum;[14] he dons Henry's clothes, presumably Henry's good clothes, to pose as a psychiatrist in scene six; in scene seven he transforms himself into a big-time gangster/businessman with a suit, "...the cruise missile of social conflict,"[15] in an attempt to match Wineva's theatre of intimidation with his own; after losing, he is cast by Wineva in the role of revolutionary, complete with beret; and it is only in scene nine, the last scene of the play, that he attempts real action, action not dependent on disguise and pretence—neither the proposed flight to Barbados nor the attempt to kill Henry are performances. Furthermore, William performs throughout the play in that his longer speeches, his flights of philosophical, political and poetic fancy, are in themselves "performed" pieces, and William is conscious of the performance context: "I weep. Look, a tear on my cheek. I have been reached personally and sincerely by this tragedy;"[16] "That was the summary. Let me rinse my mouth and give you the poetic details."[17]

While the Black Hole company concluded that his internal pain is real, or that William believes it is real, we also built into our actor's performance William's willingness to employ the pain as an element of his performance, to "use it" in an actor's sense to intensify and enlarge his "acting," sometimes with the objective of deflecting an attack from Wineva, more often as a means of including himself within the circle of Gail and Junior's love. He himself prefers to leave the pain in the realm of make-believe, rejecting Junior's advice to consult a doctor: "I've always been able to live with the possibility that these pains might be imaginary."[18] Earlier in the day, wearing the suit, he "felt entirely well:" the suit role did not require, indeed precluded, the experience of internal pain. William encourages his feelings, psyches himself up in the manner of an actor.

William comes closer to addressing the audience directly than does any other character in the play. In his 1987 production of *Zastrozzi*, Walker allowed direct address only to Michael Hogan, playing Zastrozzi himself, but encouraged the actors playing other characters to flirt with the device, to appear capable of doing so, giving Peter Blais, playing Victor, the approving rehearsal note, "He never speaks directly to the audience, but you always think he's going to."[19] In our production of *Criminals*, I encouraged Neil Lawrie, playing William, to manipulate convention in a similar manner. In scene three, in the burger joint, when William launches into the long "destiny and fate and despair" speech from which I quoted at the beginning of this essay, we had William perform not just for Gail and Junior (to Gail's acute embarrassment and Junior's delight), but also for the other, invisible customers, downstage from the booth, his performance being thus directed at and through the invisible audience in the burger joint to the real audience in the auditorium. At the beginning of scene eight, the second alley scene shortly before Wineva arrives with her bomb, Lawrie found the richest possibilities for mixing convention in this fashion on the lines:

> Some people would tell you just to think positively. These are people, of course, who have been able to spend all their summers outdoors. Probably their grandmothers had a lot of money. Others would tell you to pick yourself up by the bootstraps. These are people who have forgotten anything they might have known about life.[20]

It can be assumed that many in the audience, frustrated by Junior's passivity and Gail's paralysis in the face of doom, have been wanting the protagonists to pull themselves together, perhaps despising them for not doing so, and this moment, at the edge of direct address, is alarming, doubling convention by adding to the naive lens the possibility of confrontational accusation; the audience is in danger of being included in the dramatic action as well as in the point-of-view. Class warfare as dramatic conflict has been set up between stage and house. A similar moment occurs near the end of the play; William says:

> Other people would want to talk in terms of social patterns. Real things, like economic reform. Re-education. They'd dismiss the theory of the hanging shadow with a sneer. These are people who are members of another class. The skiing class. The long-outdoor-summer class. Historically, philosophically, they make me sick. The hanging shadow of course exists. I say fuck it, but it exists.[21]

Needless to say, we put the hanging shadow in the auditorium.

As in the case of enlargement, archetyping through point-of-view, the factor of conscious performance enters into a consideration of the young women, Sandy and Gail, as well as of the older characters, but again to a lesser degree. Sandy is obviously "acting," not very successfully, when she tries on the role of street-walker in the little dumb show which begins scene five, the first alley scene, and subsequently resorts to a "tough girl" persona from time to time in her attempts to cope with the bizarre events unfolding around her. Gail consciously rejects the larger-than-life role in which Junior has cast her in the early scenes of the play, but later resorts to pop-song, pulp novel romanticism to objectify her sense of dread: "Junior and I are doomed. It's young love gone wrong. Dead man's curve. Teenage wasteland."[22] Christine Harapiak had trouble with this speech, until she used its heightened effect as a performance intended to get the attention of William, preoccupied by Wineva's terrifying kiss until summoned back to attentiveness by a rhetoric as lush as his own. At the end of the play, Gail, more mature, has abandoned the attempt to romanticize her plight: "We're going to jail. Young lovers doomed, taking the plunge. This is that cliff, Junior. That one I read about in a dozen books…. In the books it was a bit romantic."[23]

Junior, alone, does not perform at all through most of the play. The last thing in the world he wants is to enlarge himself, to call attention to himself:

> The problem is missed opportunities. Looking back I had all these chances to get invisible. Get really small. Really really small. This big. So no one would notice. I know I was never really big but I wasn't small enough. Someone noticed I was around.[24]

It is only at the end of the play that Junior allows himself to be bigger, to give Gail the assurance she needs: "Then let's see if they've got the stomach to come in and get us."[25] He has tried before (when trying to sever the "relationship" with his father, in attempting to defy Wineva in the matter of the bomb—and here he is the first to do so, taking action before either William or Gail), but earlier attempts failed. It is only at the end of the play that we feel that there might, just might, be permanent growth. While I did not see the original production of *Criminals in Love* and cannot therefore comment on James Harrison's essentially hostile assessment of that production ("George Walker, director, betrays George Walker, playwright"[26]), I must disagree with his observation that the Junior of the script does not grow in the course of the play, that his choice of a course of action is delayed too long—Junior chooses in the second scene of the play, but is not yet strong enough to maintain the course, nor is he in subsequent attempts until finally love for Gail, stronger than the puppy love it was before being tested by events (he has, remember, risked his life for her), gives him that strength, wavering, tentative, but there.

That this growth is not large and dramatic, that a small step is taken with great effort and at great cost, is perhaps the most "realistic" touch in the portrait of the most "realistic" character in the play. That it occurs at all is another indication of change in recent Walker work; the obsessional, monomaniacal, grotesque figures of the early plays never change, and the inevitable result is the unrelievedly bleak endings of plays such as *Beyond Mozambique*. Love's little triumph at the end of *Criminals in Love* is almost mellow in comparison, in that it hints not at "hope," a word Walker dislikes, but at "possibility." He says of the recent plays:

> For me it was a matter of letting more light into my plays; just naturally, I felt I had to do that, see what sort of hope—that's not a good word; "possibility" might be better—I could find. More than anything, that's the major change I think: I'm getting more possibility, more future, into the work. The early plays don't have much hope for the future; their essential concern is "what is the world?"—what is the nature of the chaos there? Now it's more a question of how to deal with it, how to fight through it. And, if anything, it's a stronger question.[27]

At the end of *Better Living*, the family might well be strong enough to refuse to readmit Tom/Tim (or, if they do, as it transpires in *Escape from Happiness*, strong enough to assimilate him), and Mary-Ann chooses a name for her baby, a terrible name but she chooses. At the end of *Beautiful City*, it's possible that Gina Mae and Paul Gallagher, and their visions of the world, might come together. At the end of *Nothing Sacred*, the peasants might be the future. At the end of *Tough!*, Tina and Bobby might have moved closer to an understanding of each other. At the end of *Criminals in Love* it's possible that, in Walker's words, "the love which the two characters feel for each other might somehow get them through."[28]

Harrison feels that Walker strips Junior of any individuality by having Junior, finally and conclusively, choose his love for Gail over his loyalty to his father, his destiny (and in the process, he thinks, doom his father to Uncle Ritchie's fatal revenge);[29] this is necessary, given Junior's circumstances, if the concluding "possibility" is to exist, and isn't Harrison simply disagreeing with the choice Junior makes? It is the sort of extraordinarily demanding decision faced by a number of characters in Walker plays of the past decade. Power loses to Hackman in *The Art of War* because he cannot make that decision; Hackman is prepared to kill, but Power, confronted with the classic liberal dilemma, cannot, tempted though he may be. In a version of *Better Living*, Jack, priest, brother and uncle (conflicting roles all) faces the decision, and goes a step farther, threatening if not necessarily committing murder when he confronts Tom, like Hackman a fascist, whose consumer socialism, like national socialism, makes things work:

> You see what people like you force people like me to do. You force us to forget reason, our own sense of humanity.... You're a tyrant with a lot of powerful potential. So we're forced to get ourselves free. To clarify our point of view. Our idea of the world. We're taking action. That's what you are forcing us to do. Take a terrifying action....[30]

Junior and Gail, together, make a similar choice with equally terrifying implications. Destiny wins anyway, but, given the "possibility" that Walker has built into the play, its victory might not be permanent; that's the way the actors playing the roles in our production felt and played the final moment of the play, and apparently that's how the audience took the moment as well, empathizing with the "young lovers doomed" more than at any other point during the production. The moment is beautifully set up, as Walker removes characters from the stage singly and in a pair: first Henry, then Sandy, then William and Wineva together. As the older characters leave, they take their size and theatricality with them, as Walker focuses in on a quiet scene between the two realistic characters with which he began the play, finally concluding the play with the image with which he began it, Junior with his head up Gail's sweater. But Gail and Junior are not the same people they were at the beginning of the play, nor is their love the same; that it has survived the intervening onslaught of event and peril augments the "possibility" Walker speaks of. The way in which that which has intervened is presented theatrically "covers the spectrum," and that these strategies fuse in their theatrical shape presentational and representational convention, the comic and the dramatic, the philosophical, political and poetic, makes the play a more effective and satisfying theatrical model of the complexity not only of the dilemma facing the protagonists, but of the way in which Walker sees contemporary society.

Walker distrusts simplification, precise and misleading definition, easy answers. In *Beautiful City*, Jane, the witch's daughter, tells the architect protagonist: "You've lost touch with the genuinely complex nature of reality. All your friends think alike, talk alike, want the same things...."[31] That's a fairly accurate description of the world view and consequent expectations a mainstream audience takes to the theatre. Later, in the same conversation, Jane says "You're dying from a kind of simplicity.... It's like you've taken the huge throbbing life force and turned it into a piece of thread...and it's not enough to hold you together."[32]

Only through refusing to confine *Criminals in Love* within a single set of conventions, a single dramatic type, a piece of thread, and by asking questions rather than seeking to answer them, can Walker to his own satisfaction confront his audience with his version of "life force" and tell us "Junior's story. Your story. And if I may be so bold, our story.... Because aren't we all in this together.... Isn't this the absolute truth!?"[33]

NOTES

Many of my observations on *Criminals in Love* arise from rehearsals for a production of the play which I directed and in which I played the part of Henry Sr., produced by the Black Hole Theatre of the University of Manitoba at and with the Gas Station Theatre of Winnipeg in September 1988. I am grateful for the contributions and insights of the assistant director, Bruce Michalski, the set and lighting designer, Dennis Smith, the costume designer, Jamie Savage, and the cast: Guy Stewart, Junior; Christine Harapiak, Gail; Neil Lawrie, William; Cynthia Hiebert-Simkin, Wineva; and Barbara Gehring (at the time, Melnyk), Sandy.

[1] George F. Walker, *Criminals in Love*, Toronto: Playwrights Canada, 1984, 35.

[2] Jon Kaplan, "Playing Walker's Zastrozzi with passion and maturity," in *Now*, May 14-20, 1987, 35.

3 Robert Wallace, "Looking for the Light: A Conversation with George F. Walker," in *Canadian Drama/L'Art dramatique canadien* 14, 1, 1988, 31.

[4] Wallace, *Looking*, 32.

[5] Denis W. Johnston, "George F. Walker: Liberal Idealism and the 'Power Plays,'" in *Canadian Drama/L'Art dramatique canadien* 10, 2, 1984, 204.

[6] William Lane, "Introduction" to *Zastrozzi: The Master of Discipline* by George F. Walker, Toronto: Playwrights Co-op, 1979.

[7] Walker, *Criminals*, 2.

[8] Walker, *Criminals*, 18.

[9] Walker, *Criminals*, 24.

[10] Walker, *Criminals*, 70.

[11] Chris Johnson, "George F. Walker: B-Movies Beyond the Absurd," in *Canadian Literature*, 85 (Summer 1980), 87-103, and in *Contemporary Literary Criticism (CLC 61)*, ed. by Roger Matuz, Detroit: Gale Research, 1991, 424-429.

[12] Walker, *Criminals*, 8.

[13] Walker, *Criminals*, 53.

[14] Walker, *Criminals*, 15.

[15] Walker, *Criminals*, 80.

[16] Walker, *Criminals*, 33.

[17] Walker, *Criminals*, 34.

[18] Walker, *Criminals*, 88.

[19] My notes from observing the rehearsals for the 1987 Factory Theatre production of *Zastrozzi*.

[20] Walker, *Criminals*, 89.

[21] Walker, *Criminals*, 116.

[22] Walker, *Criminals*, 51.

[23] Walker, *Criminals*, 118.

[24] Walker, *Criminals*, 76.

[25] Walker, *Criminals*, 119.

[26] James Harrison, "Reporting a Criminal Act," in *Theatrum* #1, (April 1985), 11.

[27] Wallace, *Looking*, 22.

[28] Wallace, *Looking*, 27.

[29] Harrison, Reporting, 13.

[30] *Better Living*, CentreStage production script, 115. [This speech has been deleted from the published version of the play.]

[31] George F. Walker, *The East End Plays*, Toronto: Playwrights Canada, 1988, 266.

[32] Walker, *The East End Plays*, 266.

[33] Walker, *Criminals*, 35.

Paul Lefebvre

Quebec Playwriting since 1980

It was in 1968 that Quebec playwriting truly took flight, definitively rejecting the French model to define itself as North American—turning its back on literary theatre for a drama of "natural" dialogue. Starting with Gratien Gélinas—*Les Fridolinades* (1937), *Tit-Coq* (1948)—and continuing with Marcel Dubé—*Un simple soldat* (1957)—this trend became firmly established with Michel Tremblay's *Les Belles-Soeurs* (1968). Tremblay's subsequent works—for instance, *À toi, pour toujours, ta Marie-Lou* (1970), *Hosanna* (1973) and *Damnée Manon, sacrée Sandra* (1977)—confirmed his importance and made him the emblematic playwright of the new Quebec theatre. This genre of drama, in which the dialogue manifests a strong link with the spoken word, enabled Quebec theatre both to undergo an artistic explosion and to build a solid foundation among the public. In Quebec, the 1960s were the decade of the Quiet Revolution; within ten years, life changed radically: both religious practice and the birthrate plummeted, there was a rapid rise in education levels, the church and the state were separated, Quebec entered the modern age. As well, starting in the late 1960s, the theatre became a primary site for debating the collective identity. This national self-examination burned out in the mid-1970s, and until the end of the decade playwriting talents were concerned mainly with harpooning social stereotypes and describing the new confusion in private lives.

At the beginning of the 1980s, the first texts by Normand Chaurette and René-Daniel Dubois marked a clean break with playwriting over the previous dozen years. These two playwrights introduced a drama in which language no longer gave the illusion of natural speech, but was presented as unabashedly artificial. In addition, their dramatic worlds revealed great liberties both in their treatment of time and space and in their choice of cultural references. Chaurette's first well-known play was *Rêve d'une nuit d'hôpital,* a meditation on the poet Émile Nelligan (1879-1941). But the indisputable originality of his writing burst forth with *Provincetown Playhouse, juillet 1919, j'avais 19 ans (Provincetown Playhouse July 1919, I was 19)* (1981), featuring a complex structure based on bold mirror effects. Chaurette sets in motion a bizarre plot, combining elements of a police investigation and a psycho-analytic thriller, in order to examine the interchange of libidinous investments between artistic creativity and life. The structure of *Fragments d'une lettre d'adieu lue par des géologues (Fragments of a Farewell Letter Read by Geologists)* (1986) is also an investigation, this time an examination of the hegemony of scientific language (the most precise form of analytic-referential discourse) as an instrument in the search for truth. In *Les Reines (The Queens)* (1990), Chaurette takes his inspiration from the female characters in Shakespeare's *Richard III* to shed light on all the lures contained in the discourse of political power. Written in sumptuous language, constructed around uncertainties usually left unresolved (how and why did the geologist Toni van Saikin die? Is the Duke of Clarence dead?), Chaurette's wildly poetic plays attack the discourses that structure the social order, always leading to a search for the inexpressible, where language must yield to the body.

"I am a gorilla who makes pottery," René-Daniel Dubois has said. Indeed, his plays sometimes seem to result from raw logorrhea, and critics have often characterized him as "absurd" and "delirious." These epithets hardly do justice to the extreme sophistication of Dubois' writing. In *26bis, impasse du Colonel Foisy* (1983), the playwright himself forcefully shows the point to which the shopworn aspect of the dominant discourse masks a much more disturbing reality. In this play, the character of Madame, at once the author's creation and his spokesperson, after giving a few examples of this schism, declares, "So, if the absurd is naturalism and I am the object of someone's delirium, I hope you are weighing the implications of your aspirations, because the author has warned me by express mail that if there is not an immediate reconsideration, the next time he is invited to dinner by an undertaker who has a Mickey Mouse phone on his bedstand, he will eat the curtains. And his indigestion will not be a figure of speech. Have I made myself understood?"

In fact, in his work Dubois sought to update the state of existential emptiness that, for him, is the basis of human life, and to express the fundamental pain of this state, showing the point to which ambient discourses both conceal and reveal it. He expressed this search in a flamboyant fable, *Ne blâmez jamais les Bédouins (Don't Blame the Bedouins)* (1984), which involves, among other things, an Italian opera singer, a German mountain-climber, a physically unattractive genius pupil from a working-class background, two nuclear trains bristling with weapons, and an American helicopter patrol. Similarly, he denounced the ideological pitfalls of passionate love with the very realistic *Being at home with Claude* (1985).

In this mode of theatre, which distances itself from natural speech to create its own words, the plays of Jovette Marchessault and Lise Vaillancourt are also significant. Marchessault's work, such as *La terre est trop courte, Violette Leduc (The Edge of Earth Is Too Near, Violette Leduc)* (1981) and *Anaïs dans la queue de la comète (Anaïs in the Comet's Wake)* (1985), is principally devoted to the rewriting of theatre and literary history from a feminist perspective. Vaillancourt, in her plays *Marie-Antoine, opus 1* (1984) and *Billy Strauss* (1990), conducted a very complex exploration of the creator-creation tandem. *Marie-Antoine, opus 1*, for example, portrays a five-year-old girl learning to write, as written by the character herself.

Finally, there is the monstrous theatrical cycle by Jean-Pierre Ronfard, *Vie et mort du Roi Boiteux* (1981-82), a prodigious pillaging of history and of universal literature, a "grotesque and bloody epic" involving more than three hundred characters, which turns the usual facts of time and space on their head to achieve a great ludic *teatro mundi*. The theatre of these writers went beyond a reappropriation of the literary; it was also a reappropriation of the world and of the past. Whereas Quebec drama had, since Gélinas, been devoted to the theatrical transposition of Quebec points of reference and subjects, Chaurette takes us to New England, Dubois, to the Australian desert, Marchessault, to Paris, and Vaillancourt and Ronfard create a geography in which the stage is at once Montreal and Tibet, Longueuil and Hamburg.

Though some influential authors of the 1970s, such as Jean Barbeau and Jean-Claude Germain, had, in the 1980s, either commercialized their production (Barbeau) or stopped writing for the stage (Germain), this was not the case for Michel Tremblay, whose work continues to dominate the Quebec theatre scene. After leaving his characters from the Plateau Mont-Royal (a working-class Montreal neighbourhood) just long enough to write about the traditional Quebec bourgeoisie (*L'Impromptu d'Outremont*, 1980 [The Impromptu of Outremont]) and homosexuals well integrated into the new middle class (*Les Anciennes Odeurs*, 1981 [Remember Me]), Tremblay returned to the characters from his first cycle. In *Albertine, en cinq temps (Albertine, in Five Times)* (1984), one of his most powerful plays, a woman is confronted with herself at five different times of her life and makes a despairing assessment of her existence. *Le Vrai Monde? (The Real World?)* (1987) questions the relationship between a writer and those who inspired him. And *La Maison suspendue* (1990) is a key work, in which Tremblay weaves together the threads between the characters that have peopled his plays for twenty-five years. His most recent play, *Marcel poursuivi par les chiens (Marcel Pursued by the Hounds)* (1992), structured like a Sophoclean tragedy, reveals the origins of the madness of Marcel, one of the most important characters in his work.

It must be mentioned, however, that most Quebec dramatists, following in the footsteps of Tremblay's generation (and in this regard integrating with the rest of North American drama), wrote dialogue that resembled spoken language. Among the principal playwrights were Marie Laberge and Michel-Marc Bouchard. Laberge became known in 1981 for *C'était avant la guerre à l'Anse-à-Gille (Before the War, Down at L'Anse à Gilles)*, which turns the nostalgic clichés of popular culture inside out: in this play, rural Quebec of the 1930s ceases to be a sort of Eden before the advent of urban modernity, and is revealed to be a conservative, stifling society, stuck in a rigid class system. In Laberge's subsequent plays, however, she distanced herself from this genre, which the critic Gilbert David had called "epic theatre of the emotions." Plays like *L'Homme gris (Night)* (1984), *Oublier (Take Care)* (1987) and *Aurélie, ma soeur (Aurélie, My Sister)* (1988) are psychological dramas that show the devastating effects of familial snakepits in which the social façade must be preserved at all costs.

Bouchard showed how mythologies (ancient, Christian, American) influence emotional development and condition desires. He confronted his characters with pre-existing stories—parental love, the desire to have children, incest, the relationship with Mother—in order to track the mysteries of emotion and the detours of desire. Thus, in *La Contre-nature de Chrysippe Tanguay, écologiste* (1979-83), a homosexual couple who want to adopt a child hire a woman to teach them all the feminine roles the child will need. *Les Muses orphelines (The Orphan Muses)* (1988) involves four children coming to grips with the story that the two older ones once concocted to explain the disappearance of their mother. But Bouchard's best-known work (one of the great successes of Quebec theatre in recent years) was *Les Feluettes ou la Répétition d'un drame romantique (Lilies, or the Revival of a Romantic Dream)* (1987). Modelled on the great French melodramas of the late nineteenth century, *Les Feluettes* tells a story of homosexual love between a young Québécois from a rural background and a young, penniless French aristocrat (a number of loyalists took refuge in Quebec with the advent of the Third Republic), against a backdrop of Annunzio's *The Martyr of St. Sebastian* and life in a famous turn-of-the-century Lac Saint-Jean resort.

Laberge and Bouchard, like Tremblay, usually worked within the traditional scheme of Quebec theatre: a clear dramatic situation in which the audience observes the consequences on the characters. In the 1980s, a number of playwrights inverted this order, including René Gingras, Claude Poissant, and Normand Canac-Marquis. In these writers' works, the audience had to discover the nature of the situation, the conflicts that set the characters against each other, giving the image of a reality in which the stakes were not discernible at first glance. Poissant's *Passer la nuit* (1983) features a group of young adults who have invented imaginary personas and play them out every evening in a bar. In *Syncope (Breaks)* (1983), Gingras places a man in his thirties, who is not sure what he wants, between an adolescent who is seeking a father and a middle-aged businessman who is seeking a son. In Canac-Marquis' *Syndrôme de Cézanne (The Cézanne Syndrome),* one of the most stunning plays of recent years, a man reconstructs the real and imaginary fragments of his past life as he tries to rebuild the car in which his companion and child died.

The second half of the 1980s saw the arrival of a new, more aggressive generation of playwrights, who placed social, and even political, issues back on the agenda. Jean-François Caron, who studied playwriting at the National Theatre School, chose, in his own words, "to do what they taught me not to do"—to load his texts with allusions to the news. His play *J'écrirai bientôt une pièce sur les nègres... (Soon I'll write a play about Ghostwriters)* (1989) involves the three alter egos of a young writer caught in a struggle between abandoning his craft, the rejections of publishers of another generation, and his ghostwriting work for a successful playwright. *Aux hommes de bonne volonté* (1993), a text that is both terrifying and hilarious, addresses the brutality of a society that corners its teenagers between moroseness and AIDS.

Dominic Champagne, with his precise thoughts and polemical intentions, more or less took on the role of spokesperson for this young generation of artists. His most recent work, *Cabaret neiges noires* (1992, written in collaboration with François Caron, Jean-Frédéric Messier, and Pascale Rafie), draws, with exuberant ferocity, a portrait of a society that has given up dreaming. In *La Répétition (Playing Bare)* (1980), Champagne questions the nature of artistic work in his portrayal of a disillusioned actress rehearsing *Waiting for Godot* with amateurs. But his most controversial play (after some performances, audience members came to blows) is *La Cité interdite (The Forbidden City)* (1991), an exploration of terrorism in the context of the events that gripped Quebec in October, 1970.

In January of 1990, those who witnessed the creation of *Dernier Délire permis (Death, Delirium and Desire)*, by Jean-Frédéric Messier, had a feeling similar to that felt by those who had suddenly discovered the work of Chaurette and Dubois in January, 1980: Quebec playwriting was undergoing another change at the dawn of a new decade. Messier's play, inspired by Molière's *Don Juan*, introduced an elliptical theatrical language to evoke social disintegration and emotional confusion. Messier was somewhat the *enfant terrible* of the new generation, proposing a theatrical universe in which the references are explicitly and voluntarily distanced from theatre in favour of rock culture. For *Helter Skelter* (1994), Messier directed a collective of creative artists and performers; not overly concerned with formalizing the improvised language of the actors, he chose a spectacular spatial deployment to relate the imaginary biography of Sharon Tate's unborn child—the child who, in this tale, escaped the massacre perpetrated by Charles Manson and his disciples.

In the same generation as Messier are four playwrights worthy of attention: Michel Monty, Wajdi Mouawad, Yvan Bienvenue, and Daniel Danis. In *Accidents de parcours (Freak Accidents)* (1992) and *Prise de sang* (1994), Monty portrays the rites of passage of young disadvantaged characters into a world that is full of conflict and devoid of meaning. Mouawad's plays (including *Journée de noces chez les Cromagnons*, 1993 [*Wedding Day at the Cromagnons'*], and *Les Mains d'Edwige au moment de la naissance*, 1994), boldly written in unbridled language, feature colourful characters trapped in overwhelming conflicts. Bienvenue (*Histoire à mourir d'amour*, 1993; *Règlement de contes*, 1994) writes what he called "theatre of distortion:" plays with savage humour and terrifically rhythmic language, punctuated with violence and death.

Danis' two plays, *Celle-là (That Woman)* (1992) and *Cendres de cailloux (Stone and Ashes)* (1992), were received with a mixture of enthusiasm and perplexity. The author creates troubled worlds driven by madness, sexuality and death, peopled with intensely tragic characters. His texts, which imperceptibly straddle storytelling and action, pose a perpetual challenge to the director.

This brief overview of Quebec playwriting since 1980 requires some contextualization. At the beginning of the decade, Quebec suffered a double bereavement. Like the rest of the West, it mourned the passing of traditional leftist ideologies, but, after the defeat of the referendum on sovereignty in 1980, it also mourned the death of a certain form of nationalism. Subsequently, the theatre of the 1980s was built on a mistrust of words, and there was an unprecedented evolution in the disciplines of dance and image-based theatre. In the latter, creative artists like Gilles Maheu, of Carbone 14,[1] and Robert Lepage developed an open-ended dramatic form that did not present the audience with an articulated discourse. Although the 1980s did not produce a great abundance of dramaturgy in Quebec, the decade did give rise to playwrights (Chaurette and Dubois in particular) whose work challenged the prevailing norms of staging and acting in the theatre. This phenomenon is being revisited today with the surprising writing of Daniel Danis.

Also noteworthy within Quebec playwriting in the 1980s is the recurrent theme of the artist in society. In fact, some sixty plays from this decade had artistic creativity as a theme, and many of them went so far as to put the theatre itself on stage. It might be said that this was a tribal turning inward of artists who had lost contact with their community and could no longer talk of anything but themselves. However, the public responded very strongly to plays dealing with this theme. Artists and their art were often *the* major theme in Quebec theatre of the 1980s. Dominic Champagne proposes a hypothesis to explain the omnipresence of creative artists in plays: the artist is the preferred figure of the dreamer, of the one who invents other realities. During the 1980s, a decade marked by broken dreams, we needed to listen to stories of dreamers, to remind ourselves that dreaming was still possible.

As the 1990s began, Quebec playwriting was infused with new energy with the simultaneous arrival of several young writers who have caught the public's attention. It is still too early to see clearly what will emerge from this new work, but the following two tendencies can be discerned. First: it is a theatre of revolt, which, particularly in the work of Caron, Messier, Mouawad and Monty, directly tackles social issues. Second: it is a theatre that adopts the point of view of the sons; however, this does not mean killing the fathers but managing to survive in the world that was created—and then abandoned—by them. Nevertheless, this new generation is faithful to the dynamic that has driven Quebec drama since Tremblay's *Les Belles-soeurs* appeared in 1968; these new writers see their writing in relation not to foreign playwriting but to the work of other Quebec playwrights. Thus, if Quebec theatre is no longer nationalist, it remains fundamentally national. However, one may note, particularly among authors like Chaurette and Danis, a desire to explore the most stimulating trends in foreign writing, particularly those from Europe.

Original article in French;
translated by Käthe Roth

NOTES

[1] Founded in 1975 under the name *Les Enfants du Paradis*, this company, directed by Gilles Maheu, changed its name to *Carbone 14* in 1981. The company presents imagistic theatre where movement, music and set design, often based on the use of raw materials, combine to create the powerful imagery that has become the company's trademark. Their most recent productions, all of which have enjoyed extensive international tours, include: *Le Rail* (1985), *Le Dortoir* (1988), *Le Café des aveugles* (1992) and *La Forêt* (1994).

Contributors

Geraldine Anthony

Geraldine Anthony S.C. - B.A., M.A. Ph.D. - LL.D. (honoris causa, 1993) is a native New Yorker and permanent resident of Halifax, Nova Scotia. She has done post-doctoral work at Columbia University in World Drama; 17th century literature at Oxford; fellowship in Journalism at the University of Minnesota. She is Professor Emeritus at Mount Saint Vincent University, Halifax. Her numerous articles and books on Canadian dramatists include: *Gwen Pharis Ringwood* (1981), *John Coulter* (1976), both published by G.K. Hall , Boston; *Stage Voices* (New York & Toronto: Doubleday & Co., 1978); the series General Editor of *Profiles In Canadian Drama* (Toronto: Gage Publishers, 1977). She is presently historian and biographer for the Sisters of Charity of Halifax.

Susan Bennett

Susan Bennett is an Associate Professor in the English Department at the University of Calgary and the author of *Theatre Audiences: A Theory of Production and Reception* (Routledge, 1990) and *Performing Nostalgia: Shifting Shakespeare and the Contemporary Past* (Routledge, 1995). She is currently working on a project about gender, genre and women's dramatic writing.

Joyce Doolittle

Joyce Doolittle is Professor Emeritus of Drama at the University of Calgary where she established courses in creative drama and theatre for children. From 1968-1979, she represented Canada's professional children's theatres in ASSITEJ, the world organization for theatre for the young. She is currently the Drama editor of Red Deer Press.

Alan Filewod

Alan Filewod is professor of Drama at the University of Guelph, is an author of *Collective Encounters*, and has edited two volumes of Canadian Drama. He was editor of *Canadian Theatre Review* from 1988-1995. He is currently working on a study of theatre in the Trade Union Movement in Australia and Canada.

Keith Garebian

Keith Garebian holds a Ph.D. (Queen's University) in Canadian and Commonwealth Literature. He is the author of *Hugh Hood; Hugh Hood and His Works; Leon Rooke and His Works; William Hutt: A Theatre Portrait; A Well-Bred Muse: Selected Theatre Writings 1978-1988; George Bernard Shaw and Christopher Newton: Explorations of Shavian Theatre*; and detailed histories of the original Broadway production of *My Fair Lady, Gypsy* and *West Side Story*. He is also the editor of *William Hutt: Masks and Faces*. He is currently doing research for a book on Robin Phillips' Shakespearean productions.

Sarah Gibson-Bray

A specialist in English-Canadian Theatre for Young Audiences, Sarah Gibson-Bray completed her doctoral dissertation, *The Plays of Dennis Foon - A Playwright for Young Canadians*, at the Graduate Centre for the Study of Drama at the University of Toronto in 1992. She is currently compiling an index and guide to "child advocacy drama" in Canada. She lives in Perth, Ontario with her husband Carl and her one-year-old daughter, Emma.

Jennifer Harvie

A Ph.D. candidate in Theatre Studies at the University of Glasgow, Jennifer Harvie is currently teaching English, drama, and media studies at colleges of the University of London. She specializes in contemporary drama, feminist theory, and post-colonial theory and has published previously on Judith Thompson in *Theatre Research in Canada*.

Chris Johnson

Chris Johnson is Chair of the Theatre Programme and Artistic Director of the Black Hole Theatre at the University of Manitoba. He has published many articles on Canadian drama and theatre, especially the plays of George F. Walker, and has directed productions of three Walker plays, *Criminals in Love, Better Living*, and *Tough!*, for the Black Hole.

Patricia Keeney

A widely-published poet, novelist, and critic, she has specialized in the relationship between poetry and the stage. A teacher of creative writing at York University, her work has appeared in a wide range of magazines and journals including *Canadian Literature, Canadian Theatre Review* and *The Canadian Forum*.

Paul Lefebvre

Paul Lefebvre who studied at the Université de Montréal, is director, translator, and professor. He is the Literary Manager of the Nouvelle Compagnie Théâtrale (Montréal) and Coordinator of the French Directing Program at the National Theatre School of Canada. During the 1980s, he worked mostly for daily *Le Devoir*, Radio-Canada and the quarterly *Les Cahiers de théâtre JEU.*

Denyse Lynde

Denyse Lynde is an Associate Professor in the Department of English, Memorial University, where she teaches in the Drama Specialization programme. She has published widely on Canadian drama and is currently researching a variety of Newfoundland cultural activities from the 1940's to the present.

Klaus Peter Müller

Klaus Peter Müller studied English, Romance Literature and Philosophy at Düsseldorf University. He teaches at the English Department in Düsseldorf and at the University of Chemnitz. His fields of research and teaching have been English and Canadian literature, literature and cultural identity, literature and values, epistemology and literature, literary history, theories of literary criticism, translation theories and foreign language teaching. He has published a number of books and articles on these subjects, among them *Contemporary Canadian Short Stories* (Stuttgart 1990) and *Englisches Theater der Gegenwart, Geschichte(n) und Strukturen* (Tübingen 1993).

Malcolm Page

Professor of English at Simon Fraser University, Malcolm Page has been President of the Association for Canadian Theatre History and published widely on Canadian drama. His books are *John Arden* (1984), *Richard II* (1987) and *Howard's End* (1993), with nine compilations for Methuen's "Writers on File" series.

Richard Perkyns

Richard Perkyns is a professor and drama specialist in the English Department of Saint Mary's University, Halifax. He is author of *The Neptune Story*, editor of *Major Plays of the Canadian Theatre 1934-1984*, and co-editor of *Introduction to Literature*, now in its third edition. He has written numerous articles on theatre and been active in community theatre.

Richard Plant

Richard Plant teaches in the Department of Drama at Queen's University in Kingston and the Graduate Centre for Study of Drama at the University of Toronto. His many activities in the area of Canadian theatre research include co-founding *Theatre Research in Canada/Recherches Théâtrales au Canada*, co-editing *The Bibliography of Theatre Research in Canada: The Beginnings through 1984/Bibliographie au Canada: Des Débuts—1984*, editing *The Penguin Book of Modern Canadian Drama* and, most recently, co-editing *Later Stages: Essays in Ontario Theatre from World War I to the 1970s*.

Don Rubin

A Professor of Theatre at York University, Don Rubin was founding editor of the *Canadian Theatre Review* and is Executive Editor of UNESCO's *World Encyclopedia of Contemporary Theatre*.

Denis Salter

Denis Salter teaches Theatre Studies at McGill University. He has published widely on Canadian and Quebecois theatre, Victorian stage history, modern drama, Shakespeare, alternative models for historiography and contemporary performance theory. His current research is on the naturalization of (European) cultural authority within postcolonial theatrical practice and discourse.

Drew Hayden Taylor

Drew Hayden Taylor is an Ojibway writer from the Curve Lake First Nations, located in central Ontario, Canada. Aged 33, he has written television scripts for *The Beachcombers*, *Street Legal* and *North of Sixty*. His plays include *Toronto at Dreamer's Rock* for which he won a Chalmer's Award for best play for Young Audiences and *The Bootlegger Blues* which won the Canadian Authors Association Literary Award for Best Drama.

Aside from his vast experience as a journalist, Drew is the author of four books and his articles and commentaries have appeared in many anthologies.

Currently, he is working on a sequel to *Someday* and two movie projects. Drew has completed his first year as Artistic Director of Native Earth Performing Arts, Toronto's only professional Native theatre company.

Anton Wagner

Dr. Anton Wagner is a documentary film maker and Canadian theatre historian. He is the editor of *A Vision of Canada: Herman Voaden's Dramatic Works 1928-1945* (Simon & Pierre, 1993) and is the Director of Research and Managing Editor of *The World Encyclopedia of Contemporary Theatre*, based in the York University Theatre Department.